GROWING GREEN

Animal-Free Organic Techniques

by Jenny Hall and Iain Tolhurst

CHELSEA GREEN PUBLISHING COMPANY

White River Junction, Vermont

First published in the United Kingdom March, 2006.
The Vegan Organic Network
10 Charter Road
Altrincham
Cheshire
WA15 9RL, UK.
www.veganorganic.net

Published in the United States January, 2007.
Chelsea Green Publishing
PO Box 428
White River Junction, VT 05001
www.chelseagreen.com
802-295-6300

Printed in the United States of America.
First United States printing January, 2007.

ISBN-10: 1-933392-49-5
ISBN-13: 978-1-933392-49-3

Design: Sussed Design, www.susseddesign.com.
Illustrations: Jenny Hall unless otherwise stated.
Cover photo: The walled garden at Tolhurst Organic Produce by Colin Leftley.
Back cover photo: Courgettes undersown to clover by Colin Leftley.

Printed on recycled paper.

Acknowledgements

Dedicated to Keith, Alice and my dad Fred.

From Jenny - my thanks and love goes to Keith Griggs, my partner who has been supportive and given me the head space and feedback to write this book.

Firstly, the authors would like to thank Harold Bland, Peter Corden and Nick Gale of the Cyril Corden Trust for providing a grant for this book. Thank you to the Vegan Organic Network for sponsoring the book. For their constant love, support and inspiration we thank David and Jane Graham and Peter and Diana White. For the technical and proof reading we thank Dave - Organic Growers of Durham, Pauline Lloyd, Nick Fox, Stephane Groleau, Michaela Altman, Helen Lear and Paul Robertshaw. For allowing Jenny the opportunity to take time off work we would like to thank Lancashire Wildlife Trust. For help with various sections and illustrations we thank Graham Burnett. For support with logistics we thank Patrick Browne, John Curtis, Ziggy Woodward, Graham Cole and Rochelle Gunter. For organising photos we thank John Walker and Colin Leftley. For their inspiration and permission to use information about their businesses Jenny thanks Alan and Debra Schofield, the workers co-operative Growing with Grace and Sue Morris and Trevor Warman from Le Guerrat. We thank Johnny's Selected Seed for sending information about green manuring. We would like to thank Mick Marsden and Alasdair Smithson of the Soil Association for proof reading individual chapters. We would like to thank the Soil Association for allowing us to look at back copies of the Organic Farming magazine and reproduce information from them. We would like to thank Tim Deane for his foreword. Finally, a massive thank you goes out to all the members of the Vegan Organic Network.

Foreword

Iain Tolhurst has been in the forefront of organic horticulture for twenty five years and more. I first met him at the Organic Growers Association conference at Cirencester in January 1983 when he was already respected for the dynamism and innovation of his growing, at that time in almost impossibly inhospitable conditions among the Cornish clay hills. During our first conversation he told me that farm workers were overpaid. As I was then a farm worker, and a branch secretary of the now long defunct NUAAW to boot, this opinion did not go down well. Later we got to know each other better. Becoming a self-employed grower myself, and with the inevitably much reduced income which this move entailed, I was able to gain a little (but not much!) sympathy for his view. Probably he never meant it that seriously. In any case I soon came to understand that in anything to do with horticulture Tolly's views are worth taking note of – this because they come from a keen intelligence combined with the practical skills of a craftsman.

The OGA set out to show a credible and commercially viable alternative to "conventional" agriculture, and was the catalyst for the gradual recognition of at least the validity of the organic approach to food production. It was organic vegetables that led the scarcely believable growth of the organic market. Inevitably, given the increased demand, the shape and nature of organic horticulture have changed. From being a fringe activity conducted on the margins (West Wales, the Westcountry) the greatest area of organic vegetable production is now to be found alongside that of non-organic production in recognised horticultural districts. It is of course all to the good that an ever-increasing area of vegetable ground is managed to organic standards, as it is that more and more organic food is available. On the other hand the bulk of the organic market is in the hands of large commercial organisations and depends on the same system of distribution and finance as its non-organic equivalent. This does not inspire confidence that simply producing food within the organic regulation is doing much to improve our relationship with the Earth.

In essence the philosophy which underlies organic production is radical – in a literal sense in that it looks to the roots of fertility within the soil. It is even revolutionary because, by recognising those roots, it turns its back on external inputs. In this way it can begin to free itself from an economic system which, seeing food as a commodity and ever-increasing consumption as the only good, is fundamentally at odds with that philosophy.

In this book you will see what organic horticulture can achieve, when it doesn't merely aim to substitute acceptable inputs for prohibited ones. It looks far beyond this - to the production of food as a continuum, as a means of survival in balance with the ecosystem that sustains our lives.

It used to be that the refinements to the techniques which enable organic horticulture to be commercially practical could only come from within the community of organic growers. Apart from our relatively small, but somehow usually adequate number of customers, nobody else was interested. Now there is official recognition and a good deal of funded research, which is something to be thankful for. However the Organic Growers Association is no more and some of the sense of being part of a community has gone with it. The most valuable and directly useful knowledge of organic growing always comes from making a living out of what the soil produces. A community of common purpose allows the knowledge to be shared. Growing Green is an expression of that common purpose.

For this book is not written by Tolly alone, nor derived solely from his own experience. The wealth of knowledge and information within it is drawn not just from what has been achieved at Hardwick but from many other sources. These are also intimately connected with the real nature of organic growing. I have chosen to emphasise Tolly's role because his trajectory epitomises what the OGA at least partly set out to do, and that was to change the world. Anybody with an intelligent interest in how food is produced can see that this is necessary and that the present wasteful systems cannot long be continued. If you want to make a real difference producing decent food on your own small but significant portion of the world - the following pages will tell you most of what you need to know.

Tim Deane
August 2005

Contents

Chapter 3 - Soil fertility

Chapter 10 – UK vegetable crops

Chapter 12 – Season extension and crop storage

Chapter 13 – The marketing of stockfree-organic produce

Stockfree-Organic Growers and Farmers Mission Statement

"We aim to establish commercial stockfree-organic food production systems that optimise land use by growing crops for direct human consumption leaving marginal lands for wildlife conservation and forestry. This will enable us to feed, clothe and shelter present and future world populations.

We aim to farm in the most environmentally sound way possible taking a systems-based approach. This means we will create the majority of the fertility on the holding using green manures, plant-based composts, mulches and chipped branch wood so that we do not rely on large acreages and animal manures to close the system. We aim to achieve sustainable pest control by encouraging the natural flora and fauna of the area and by using barriers where necessary.

We are always conscious of our ecological footprint and aim to reduce pollution and waste from the farm by using appropriate technology, reusing where possible and ensuring that we recycle water and organic wastes on the holding. We will also take responsibility for our off-farm environmental impact and will avoid using fossil-fuel-intensive inputs that create pollution elsewhere. We aim to sell fresh stockfree-organic produce as near to the organic farm as is possible to reduce the food miles. Finally, we believe that it is essential that the organic farm provides a living income to ourselves and that we strive to achieve a life / work balance and devote enough time to our family and achieving personal fulfilment."

Chapter One

Introduction to Stockfree-Organic systems

1.1 Introduction

This book compiles information gathered from many sources and is a practical reference guide on how to grow food. Until now there have been no comprehensive guidelines for the adoption of stockfree-organic growing techniques at the three different scales of commercial vegetable growing:

- Field scale e.g. using tractors.
- Market garden scale using small machinery and hand tools.
- Protected cropping (greenhouse and polytunnel) scale using small machinery and hand tools.

This is the first UK edition. It is hoped that this will be regularly updated for the UK and editions will be written for other countries particularly, countries with tropical and subtropical climates.

1. 2 Defining sustainability

Sustainability depends on three things: perpetuity, reproducibility and information dissemination. A practice needs to have the ability to continue forever, to apply in different situations and to be easily copied and the information has to be accessible to many. Setting up structures for sustainability has been the motivation for this book.

1.3 Defining stockfree

Stockfree as a term was introduced in 2000. It is a description of an organic method of growing food without the use of animal inputs. It is an adaptation of the word 'stockless' commonly used by organisations like the independent Elm Farm Research Centre (EFRC) based in Newbury, Berkshire, to denote all arable farming.

Research into commercial stockfree-organic agriculture arose not for compassionate reasons but through economic necessity. This becomes a common theme in understanding the importance of UK-wide (macro) stockfree adoption. The Elm Farm stockless trials came about in the early 1990s because of the lack of farmyard manure in the arable eastern counties like Norfolk and South Lincolnshire. The lack of livestock inputs was proving a significant barrier to getting farmers to convert to organic grain production.

The Stockfree-Organic Standards[1] were agreed in 2004 and they provide the first guidelines for stockfree-organic systems and are further elaborated upon in this book. Stockfree-organic production offers two complementary techniques for maintaining soil fertility: (1) green manuring and (2) adding organic amendments.

What the Elm Farm trials proved (and the findings were latter backed up by the ADAS Terrington trials[2] and Co-operative Wholesale Society[3] in Leicester) was that it was possible to grow grains organically without animal inputs. Fertility was provided by a green manure ley (usually red clover) incorporated into the rotation. This production system was also shown in trials to give better financial returns (taking advantage of available subsidies) than conventional farming using synthetic fertilisers.

It is the opinion of many of the growers featured in this book that additions of plant-based composts and chipped branch wood, as well as green manures, are essential to replenish organic matter lost through cropping and to encourage high levels of soil microbial activity.

1.4 Are animal inputs necessary in organic systems?

Among organic farmers and growers and their supporters there is an almost universal belief in the following myth:

It is not possible to build up soil health and grow organically without animal manure.

The trials mentioned above have proved this to be untrue. In fact it would be thermodynamically impossible for all fertility to originate from animals. Animals do not have the ability to produce new plant fertility. Plants alone are the producers of food energy and of soil humus and all animals, including humans, are net consumers. We may convert and concentrate food energy, and thus fertility, in our bodies and wastes, but we are net destroyers of it.

No one is denying that animal manures and slaughterhouse by-products fertilise the soil and yield crops. However, the fertility does not originate from these residues, but rather from the grass and grains which the animals ate. The animals destroy the greatest part of that food energy by their digestion, metabolism and other life processes. Only a small portion of that energy is preserved within the meat, milk products or manure of that animal[4].

1.5 Defining organic
In the Stockfree-Organic Standards 'organic' is defined as

... a method of producing food by promoting soil fertility and soil life through the addition of biological (non-synthetic) substances to the soil to replenish any organic matter lost through cropping. Organic growers minimise their reliance on imported inputs and utilise all the resources on the registered holding.

No inputs, as the sole source of fertility, are allowed into an organic system that may adversely affect the soil ecosystem. Soluble fertilisers are not permitted, as they by-pass the soil and feed the crops directly. Synthetic fertilisers, synthetic pesticides and weedkillers are not permitted in an organic agricultural or horticultural system. The registered grower is not permitted to use genetically modified organisms (GMOs) or any products derived from such GMOS.

The organic production system makes a positive ecological impact on the registered holding by conserving wildlife habitats as well as attempting to prevent harmful impacts on the wider environment. Reliance on non-renewable resources like fossil fuels is discouraged.

The need for a positive ecological impact is essential for the perpetuity aspect of sustainability. In an attempt to replicate the closed nature of natural ecosystems the organic grower attempts to utilise natural resources available on the holding or in the garden to enhance soil fertility and not rely on brought-in products.

Just because a single technique for food growing falls within the definition of organic, it does not necessarily mean that it will have a positive ecological impact. The organic system of growing food has to be seen as a holistic system. The grower needs to adopt a systems-based approach using all beneficial practices and not being selective. An example is the treatment of soil fertility. Growers may abandon the use of synthetic fertilisers and pesticides (which require high fossil fuel inputs), but, if they do not replenish the organic matter levels, the soil will degrade within a few years, which will be reflected in the health of the crops.

There are many practices that a grower can adopt to create a positive ecological impact. From a stockfree-organic growing point of view the most important are composting, green manuring and encouraging beneficial wildlife. These will do much to improve the health of the soil and organic system.

1.6 Wider principles for sustainable food production
The genesis of the organic movement occurred in the earlier part of the 20th century, before opposition to pesticides. The movement was more concerned with health than the environment. The pioneers set out to find the causes of good health. In the UK Lady Eve Balfour was the force behind the foundation of the Soil Association and she wrote in her seminal work The Living Soil (1943; reprinted 1975):

The health is part of a continuum through soil, plant, animal and man; and that by recycling nutrients through this chain, productivity can be maintained over time and health can be enhanced at all stages; as long as the food is consumed fresh, for the most part whole and subjected to little or no processing and to no chemical intervention at any stage[5].

The International Federation of Organic Agricultural Movements (IFOAM) had its first conference in 1977 and charged itself with laying down the fundamental principles of organic systems. These were later agreed in 1982.

The IFOAM principles of organic agriculture are:
1   to work as much as possible within a closed system and draw upon local resources.
2   to maintain the long-term fertility of soils.
3   to avoid all forms of pollution that may result from agricultural techniques.

4 to produce foodstuffs of high nutritional quality and sufficient quantity.

5 to reduce the use of fossil energy in agricultural practice to a minimum.

6 to give livestock conditions of life that conform to their physiological needs and to humanitarian principles.

7 to make it possible for agricultural producers to earn a living through their work and develop their potentialities as human beings.

8 to use and develop appropriate technology based on an understanding of biological systems.

9 to use decentralised systems for processing, distribution and marketing of products.

10 to create a system which is aesthetically pleasing to both those within and those outside the system.

11 to maintain and preserve wildlife habitats.

The stockfree-organic system is also based on these principles with the exception of no. 6. However, as will be argued, the rearing of livestock to promote organic agriculture could be at odds with principle 3 (because cattle produce methane), principle 4 (producing sufficient food for world populations) and principle 5 (minimising the use of fossil fuel).

1.7 Food sufficiency

According to the State of the World Report the world's population has passed the 6 billion mark. The UN predicts 4.6 billion more will be added to this in the 21st century. Not only is the overall global population increasing, but the increase is taking place in the developing countries. By 2050 another 600 million people will live in India, another 300 million in China. Yet 2 billion people are presently malnourished[6].

More and more people will live in urban centres. As economic conditions improve, people demand more animal products in their diets. A study commissioned by the Commission of the European Union, World Bank and various governments shows[7] that urban populations consume more meat per person than rural populations. The overall human demand for animal products is expected to triple or even quadruple in the next 30 years.

It is questionable whether it would be physically possible for all the world's estimated future population to eat animal products at the same level as, say, the people of the USA today. The State of the World Report in 1999 estimated

that, for 10 billion people to eat a US diet, we would need 4 planets the size
of Earth to produce the extra 9 billion tons (US) of grain required. At present
livestock consume 38% of the world's cereal production[8]. In the UK about
60% of the 6.7 million hectares of arable land is used for producing food for
farm animals instead of crops for human consumption.

The most obvious way of tackling world hunger is for humans to eat more
efficiently and lower down the food chain, i.e. all arable land should be used to
produce food for human consumption. It has been estimated that it would take
0.07 hectares of land to feed a person on a plant-based diet[9] and 8.85 times
more that that (0.62 hectares) to feed someone on the average US diet[10].

Lawrence Woodward, the Director of the Elm Farm Research Centre, has
written a briefing paper 'Can Organic Farming Feed the World?' Although he
is not looking at this from a stockfree-organic viewpoint, the following
passage is instructive.

*'During a recent exchange we had with the Department of Agriculture in Malawi, they
rightly pointed out that organic farming has little to offer intensive maize plantations
or any other capital intensive monoculture commodity production system used to trade
and raise foreign exchange. Organic farming was therefore dismissed 'as only good for
small scale, local vegetable production'. But this is what feeds people.*

*It is easy to dismiss this approach as extreme and forget that the 'Dig for Victory
campaign during the [second world] war was a very important part of the British
Government's efforts to ensure food security and health. The garden and, in particular,
biologically-intensive gardens are more productive in terms of nutrients per hectare than
any farming system.*

*Organic farming based on locally adapted, intensive biological systems works extremely
well and can be highly productive, particularly across a range of basic food crops.
[Organic methods] are stable and relatively secure on vulnerable soils and in volatile
climatic conditions due to their focus on living organic material, which provides a buffer
for soil and water. As such they are very appropriate to Southern countries. There are of
course problems in some regions. Pests and diseases are a threat. In such cases, cropping
diversity reduces the threat and spreads the risk, thus ensuring stability and security.
Organic farming founded on a technical level can be seen to provide adequate food in
all parts of the world. Where it doesn't, issues such as access to land and political*

problems, including the role of women, are often the major obstacles. [These are] matters of power and economy, not technical issues'[11].

1.8 Are plant-based diets suitable for people?

The other barrier to the widespread adoption of stockfree-organic methods as the basis of a food policy is that many people object to plant-based diets. 'Where do you get your protein?' Studies discussed in Gill Langley's 'Vegan Nutrition' (1995)[12] show that wholefood vegan diets provide the amounts of protein, carbohydrates, vitamins and minerals recommended by the World Health Organisation. On the other hand, many omnivores and lacto-vegetarians eat more protein and undesirable fats than guidelines recommend. Dr Stephen Walsh's book 'Plant based nutrition and health'[13] is a comprehensive guide ensuring that vegans can achieve a complete and healthful diet.

1.9 Fossil fuel use in agriculture

The workers' co-operative Organic Growers of Durham has dedicated much effort over the last ten years to defining and measuring efficient agriculture. Generally, the industrialisation of farming has shown an increase in productivity but not an increase in efficiency. Productivity means the amount produced per unit of land or per person employed, whereas the efficiency of a system means the ratio between the work or energy got out of it and the work or energy put into it. Output / input ratios are a good measure of the extent to which an agricultural system is using up the earth's energy resources. They relate the energy put out in the form of crops or animal products to the energy put in as fossil fuels, labour and manufactured goods. If the output is less than the input, then energy is being lost. These concepts are further discussed in section 10.4.

Köpke and Haas[14] reported that organic farming is more efficient, using a third of the energy per unit area of land than conventional farming. According to many studies (e.g. Steinhart and Steinhart[15]) intensive beef production is the most inefficient form of farming, having an output/input ratio of about 0.08.

1.10 The economic cost of current agricultural policies

The livestock industry has a quadruple subsidy. The first two subsidies are direct:

1   fish, meat, dairy and

2   livestock feed grains

all of which attract substantial agricultural subsidies from the European Union.

Despite the subsidy farmers and fishermen struggle to make living incomes. There are also the indirect subsidies in the form of:

3   environmental and livestock welfare crisis incidents e.g. slurry in water courses, foot and mouth and BSE.
4   costs to the NHS, e.g. the National Audit Office found that obesity costs the NHS at least £½ billion a year[16].

These indirect subsidies are ultimately paid by the taxpayer and water customer. If livestock farmers internalised their external costs, vegetables would seem fairly priced in comparison with meat and dairy products. One of the biggest barriers to getting people to eat fruit and vegetables is that they are considered to be too expensive. It appears contrary to good health that animal feeds should be subsidised when vegetable and fruit growing is not.

With morale in farming being at an all time low and with farmers struggling in an age of international trade and globalisation, the essence of farming needs to be addressed. Some proposals for agricultural policy changes have included:

1   removing subsidies from livestock enterprises;
2   introducing subsidies to encourage legume leys in rotation;
3   rewarding farmers for their efficiency (see section 10.4);
4   ensuring a more equitable distribution of incomes between farm workers and office workers.

1.11 Local food

In the market place organic crops cannot compete with conventionally grown crops where the consumer wants cheap food. Direct links with consumers have become a lifeline for many organic growers, as they take back control from the wholesalers and supermarkets over the marketing of food. Cutting down the number of links in the food marketing chain is clearly in the financial interests of the farmer and consumer and increases the freshness of the food.

Community Supported Agriculture, in the form of farm shops, subscription schemes, box schemes and farmers' markets, has increased since the early 1990s. These schemes reinforce the local link. Box schemes present the consumer with a fixed amount of seasonal vegetables. The great advantage of this system for planning horticultural production is that it gives the grower a fixed weekly order and a guaranteed income. This book is geared towards educating growers about the cropping regimes, direct marketing and economic techniques necessary for making a successful box scheme. It also offers techniques in environmental accounting so that growers have a yardstick for measuring their year on year improvements.

1.12 Conclusion

This chapter has presented reasons for adopting stockfree-organic food systems. The rest of the book is dedicated to describing the techniques to put this approach into practice. The book does not claim to be exhaustive and new techniques will evolve and gain new importance. The book attempts to provide comprehensive information, which will lead to describing practices that are in opposition to one another. For example, on the one hand it describes 'primary cultivations to turn under green manures' and, on the other 'zero tillage mulching systems.' Both systems are currently used on different stockfree-organic holdings and it is for you, the reader, to choose what suits your particular circumstances.

1 Copyrighted to the Vegan Organic Trust, registered charity no 1080847. Anandavan, 58 High Lane, Chorlton, Manchester. M21 9DZ.

2 COMACK WF, ADAS Terrington, Terrington St Clement, King's Lynn, Norfolk, PE34 4PW

3 LEAKE A, CWS Farms Group, Farmworld, Gartree Road, Leicester LE2 2FB.

4 Adapted from BONSALL, W (1996) The Khadigher Community – Ethical Farming in Action VOHAN News 1: 6

5 A compilation of her central ideas quoted in BESSON, JM and VOGTMANN, H (1978) Towards a Sustainable Agriculture.

6 The statistical information is taken from the D'SILVA, J (2000) Factory Farming and Developing Countries. Compassion in Wold Farming Briefing Paper.

7 This study is reported by CEES DE HAAN et al (1996) Livestock and the Environment - finding a balance.

8 DURNING, AH and BROUGH, HB (1992) Reforming the Livestock Economy in BROWN, LR (ed) State of the World. WorldWatch Institute.

9 SPEDDING, CRW (1996) Agriculture and the Citizen.

10 PIMENTEL, D&M (1996) Food, Energy and Society. Resources & Environmental Science Series.

11 Full briefing paper available from Elm Farm Research Centre.

12 LANGLEY, G (1995) Vegan Nutrition. Vegan Society.

13 WALSH, S (2003) Plant Based Nutrition and Health. The Vegan Society.

14 KÖPKE, U and HAAS, G (1996) Fossil Fuels and CO_2 New Farmer and Grower spring 1996.

15 STEINHART, JS and STEINHART, CE (1977) cited in Geographical Review vol. 67.

16 REPORT OF THE COMPTROLLER & AUDITOR GENERAL (2001) Tackling Obesity in England. National Audit Office.

Chapter Two

Understanding soil protection

2.1 Understanding soil protection

Preserving soil for future generations is necessary for life on this planet. The main danger for world soils is that, by applying the principles of industry to the biological cycles of the soil, farming methods more closely resemble open cast mining than good husbandry.

2.1.1 UK trends –loss of organic matter

Even in the 1970s, when MAFF commissioned the Strutt Report, Modern Farming and the Soil, the phenomenon of soil degradation was well known. The Strutt report concluded that:

'Some soils are now suffering from dangerously low organic matter levels and could not be expected to sustain the farming systems which have been imposed upon them.'

Up to the prohibition on straw burning in 1993, the trend became worse. Even now crop yields can be increased at the expense of soil organic matter levels and balanced nutrients. The biological activity of the soil, which depends on the availability of soil organic matter, also declines. Mats of organic matter at the surface, mottled layers of soil and hard pans all suggest poor structure, poor drainage and a lifeless soil.

2.1.2 UK trends – soil erosion

It is unnatural for soil to be without plant growth and totally exposed to the elements. Soil erosion, and particularly water erosion, has proved to be of great concern. When soil particles are washed down a slope into water bodies, nutrient enrichment (eutrophication) can result in algal blooms, which use up the oxygen in the water and kill aquatic life. Reading University's Environmental Challenges in Farm Management has listed the modern UK farming practices that cause erosion:

- Autumn crops are one of the principle causes of erosion in the UK, as the ground is left clear of developed vegetation during the higher rainfall winter months.
- The creation of tramlines created by the wheels of the spraying machinery.
- Other tractor wheelings.
- The need for fine, flat seedbeds for both arable and vegetable crops to aid establishment and pesticide efficiency.
- Increase in the length of slopes through hedgerow removal.
- The substitution of maize silage for grass in some areas of the country.
- Out wintering and supplementary feeding of livestock.
- Outdoor pig units on unsuitable sites.
- Ploughing and/or reseeding of grassland on slopes.
- Damage to river banks by grazing livestock.

Poor soil management could also occur in stockfree-organic systems if the grower does not take care. The grower is warned in 2.1 of the Stockfree-Organic Standards that soil can suffer when exposed to:

- drought conditions;
- heavy rain leading to erosion;
- strong wind leading to erosion;
- heavy machinery leading to compaction;
- inappropriate cultivation leading to structural damage and organic matter losses;
- frost shattering action on unprotected bare soils and
- deforestation.

Recommended practices will help alleviate the worst effects of soil erosion. To understand soil management it is necessary to understand the physical nature of soil.

2.2 Soil structure and physical components

An optimum soil structure has been described as:

a water-stable, organically enriched, granular structure where all the water reserves within aggregates can be fully exploited by root hairs and the space between aggregates is large enough to allow rapid drainage, to admit air and to facilitate the deep penetration of roots[1].

The mineral components of soil are derived from rocks, which are weathered into all sorts of sizes from the largest boulders through to stones, sand, silt and the tiniest particles of clay. Soils vary widely in their relative contents of sand, silt and clay, but a good proportion is around 20% clay, 50% sand and 30% silt. Such mixtures are known as loams.

All soils need careful management, especially the timing of cultivations, which should be carried out when the soil moisture content is just right – not too wet and not too dry.

Sandy soil – is the easiest to work, warming quickly in spring and draining easily. However, it tends to be slightly acidic and can dry out easily in the summer. It has large pore spaces and, if the soil is not carefully managed, rapid water movement through the sand will leach nutrients, leading to fertility deficiencies. Also, the larger air spaces mean that organic matter is more likely to be oxidised and lost. Sandy soils need organic matter to bind particles together.

Silty soil – is a fragile soil that can cap at the surface. The pores are small and can remain completely waterlogged in wet conditions or can become dusty in dry conditions. Even if some form of structure with large air pores can be achieved, it can disintegrate easily with a packing down effect leading to compaction where the soil becomes airless. Silts benefit from the addition of organic matter to open up pore spaces.

Clay soil – is late to warm in spring, heavy to work and has poor drainage. It is sticky when wet and tends to bake hard in summer. As the soil is wetted and dried the clay particles can expand and shrink, causing cracking. Clays benefit from the addition of organic matter, which opens up the air pores and makes the soil less dense.

The characteristic behaviour of clay particles is very different from that of sand or silt. The latter are chemically inert and only affect water retention and drainage. In contrast, clay particles, the smallest particles of rock, are electrically charged and can attract, hold and make nutrients available to plants.

Peaty soil – is organic, as opposed to mineral, in origin. An example of its formation is when, millennia ago, seas flooded established forests and in recent times such land has been reclaimed from the sea. Such soil can look and feel just like compost or peat. These soils tend to be too acidic for earthworms. They can also be boggy in places and need careful attention to drainage.

Organic matter – The average content of organic matter in arable land is around 2%. A lower organic matter content will give rise to greater structural stability and hence greater susceptibility to erosion. High organic matter levels e.g. over 10% in non-peaty soils will generally indicate low levels of biological activity. This may be due to acidic pH levels and / or poor drainage.

2.3 Recommended practice – adding plant-based compost to soil
Topsoil is a mixture of disintegrating mineral rock and organic matter. Organic matter is material of once living origin: plant debris, manures and dead bodies of all animals and microscopic creatures. Organic matter is continually decaying, feeding the soil biota (billions of soil bacteria, fungi, microscopic soil animals and larger animals like worms). Replenishing organic matter lost through oxidation (accelerated by tillage) will improve soil structure. Organic matter retains moisture, binds sands and opens up clay soils, making all soils more easily worked. Earthworms are the most significant species for soil structure, as their burrows provide air and drainage channels. Earthworms require plenty of organic matter and do not like acidic conditions, poor drainage or frequent tillage.

If you follow the guidelines for making good compost in chapter 4, then you should be left with friable dark compost that crumbles in your hands and smells pleasantly earthy.

2.3.1 Applying compost on a field with machinery
• Recommended time: early spring, as soon as ground conditions allow, which in the southern UK may be March and in the north late April.

Stockfree-Organic Standard 2.2(a) - adding plant-based compost to soil

Wider environmental impact	Soil rendered inert without organic matter. Organic matter (carbon) locked in the soil and not released into the atmosphere where it would be adding to greenhouse gases. Organic matter returned to soil and not ending up in landfill.
Advantages for the grower in terms of structure	Replaces losses through oxidation. Improves all soil structures - binds sands / open clays. Increases earthworm populations whose burrows provide air and drainage channels.
Disadvantages for the grower	Finding enough. Managing a heap can be time consuming. May need to buy in materials (see 3.7).

- It will be necessary to get a fore-end loader (or similar loader) to load a muck spreader.
- The muck spreader should only pass onto the land in suitable weather conditions, i.e. when the land is dry enough.
- In accordance with the manufacturer's specification, the muck spreader should be calibrated to deliver up to 25 tonnes a hectare / 10 tonnes an acre of plant-based compost.
- Application should be according to rotation (see chapters 6 and 11).

2.3.2 Applying compost by hand
- Recommended time: early spring, as soon as ground conditions allow - usually March.
- A wheelbarrow should only pass onto the soil in suitable weather conditions, i.e. when the land is dry enough.
- Apply one barrow load per ten metres square every other year.
- Tip the compost from the wheelbarrow in one load and then rake evenly and thinly onto the soil surface.
- Application should be according to rotation (see chapters 6 and 11.)

2.4 Recommended practice - green manure leys

Green manures are plants that are grown specifically to benefit the soil, replacing nutrients, improving soil structure and increasing organic matter content. The different green manures and their establishment are discussed in section 3.5.

A ley is an area of land taken out of cropping production and replaced with growing green manures for fertility building. Some green manures are from the legume family and have the ability to take up nitrogen from the air, tapping a free source of soil fertility. Red clover, sweet clover and lucerne are the usual nitrogen-fixing green manures chosen for the ley. At Tolhurst Organic Produce we use pure stands although mixtures including these and grasses are also widely used.

The green manure ley may grow for several years and has the benefit of improving soil structure, as the deep roots of a green manure like clover penetrate and break up the soil and the subsoil and the root channels remain

Stockfree Organic Standard 2.2(b) - green manure leys	
Wider environmental impact	Less erosion.
	Avoids transporting bulky organic wastes.
Advantages for the grower in terms of structure	Mowing and mulching provides conditions for earthworm breeding.
	Improves all mineral soil structures.
	Mowing and mulching returns organic matter to the soil.
	Biological subsoiling with deep roots.
	Root channels remain long after the green manure decomposes.
	Organic matter added when incorporated.
Disadvantages for the grower	Need to learn green manure management skills.
	Land out of production.
	Seed can be expensive.
	Finding ideal conditions for establishment e.g. adequate soil moisture and weather conditions.
	May need to irrigate.

long after decomposition. A grower cannot create such a complex and intricate network of tiny air pores and drainage channels with cultivation equipment. A subsequent crop will be able to take advantage of this improved soil structure[2].

2.4.1 Incorporating a green manure with machinery

To maximise improved soil structure when turning under a green manure ley, you should allow the channels created by the deeper roots to remain. The key to successful use of green manures lies in how effectively they are worked into the soil. The major aim should always be to achieve a gradual complete aerobic decomposition of the material[3]. Before incorporation, the green manure should be chopped and shredded at ground level several days before to allow wilting to take place.

There are two options open to the stockfree-organic grower using machinery:

* *Technique 1* - bury the green manure ley and at a later date use a secondary cultivation to create a seed bed. Typical equipment: mouldboard plough (ploughing no deeper than 15cm) and power harrow (see section 2.7.2).
* *Technique 2* - distribute the chopped green manure throughout the topsoil profile in one action. Typical equipment: a tractor-mounted rotary cultivator, spader or pedestrian-operated rotovator (see section 2.7.3 and 2.7.4).

2.4.2 Incorporating a green manure by hand

* The green manure should be chopped and shredded at ground level several days before incorporating to allow for wilting to take place. (As rye can be particularly difficult to kill, the green manure can be pulled up, laid flat on the soil surface to wilt and then dug in).
* A green manure can be incorporated by inverting the soil using a 'turfing' technique.
* Cleanly cut the edge of the turf with a spade.
* Under cut the green manure turf at a depth of at least 10cm until it breaks.
* Turn the turf over by hand ensuring that no greenery is present on the surface.
* Leave for at least two weeks before trying to create a seedbed with a rake.
* If the green manure regenerates turn it in again.

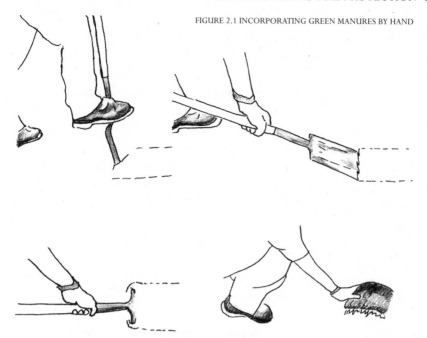

FIGURE 2.1 INCORPORATING GREEN MANURES BY HAND

2.4.3 Avoiding nitrogen lock-up

How quickly the green manure breaks down will be affected by soil temperature, moisture content and the carbon:nitrogen (C:N) ratio of the green manure. When green manures are incorporated into the soil, soil organic matter is one of the products of their decomposition. When a carbon-rich green manure such as a cereal (see sections 3.5.2 and 3.5.3) is turned in, the soil micro-organisms multiply rapidly to feed on the organic matter, decomposing it but also consuming a lot of nitrogen doing so. This process leaves less available soil nitrogen (nitrogen lock-up) for subsequent crop growth, until breakdown has completed and the microbes begin to die and release their nitrogen to the soil. A general rule of thumb is to leave the soil for at least two weeks after turning in the green manure, before attempting to create a seedbed for another crop. If you were to turn something in with an even higher C:N ratio than a green manure, for example sawdust, this might cause nitrogen lock-up for several years and should be avoided.

2.4.4 Green manure leys and zero tillage

The Organic Growers of Durham have shown that green manures leys can be managed in a different way than cutting, mulching and incorporating them.

They favour zero tillage mulching systems - see 2.9.1 and 3.6.2 for a description of these techniques.

2.5 Recommended practice - overwintering green manures

Wind and water erosion may be prevented by using green manures, as 'cover crops'. Since adverse weather conditions tend to be in winter, bare soil at this time is bad practice. The overwinter green manure roots hold the soil and the top growth prevents most damage from splashing and surface run-off. Whilst the commonly used green manures like the clovers and vetches need to be sown by late August, the cereal green manures can be sown later (see section 3.5.3).

Stockfree Organic Standard 2.2(c) - overwintering green manures

Wider environmental impact	Reduces erosion.
Advantages for the grower in terms of structure	Maintains soil structure over winter. Prevents worst damage from rain.
Disadvantages for the grower	Green manure needs to be established before winter, but crops may be growing at this time. Possible need for autumn cultivation, which can lead to its own erosion problems.

2.6 Recommended practice - undersowing green manures

When using overwinter green manures clovers and vetches need to be sown by August to get good establishment. There is a conflict of land use, as crops may be growing at this time.

One way of getting around this problem, popularised in the UK by the author, Iain Tolhurst, and in the US by Eliot Coleman[4], is the technique of undersowing. Undersowing is where the green manure seed is sown underneath the growing crop. It is getting the best of both worlds - cropping and soil protection. The undersown green manure provides places for foot traffic and other compaction damage when harvesting the vegetables. The role of undersowing to improve soil fertility is discussed in section 3.5.10.

Stockfree Organic Standard 2.2(d) - undersowing green manures under existing crops (also known as living mulches)

Wider environmental impact	Reduces soil erosion.
Advantages for the grower	Maintains soil structure over winter. Places for foot traffic.
Disadvantages for the grower	Timing is critical (see 3.5.10) sow too early and the green manure can overwhelm the crop, sow too late and there might not be enough time to get establishment before winter.

2.7 Recommended practice - timing cultivation

Soil cultivations should aim to provide a soil structure that will allow for deep rooting crops. Soil cultivations can be made with the following equipment:

- tractor-mounted equipment;
- pedestrian-operated rotovator.

2.7.1 Suitable soil conditions

The mineral particles in the soil are held together in aggregates or 'crumbs' with pores between them. The pores are very important as they allow for drainage, aeration and root growth. In organic systems the plant roots need to spread easily to get full access to the soil profile and to grow deeply and not stop at areas of compaction. Unlike growing with chemical soluble fertilisers, which are applied

Stockfree-Organic Standard 2.2(e) timing cultivation to avoid tillage in wet or dry weather

Wider environmental impact	Reduces soil erosion.
Advantages for the grower	Retains soil structure. Avoids compaction.
Disadvantages for the grower	Waiting for suitable conditions may take weeks. Any cultivation can damage soil structure if not correctly carried out.

to the soil surface, crops in organic growing systems need to have extensive rooting systems that are in contact with as much soil as possible to maximise access to moisture and nutrients. Soils, therefore, need to be cultivated correctly.

Tillage can have a destructive effect on soil structure if wrongly carried out.

- Tilling dry soil can turn it into dust, which can be blown or washed away in subsequent rain.
- Tilling wet or frozen soil can result in panning and compaction.

Sands are free draining soils. Clays and silts are prone to waterlogging. Consequently, after heavy rain a sandy soil can be worked more quickly than clay, but after a dry spell the sandy soil is more likely to be blown about. The stockfree-organic grower will get a feel for their soil, learning by experience when the soil is too wet or too dry to work. Until that time it will be a matter of doing a physical examination by taking a handful of soil and observing how wet it is.

2.7.2 Primary cultivations using tractor-mounted machinery

The stockfree-organic grower needs to understand the difference between the topsoil and subsoil. The topsoil is host to organic matter and the soil biota and is usually darker. With a well-managed soil the topsoil is about 30cm deep. The stockfree-organic grower should not invert the subsoil, burying the topsoil and bringing the subsoil to the surface.

Whether using the traditional mouldboard plough mounted on a tractor or the humble spade, the stockfree-organic grower should not need to turn over the soil any deeper than 15cm. Ploughing was, traditionally, to a depth of 30 - 35cm but this is not suitable in stockfree-organic systems. Shallow ploughing is beneficial in terms of retaining soil structure, soil biological activity, nutrient dynamics and soil moisture conservation.

When dealing with tractors safety must remain paramount. Carelessness with machinery kills and maims many agricultural workers each year, making farming more dangerous than mining. The Health and Safety Executive has produced the document 'Farm wise: your guide to health and safety in agriculture' available free from their website www.hse.gov.uk

The plough has been used in its different forms for many centuries and is still the primary tool used for burying vegetation. The plough is an implement with one or more mouldboards, which cut and turn furrow slices. It has a high power requirement and using it is a skilled job[5]. In stockfree-organic systems, with their emphasis on the use of green manures, the plough may prove useful for turning them in. However, ploughing alone is not sufficient to form a seedbed and will always require a secondary cultivation.

2.7.3 Secondary cultivations using tractor-mounted machinery
Secondary cultivations are used for:

* the creation of seed beds;
* chopping and mixing green manures and surface vegetation throughout the topsoil;
* mixing both organic and mineral amendments uniformly in the soil profile[6].

The disadvantages of secondary cultivations are that they can:
* rapidly aerate the soil, hastening losses of organic matter to the air through oxidation, which can be good if the idea is to break down a carbon-rich green manure but undesirable if the organic matter levels of the soil are already depleted;
* kill earthworms and other soil micro-organisms;
* cause panning and smears at the base of the cultivation level and
* exacerbate perennial weed problems by chopping and spreading weed roots.

Tractor-mounted power harrows – have vertical rotating tines fixed to a series of rotor heads across the full width of the machine, which can be from three metre to eight metre wide. The drive is taken from the PTO shaft through a gearbox and system of gearing to the tine rotors. A basic model has a lightweight frame to support the gears and rotors. A levelling bar and simple crumbler roll is attached to the frame at the rear. A fine tilth is achieved with a low tractor gear and high rotor speed.

Tractor-mounted rotary cultivators - are made in working widths from one metre to more than five metre depending on the draught power of the tractor pulling it. The rotary cultivators are mounted on the three-point-linkages and are powered by the PTO shaft which rotates L-shaped blades. The blades throw the soil against a hinged flap at the rear of the machine, which shatters the clods.

Tractor-mounted spader – is designed to produce results much like those achieved by manual double digging. Spaders lift and aerate the soil and can help to introduce humus to deeper layers in the soil. The spader's ability to incorporate dense vegetable matter in a single pass makes the machine ideal for systems that incorporate green manures. A spader can loosen topsoil, mix surface vegetation and open up the subsoil without panning at the cultivation level. The problem with rotary cultivations is that tines pulverize a dry soil or create a smear in a wet one. The absence of compaction pans is one of the principle advantages of the spader.

2.7.4 Consolidating the seedbed with a tractor-drawn roller

The soil surface should be fine and firm, to conserve soil moisture. The soil needs to be moist 3cm to 7cm below the surface and should not have a fluffy tilth. Rollers going before cultivation will assist with breaking up large clods and rollers after cultivation will consolidate the seedbed and conserve moisture.

- Cambridge ring rollers are better at consolidating the soil after drilling as this helps to prevent capping on some soil types.
- A flat roller provides a firmer surface and is beneficial before the surface is disturbed again, e.g. before transplanting as the firmer surface aids the planter.

A good way to determine whether the seedbed is firm enough is to walk on it. If an entire footprint is visible but does not go deeper than 1cm, the seedbed is probably adequate.

2.7.5 Cultivations using pedestrian-operated machinery

Rotavator – The pedestrian-operated rotovator is a popular and affordable machine with small-scale growers. A powered axle rotates L-shaped blades, which till the soil, creating seed beds and chopping plant-based materials into the topsoil. However, because it is difficult to change the depth of the cultivation level it can lead to panning problems.

2.7.6 Consolidating the seedbed with a hand-pulled roller

On an intensive scale, a hand pulled garden roller will be useful after rotavating in order to consolidate the seedbed and conserve moisture.

2.8 Recommended practice - varying the depth of cultivation to prevent panning

As stated in 2.7.1 soil is composed of crumbs surrounded by large air pores. The larger pores promote rapid water drainage, aeration and root growth. If compaction occurs the crumbs break down and small pores dominate. Machinery wheelings, and even walking on the soil in wet conditions, are responsible for soil compaction. Panning tends to seal off the vertical channels in the soil, preventing roots growing any deeper into the soil.

Traditionally a commercial grower uses subsoiling equipment and a gardener uses double digging to remedy compaction and panning. However, the need to subsoil should be perceived as an exceptional measure to be used in the early years if you inherit a soil with these problems. After adopting the use of green manure leys in a growing system, the stockfree-organic grower should find that careful cultivations, green manure roots and enhanced earthworm populations make compaction a thing of the past. The roots of chicory for example, have the ability to penetrate event the thickest of hardpans.

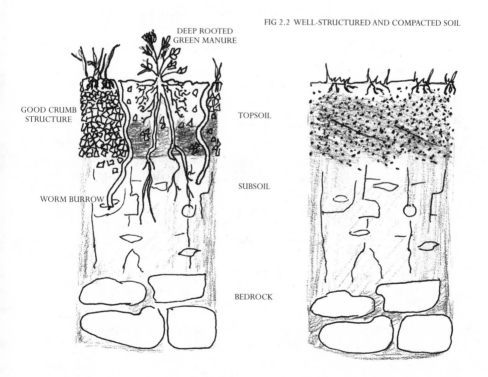

FIG 2.2 WELL-STRUCTURED AND COMPACTED SOIL

DEEP ROOTED GREEN MANURE

GOOD CRUMB STRUCTURE

TOPSOIL

WORM BURROW

SUBSOIL

BEDROCK

Stockfree-Organic Standard 2.2(f) varying the depth of cultivation to prevent panning

Wider environmental impact	Not quantified.
Advantages for the grower	Retains soil structure. Allows for deep rooting crops.
Disadvantages for the grower	Cost and high draught requirement of subsoiling machinery.

Even if the structure of the topsoil is adequate, soil compaction problems can occur lower down in the soil profile because of faulty cultivations or soil types that are generally difficult to manage, like fragile silt soils. The reoccurrence of compaction and pans suggest poor soil management.

If problems continue in an organic system, it is time to consider:

- avoiding cultivating, harvesting and standing on the soil in wet conditions;
- limiting autumn cultivations, which expose a smooth fine seedbed with minimum crop cover to adverse weather conditions;
- increasing the levels of organic matter, as this has a stabilising and preventative effect and
- reducing the weight of agricultural machinery.

2.8.1 Using tractor-mounted subsoiling equipment

Subsoilers are used to break areas of compaction, allowing the free passage of air and water. They typically work to a depth of 40cm and have a high power requirement. Subsoiling should be carried out at right angles to the direction of the primary cultivations, when the ground is dry between August and October. Mounted on the three-point linkage, subsoilers have from one to five legs, fitted with shares, which are pulled through the soil.

2.8.2 Using Eliot Coleman's broad fork

Designed by Eliot Coleman, this useful tool can be imported from the US through Johnny's Selected Seeds[7]. The broad fork is used prior to creating seedbeds, and preferably in the autumn. It allows aeration without the mixing of soil layers. It consists of a 60cm wide steel fork base with 25cm long tines and two handles, which allows you to cover a lot of ground quickly. It is designed so that body weight is used to insert and manoeuvre the tool instead of the back and arms.

2.9 Recommended practice - keeping the soil permanently covered

Many soil scientists and stockfree-organic growers including the Organic Growers of Durham and Plants for a Future[8] have argued that tillage is bad practice because it:

* disturbs the natural balance;
* results in the loss of organic matter;
* reduces soil life;
* breaks down the soil structure;
* increases erosion;
* increases nutrient loss.

In their experience it is not necessary to incorporate plant material into the soil, as decaying mulches laid on the surface will be eventually drawn under by earthworm activity. Plant nutrients will be available at the root level and not be buried.

Mulching is a method of applying a constant supply of uncomposted plant-based material to the soil surface, thus suppressing weed growth. Thick mulching provides favourable conditions for earthworms. The mulch retains

---

Stockfree-Organic Standard 2.2(g) - keeping the soil permanently covered with decaying plant material in the form of a mulch

Wider environmental impact	Reduces soil erosion. Transport of bulky mulching materials.
Advantages for the grower	Retains soil structure. Possibly reduces weeding. No need for tillage equipment.
Disadvantages for the grower	Access to suitable mulching materials and lack of mechanisation may limit the scale. Probably need to buy in restricted materials. No plant roots in the soil to check nutrient leaching over winter. Mollusc control in damp climates.

moisture and protects the earthworms from high temperatures in summer and, in the case of a sudden frost in autumn, can provide insulation. Under a cover of mulch the worms come to the surface even in the daytime and can also stay active longer in the cold season.

2.9.1 Organic Growers of Durham's zero tillage system

Organic Growers of Durham have adapted Ruth Stout's[9] mulching techniques to commercial growing on a five-acre site, of which 2.5 acres is for vegetable production. Whilst Ruth Stout recommended mulching at least once a year, this has proved too labour intensive, especially when placing mulch around individual plants. Instead OGD are testing a system whereby the mulching is done every four years. To do this they have 50% of the market garden set aside for legume-rich hay production (see 3.6.2) and have devised a strip mulching rotation (see 6.7) for vegetable production.

The main difficulty is correctly judging the initial thickness of the mulch:

- If it is too thin, it will rot down too fast and will leave the soil bare in last course or two of the rotation.
- If it is too thick, it may impede the growth of crops.

The depth currently being used is about:

- 10cm of legume-rich hay laid on the soil to provide the fertility;
- and about 30cm of cereal straw (bought in) placed on top of the hay.

The hay and straw are brought into the vegetable growing area in the form of round bales. These are rolled out onto the beds to provide the layers of mulch. A bed width of 2.4 metre has been adopted, which is just twice the width of a standard round bale. So two bales, side by side, can be applied to each bed.

- First the hay is rolled out to the required depth.
- Two bales of hay are sufficient for a 50m bed.
- Then the straw is rolled on top of it.
- Four bales of straw are sufficient for a 50m bed.

Hay is made and baled up fairly loosely into round bales. If the bales are tight, they are too heavy to roll by hand and, when used as mulch, the hay is too compact for the crops to grow through. However, if the hay is too loose the bales will sag and become impossible to roll.

2.9.2 Laying the first mulch on cleared ground

- Mulch for vegetable growing should be laid when the soil is warm to about 20cm. It is usually left until the following year before being planted into.
- According to Ruth Stout[10] the first mulch should not be laid onto cold, wet ground, e.g. in the early spring, since the mulch will insulate the cold conditions for several months.
- If beginning in spring, it may be necessary to clear the ground through tillage and then plant into bare soil. The mulch can then be brought around the small plants. It should not be necessary to till again.

2.9.3 Basic horticultural techniques with mulching

- Seeds can be directly sown into the soil. The mulch is raked back and remains removed until the seedlings have reached a size whereby the mulch can be placed back around them by hand.
- Transplants (see chapter 5) can be planted into the soil. The mulch is raked back, the transplants are planted into it and the mulch is placed back around the plants by hand.
- Perennial weeds like dandelions, thistles and docks may push their way through the mulch and may need to be dug out.
- Green manures (see 2.4 and 3.5) can also be used within the mulching system, the mulch being raked back to sow the seeds. When it comes to incorporating the green manure, chop down the plants to soil level and cover with a light-excluding mulch.
- Soil moisture levels are consistently higher under mulch treatments than in tillage systems because of the prevention of evaporation from the soil surface. This is an advantage in drought-prone areas over the undersowing green manures techniques (see 2.6).

2.10 Recommended practice - minimising tillage

Popularised by one of first stockfree-organic growers, R Dalziel O'Brien[11] in the 1950s surface cultivation is a method of minimising tillage. For nearly twenty years

Eliot Coleman[12] has adapted this surface cultivation system in his greenhouses.

2.10.1 The surface cultivation - permanent bed system

A permanent bed system is set up where the beds (which can be one metre wide) are never walked on but can be straddled for ease of picking.

Paths of at least 30cm are set up between each bed for foot traffic.

- Add compost to the surface of the beds prior to the planting of a new crop.
- Instead of tilling, shallowly cultivate the top 1cm of the soil using only a hoe to root up weeds and crop residues. Leave either in situ or removed to the compost heap if bulky.
- Use green manures that are killed by the winter frosts e.g. buckwheat and mustard, which can be hoed aside in spring.
- It would be difficult to use deep-rooting green manures like clover in this system.

Stockfree-Organic Standard 2.2(h) - minimising tillage

Wider environmental impact	Reduced soil erosion.
Advantages for the grower	Retains soil structure. No need for tillage equipment.
Disadvantages for the grower	Does not deal with established weeds.

---

1 ELM FARM RESEARCH CENTRE (1984) The Soil.
2 COLEMAN, E (1995) New Organic Grower. A Master's Manual of Tools and Techniques for the Home and Market Gardener. Chelsea Green publishing.
3 COLEMAN, E (1995) New Organic Grower. A Master's Manual of Tools and Techniques for the Home and Market Gardener. Chelsea Green publishing.
4 COLEMAN, E (1995) New Organic Grower. A Master's Manual of Tools and Techniques for the Home and Market Gardener. Chelsea Green publishing.
5 It is suggested that you contact your local agricultural college to learn ploughing, plough maintenance and secondary cultivation skills.
6 COLEMAN, E (1995) New Organic Grower. A Master's Manual of Tools and Techniques for the Home and Market Gardener. Chelsea Green publishing.
7 Johnny's Selected seeds, 184 Foss Hill Road, RR 1 Box 2580, Albion, Maine, 04910-9731. USA. www.johnnys.com
8 FERN, K (1997) Plants for a Future. Edible & Useful Plants for a Healthier World. Permanent publications.
9 STOUT, R (1961) Gardening Without Work.
10 STOUT, R (1961) Gardening Without Work.
11 DALZIEL OBRIEN R (1956) Intensive Gardening. Faber.
12 COLEMAN, E (1995) New Organic Grower. A Master's Manual of Tools and Techniques for the Home and Market Gardener. Chelsea Green publishing.

Chapter Three

Soil fertility

3.1 Understanding soil fertility

Promoting sustainability is the motivation for this book. As Lady Eve Balfour (founder of the Soil Association) has argued, it is wrong to equate productivity and fertility, because short-term high yields may be at the expense of long-term fertility. So, nowhere, is the concept of sustainability more easily understood than in the context of soil fertility.

If you are working within a closed system; enhancing your soil fertility from resources on your holding, then you are instantly lessening your wider environmental impact. It is doubtful whether most supporters of stockfree-organic systems would want a crop production system that is totally out of their control, depending on purchased materials involving great costs, suppliers and transport networks. This book argues that it is better to be self-reliant, creating a system that does not rely on bought-in products.

The key characteristics of a soil fertility system that will continue indefinitely are:

* maintaining organic matter levels, which will encourage soil biological activity;
* providing crop nutrients indirectly, using relatively insoluble sources, from which nutrients are made available to the plants by the action of soil micro-organisms;
* nitrogen self-sufficiency through the use of legumes and
* effective recycling of organic wastes including crop residues, straw and compost.

The stockfree-organic grower can minimise losses of fertility by preventing erosion (see chapter 2) and nutrient leaching (see 3.5.9) and make the full use of natural recycling processes and biological nitrogen fixation. Unfortunately, the recycling of the nutrients in an organic system can never be one hundred per cent efficient, even if all wastes were returned to the land, as losses from the system are inevitable at points of the cycle. Where these losses are not balanced by the following natural processes:

- chemical weathering of the bedrock;
- rainfall;
- photosynthesis - capturing carbon that will be returned to the soil as organic matter;
- biological nitrogen fixation;
- deep rooting crops accumulating nutrients from the subsoil;

some import of plant nutrients may be necessary. However, the majority can be generated on the holding.

3.2 Role of plants in fertility
Fertility is a term that should be applied to the soil and plants together. Organic matter is captured in the aerial parts of plants that are later returned to the soil and therefore soil derives its capacity for producing life from the plants as much as plants derive their capacity for growth from the soil.

Plants have three ways of feeding through their roots[1]:

1. *Minute hairs* - along every root there is a constant growth of minute hairs, which live for only about three days. As they die, they release proteins and carbohydrates, on which the beneficial soil micro-organisms can feed and in the process make plant food minerals available for absorption by the living rootlets.

2. *Symbiotic fungi (mycorrhizal association)* - live with one end of their bodies reaching in through the bark of the larger roots, extracting sap and energy-providing food and the other gathering nutrients from the soil, which they pass on to the plant that feeds them. One gram of mycelium (dry weight) occupies an area of 4 square metres that gives an assimilating

surface one hundred times larger than that of the roots by themselves. The phosphate intake of roots is three to five times more efficient when they are infected with the fungus.

3. *Main roots (transpiration system)* - absorb moisture-containing plant nutrients directly from the soil without the interaction of soil micro-organisms (bacteria and fungi).

When crops are fed artificially, the plant absorbs the soluble nutrients through the main roots. This can be a wasteful system, since half of the artificial nitrogen fertilisers applied to the soil never makes it into plant tissues. Instead they evaporate or are washed out of the soil, leading to possible nitrate pollution. Feeding plants directly can be compared to a drug addiction, because the crops always require a 'fix' of artificial fertilisers and the soil is merely an inert medium for anchoring crop roots. When the soil micro-organisms have no role, they die and therefore crops in conventional systems can lose their ability to feed indirectly. The manufacture of artificial fertilisers is also very fossil fuel intensive.

By contrast organic systems emphasise the cycling of plant nutrients instead of a linear throughput. Plants in stockfree-organic systems obtain their nutrition using all three methods, with soil micro-organisms releasing nutrients from organic matter and occasional low solubility mineral amendments. It is a slower system but one that can produce bountiful crops without being so dependent on fossil fuels.

3.3 Plant nutrients

A good soil for arable and vegetable production has a good depth of light topsoil, is stone-free, is not too sloping, (but south facing if there is a slope), contains plenty of organic matter, nitrate, phosphate and potash and has a pH value of 6.7. Most growers will not have the ideal soil but, through careful management, they can produce adequate crops.

The Organic Advisory Service at Elm Farm Research Centre[2] offers a soil and compost analysis service. It is important for a stockfree-organic grower to understand the nutrient status of the soil.

Critical nutrients
- Nitrogen (N), phosphorous (P), potassium (K), calcium (Ca), magnesium (Mg), sulphur (S) and chlorine (Cl).
- Up to half a tonne per hectare required.

Macronutrients
- Iron (Fe), manganese (Mn), zinc (Zn), boron (B), copper (Cu), molybdenum (Mo).
- From a few to a few hundred kilograms per hectare required.

Micronutrients or trace elements
- Sodium (Na), silicon (Si), and cobalt (Co).
- Few grams per hectare required.

N,P,K are the most critical elements for crop production. For example, nitrogen is contained in all living things – in proteins and nucleic acids. When crops are sold or eaten away from the holding, the nutrients from the closed cycle are lost.

Table 3.1 Average take-off nutrients levels[3]

	%N	kgN	%P	kgP	%K	kgK
Potatoes 30t/ha	0.32	96	0.06	18	0.4	120
Onions 30t/ha	0.24	72	0.036	11	0.157	47
Carrots 30t/ha	0.18	54	0.036	11	0.341	102
Cauliflowers 30t/ha	0.43	129	0.056	16.8	0.259	78
Courgettes 33t/ha	0.175	58	0.029	10	0.202	67
Lettuce 10t/ha	0.19	19	0.026	2.6	0.265	26.5
Cabbage 40t/ha	0.25	100	0.03	12	0.5	200
Tomatoes 250t/ha (long season, heated)	0.175	438	0.027	67.5	0.244	610
Peas 6t/ha	1	60	0.02	1.2	0.316	19
Grass/clover 45t/ha	0.48	216	0.065	29.3	0.45	202

It is, therefore, important that the stockfree-organic grower can replace lost nutrients. Nutrients are usually absorbed into the plants in the form of small charged particles called ions, because these usually dissolve in water.

Nutrient ions are of two kinds:

Anions, which are negatively charged:
Phosphate (phosphorus combined with oxygen, $PO_4{---}$), sulphate ($SO_4{--}$), nitrate (NO_3), nitrite (NO_2-), and chloride ($Cl-$).

Cations, which are positively charged:
Calcium ($Ca++$), magnesium ($Mg++$), sodium ($Na+$), potassium ($K+$) and iron ($Fe++$ or $Fe+++$) and also ammonium (NH_4+).

The anion nitrate is prone to leaching, as there is no physical force to hold it in the soil. By contrast, the positive cations are held in the soil by negatively charged sites. These absorptive sites are referred to as soil colloids. The ability to exchange the nutrient ions (in a neutral solution) is called the cation exchange capacity (CEC). There are two contributors to the soil's CEC:

• clay particles and
• humus.

Humus is the generic term to describe any organic matter in the soil that has broken down into its later stages of decomposition, for example:

• organic residues reprocessed by soil micro-organisms; protein-like substances, organic acids, carbohydrates, gums, waxes, fats, tannins and lignins;
• high molecular weight humic substances: fulvic acids, humic acids and humin, which are generally resistant to further biological decomposition.

Organic systems that tend to raise humus levels also enhance the CEC of the soil, unless that soil has a large clay fraction with a high CEC anyway. The benefits of a high CEC are that it acts as a bank account, holding large reserves of nutrients and preventing leaching. Humus also ties up certain ions, which otherwise tend to make phosphates insoluble. So, whereas plant-based compost itself does not contain large amounts of major nutrients (typical analysis of

1.5% nitrogen, 1.2% phosphates and 2.1% potash), the humus that is formed from it has an important role to play in making plant nutrients available.

3.3.1 Managing nitrogen

Nitrogen in the soil has six possible routes[4]. The stockfree-organic grower wants to manage the first three and avoid the others.

1. *Mineralisation and use by a subsequent crop* - in relation to plant nutrients mineralisation of elements like nitrogen and phosphorus means the conversion of relatively complex insoluble organic compounds into relatively simple water-soluble inorganic compounds, which can be absorbed by plant roots or leached out of the soil. In organic systems the soil micro-organisms account for about 37% of nitrogen mineralisation[5]. Mineralisation is most active when the soil is at its warmest in the summer months.

2. *Immobilisation* - occurring all the time, nitrogen becomes bound by the soil micro-organisms into proteins and is mineralised later.

3. *Excess mineralisation* - occurs when there is not enough organic matter in the soil. The carbohydrate content of humus provides the energy source for the soil micro-organisms and, if there is insufficient carbohydrate there will be a stage when excess nitrogen ions become available, known as net mineralisation. The crops will have sappy, leggy growth and will be more likely to suffer from pest and disease attack.

4. *Nitrogen lock-up (excess immobilisation)* – a temporary event, lasting for a couple of weeks when turning in a carbon-rich green manure like a cereal (see 2.4.3) or for several years when turning in sawdust with a high C:N ratio.

5. *Leaching* - If there are no plant roots to take up the nitrogen, it will leach away. Nitrate ions are very soluble in water and are quickly leached from the soil by rain or irrigation water. In this way, nitrate is rapidly carried deep down into the soil, where it can no longer be reached by plant roots, or is carried to waterways where it can become a pollutant.

6. **Denitrification** - This typically occurs in anaerobic conditions, where there are no air spaces in the soil because it is either waterlogged and/or compacted. The nitrate ion is converted by denitrifying bacteria into nitrogen gas that then drifts off into the atmosphere. The bacteria are responding to a lack of oxygen for respiration by breaking down the nitrate to meet their oxygen needs.

3.3.2 Recovering P and K

A criticism levelled at stockfree-organic systems is that they do not address phosphate P and potash K shortages.

The problem with phosphorus is lack of mobility. Phosphate has to be in an acceptable form to a plant and, as it cannot move in the soil, the roots have to move to the P. This explains why mycorrhizal association (see section 3.2) will help improve phosphate uptake.

Fortunately potassium is one of more common elements in rocks. Clay soils will usually contain adequate potassium. Sandy and peaty soils have much lower reserves.

In most organic farming publications animal manures are cited as the best available sources of P and K. When using animal manures, it must be remembered that the P and K comes from the grass and animal feed and therefore, whilst improving P and K levels on an individual farm, if the feed is grown off the farm, there is a shortfall somewhere else. Increasing the levels of P and K on one farm simply results in lowering levels on another farm.

The long-term strategy must be to work within closed systems on the individual farm, ensuring that soils have high humus levels, to encourage micro-organism activity to release the nutrients. In stockfree-organic systems:

- adding straw to compost heaps will help improve P and K;
- adding wood ashes to compost heaps will help improve K;
- using deep rooting green manures like lucerne, red clover, lupins and chicory will help bring P and K up from the subsoil;
- mulching and zero tillage present better daytime conditions for crops to take up P and K (see 2.9, 3.6.2 and 6.7);

- the soil pH should be kept between the values of 6.0 and 7.0 to encourage the maximum uptake of P and K;
- mineral amendments (see 3.10) can be used to address shortfalls (with permission from the certifying body);
- potash boosts in the form of liquid comfrey feed (see 3.9.1) can be used for fruiting vegetables but this is prohibited as the main source of fertility.

3.4 Recommended plant-based composts

Soil organic matter is the product of living matter and the source of it. It is an end product of all life processes: animal and human faeces, food processing wastes, domestic wastes, crop or vegetable residues, even dead bodies yet at the same time through the agency of soil micro-organisms it is the beginning of new life.

The stockfree-organic grower can increase the organic matter content of the soil by:

- managing a compost heap outside the cropping area and applying finished compost to the cropping area;
- turning in carbon-rich green manures (see 2.4.1 and 2.4.3) and other plant materials;
- applying mulches (see 2.9, 3.6.2 and 6.7);
- applying chipped branch wood (see 3.8);
- reducing tillage.

Composting organic waste is an important task of the stockfree-organic grower, because the health of the soil depends on the growing treatment it receives.

- See section 2.3 as to how compost improves soil structure.
- See section 2.3 for applying compost.
- See chapter 4 for composting procedures.

3.4.1 Compost application rates

- Plant-based compost should be applied at a rate of up to 25 tonnes per hectare / 10 tonnes per acre / one barrow load per ten metre square each year, according to rotation.

Stockfree-Organic Standard 3.2(a) - Plant-based composts made from materials from the registered holding

Wider environmental impact	Soil rendered inert without organic matter.
	Organic matter (carbon) locked in the soil and not in the atmosphere where it would be adding to greenhouse gases.
	Organic matter returned to soil and not ending up in landfill.
Advantages for the grower in terms of fertility	Adds to the soil humus fraction.
	Enhances CEC, banking a reserve of nutrients.
	Energy for the soil micro-organisms.
	Encourages earthworm populations.
Disadvantages for the grower	Finding enough.
	Managing a heap can be time consuming.
	May need to buy in materials (see section 3.7).

Compost applied to the soil has the indirect benefit of becoming the food source for earthworms and the energy in general for the soil micro-organisms. Earthworms have been burrowing through the earth for about 200 million years. Through their burrows, which may go down as far as seven metres below the surface, they bring up nutrients from the subsoil and keep the soil structure open, creating a multitude of channels which allow the processes of both aeration and drainage to occur.

The earthworm will pull down any organic matter deposited on the soil surface (e.g. compost or plant residues) either for food or when it needs to plug its burrow. In huge numbers they swallow semi-decomposed organic matter and transform it in their gut, with the aid of tiny pieces of grit, into worm casts. Worm casts are up to five times richer in available nitrogen, seven times richer in available phosphates and eleven times richer in available potassium than the soil itself[6]. Surface castings prevent crusting. In conditions where there is plenty of available humus, the weight of casts produced may be greater than 4.5kg per worm per year. The casts contain silicic acid, which is essential to plants for the healthy growth of cell walls.

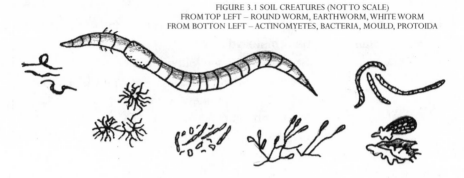

FIGURE 3.1 SOIL CREATURES (NOT TO SCALE)
FROM TOP LEFT – ROUND WORM, EARTHWORM, WHITE WORM
FROM BOTTON LEFT – ACTINOMYETES, BACTERIA, MOULD, PROTOIDA

Year-old compost will also inoculate the soil by adding a whole range of micro-organisms. The role of the microscopic soil life is poorly understood. It is still not even possible to obtain an accurate survey of soil fungi populations. But at least it is known that there are four tonnes of micro-organisms in one acre of fertile soil. The microbes have a role to play in decomposing organic matter, mineralising plant nutrients, making trace elements available to plants, nitrogen fixation, producing substances beneficial for plant growth and helping plants resist attack.

3.5 Recommended – cut and mulched green manure strips, areas or leys[7]

This section outlines green manures that are cut and mulched in situ and then are later incorporated (see 2.4.1 and 2.4.2). Section 3.6 examines green manure areas where the hay is removed.

All soil fertility cannot be derived from plant-based compost. Shortages of raw materials and the problem of selling crops off the holding, combined with

FIGURE 3.2 LEGUMINOUS GREEN MANURES (FIXERS)
LUCERNE AND RED CLOVER

Stockfree-Organic Standard 3.2(b) Recommended - cut and mulched green manure strips, areas or leys

Wider environmental impact	Avoids transporting bulky organic wastes. Organic matter (carbon) locked in the soil and not in the atmosphere where it would be adding to greenhouse gases.
Advantages for the grower in terms of fertility	Nitrogen fixation. Mowing and mulching returns organic matter to the soil. Mowing and mulching provides ideal conditions for earthworm breeding and increases soil micro-organism activity. Deep roots recover P and K from the subsoil.
Disadvantages for the grower	Need to learn green manure management skills for stockfree systems. Possible nitrogen lock-up. Land out of production. Seed can be expensive. Establishment and regular mowing costs.

losses due to leaching and oxidation means that there will always be a shortage of compost available[8]. To maintain short-term organic matter levels in the soil, therefore, growers must also rely on extensive use of green manures, particularly legumes, for nitrogen and deep rooting green manures for the recovery of phosphate and potash from the subsoil.

3.5.1 Legumes for building nitrogen supplies in the soil[9]

Nitrogen-fixing micro-organisms on the roots of clover are the single most important input of nitrogen into organic farming systems in the UK. Nitrogen-fixation is essential to the cycling of nitrogen out of the atmosphere and into the environment occupied by living organisms. There are a group of nitrogen-fixing bacteria called rhizobia that have a special intimate relationship with leguminous host plants – clover, lucerne, trefoil, vetches, peas, beans and pulses.

The rhizobia live in a free-state in the soil and exist quite happily in this way until a legume is planted into the ground close to where they are living. As the legume seedlings develop, their roots start to secrete substances into the soil, which attract the rhizobia nearby. The bacteria eventually enter the roots and stimulate the formation of swellings, called nodules, inside which the microbes multiply. At the same time, the bacteria take on different shapes to such a degree that they no longer look much like the soil rhizobia from which they came. For this reason, in the roots they are called 'bacteroids' and these now have the ability to fix nitrogen from the air.

Nitrogen fixation by different legumes in ideal conditions (kg/ha)[10]:	
Lucerne	300-550
Red clover/grass	230-460
Field beans	155-285
White clover/grass	150-200
Field beans	150-390
Peas	105-245
Lupin	100-150
Vetches	60-90

In exchange for a share of the legume's sugars manufactured by the leaves and stems of the plants, the bacteroids pass on nitrogen in a usable form to the host plants and to adjacent plants. In the case of green manures they will leave a surplus in the soil to be taken up by subsequent crops via rotation.

3.5.2 Carbon-rich green manures for building humus

Incorporating young lush green manures will add immediate nitrogen and stimulate activity in the soil, but will not generally boost the organic matter levels. On the other hand, mature, dry and carbon-rich residues like cereals and straw will take longer to break down and will release nitrogen over a longer period of time. Carbon-rich green manures will decompose faster if they are chopped, shredded and kept moist before incorporation (see 2.4.1 and 2.4.2). To improve long-term recalcitrant organic matter levels chipped branch wood (see 3.8) and green waste composts (see 3.7.1) provide complementary techniques to green manuring.

3.5.3 Green manures for all occasions

Green manures increase fertility and get life back into the soil. Like any organic crops, green manures should not be grown in endless monoculture, as they have their advantages and disadvantages for following crops in rotation.

As well as the nitrogen fixing green manures there are the non-legume green manures that are known as 'lifters'. They mop up available nitrogen directly from the soil, which is later released back into the soil after incorporation.

Table 3.2 Different green manures

Ley before heavy feeders	Red clover, lucerne (pure stand)
	Grass mixes not before potatoes
Maximising nitrogen fixation	Crimson red clover, Vetch
Resistance to foot traffic	White clover, yellow trefoil
Paths	White clover various types
Undersowing vegetables	Red clover, lucerne, vetch, yellow trefoil, cereals
Undersowing protected crops	Yellow trefoil, kent wild white clover
Winter killed	Buckwheat, mustard
Late autumn sowings	Cereals in general especially rye
Weed suppression	Phacelia, rye and buckwheat
Reducing wireworm	Mustard

FIGURE 3.3 NON-LEGUMINOUS GREEN MANURES (LIFTERS)
MUSTARD AND BUCKWHEAT

Table 3.3 Recommended 'fixers' by growers

Green manure	Suitability dates	Field sowing per acre	Hand sowing per metre squared
Lucerne	April - July	5kg	2 grams
Good perennial ley up to 5 years that is drought resistant. Needs a high pH, well drained soil and inoculum to establish. Can be grown as a pure stand.			
Red clover	April - E Sept	3kg - 5kg	1 – 2 grams
Good perennial ley up to 3 years that can tolerate wetter conditions. Roots have many branches and a taproot, high yielding in terms of green material, rapid recovery after mowing. Ensure eelworm free. Can be grown as a pure stand.			
White clover	April - E Sept	2.5 - 4kg	1 – 2 grams
Shallow rooted, low growing clover suitable for paths for up to 9 years. Need strong growing varieties to recover from mowing. Best established in Spring.			
Crimson red	July - E Sept	2.5 - 4kg	1 – 2 grams
Annual, best for N fixing between crops and is usually only grown for 2 – 3 months.			
Vetch	April - E Sept	25 – 50kg	8 – 15 grams
Deep rooted, quickly produces a large weight of green material especially in early spring. Suitable for undersowing when it is to be incorporated the following spring. Does not recover from constant mowing and should only be lightly topped once to control the first flush of weeds.			
Kent W W Clover	April - E Sept	2.5 - 4kg	1 – 2 grams
Low growing clover suitable for undersowing greenhouse crops. Trim with shears.			
Yellow trefoil	April – E Sept	2.5 - 4kg	1 - 2 grams
Low growing annual suitable for undersowing greenhouse crops and very tolerant of shade.			

Table 3.4 Recommended 'lifters' by growers

Green manure	Suitability dates	Field sowing per acre	Hand sowing per metre squared
Cocksfoot grass and chicory	April – late Aug	9kg	3 grams
Strong tap rooted species for improving soil structure and building humus. Can be grown in a ley with red clover or lucerne.			
Ryegrass	Sept -Nov	6kg	2 grams
Aggressive quick growing grass should be mulched back or incorporated before seed heads appear. Good for foot traffic. Often included in ley with red clover.			
Cereal rye	Sept -Nov	75kg	23 grams
Most winter hardy of cereals which will germinate at 3°C. Best root system of annual cereals, can reduce N leaching by two thirds. Incorporate in April when the seed head can be felt at the base of the stem.			
Barley	Sept - Nov	50 –100kg	15 - 30 grams
Less hardy than cereal rye or winter wheat. Likes cool and dry conditions. Produces more biomass than other cereals and seeds are inexpensive			
Oats	Sept -Nov	50 –100kg	15 - 30 grams
More sensitive than barley, but can tolerate wider pH, good on all soil types, fibrous roots.			
Buck wheat	April - E Sept	20 kg	6 grams
Good for summer use and grows quickly, incorporate before it goes to seed. Will grow on infertile soil, frost sensitive.			
Rape	Mar – Sept	6kg	2 grams
Superior at mopping up nutrients, frost sensitive, brassica family and can carry club root.			
Mustard	Mar – Sept	6kg	2 grams
Frost sensitive but provides large quantities of green material in 6 - 8 weeks. Brassica family and can carry club root, can be used to suppress wireworm populations in appropriate rotations, incorporate before flowering.			
Phacelia	April - August	4kg	1 grams
Fern-like leaf for weed suppression. Flowers attractive to beneficial insects especially bees. Incorporate after 2 months.			

3.5.4 Sowing a green manure ley using machinery
Irrespective of scale the ideal sowing conditions for green manures is that the soil should be:

- cleared of any residues;
- made into a fine seedbed which is consolidated with a flat roller before sowing. If the soil is too dry, it will not roll firm enough and there will be insufficient moisture to germinate the seed. If it is too wet, it will not work down fine enough and will give too hard a surface and the seedlings will find it difficult to emerge.
- From the authors' experience, to achieve effective weed control, drilling should be avoided and broadcasting is the best method using spinners or a seed fiddle.

3.5.5 Sowing a green manure area by hand
Timing of sowing:

1. At the beginning of the sowing period (e.g. early May) generate a stale seedbed prior to sowing (see 7.3) and broadcast the seed at the higher seed rate.
2. At the height of the sowing period (summer) e.g. June and July, broadcast the seed at the lower seed rate.
3. At the end of the sowing period (late summer / early autumn) e.g. August and early September broadcast the seed at the higher seed rate.

With all three timings:
- Rake the seed gently into the soil.
- Pat the soil down with a roller, your feet or the end of the rake.

3.5.6 Mowing a green manure ley - 'cut and mulch' technique
The good news is that green manures can generally out-compete the weeds, as long as they are sown evenly. It may be necessary to rogue the odd perennial weed. When managing an area including clover or lucerne it is necessary to have a regime of mowing. The first mowing prevents the annual weeds from going to seed. Subsequent mowing depends on how quickly the plants are growing. It is important to prevent the green manure growing too long or there may be too much material for the mower to process and it might lie on the ground and be difficult to cut. Frequent mowing will ensure

that the mulched material rapidly assimilates into the soil. However, it is a good idea to let strips of the green manure flower to encourage natural predators (see 8.1.1).

Depending on the scale of growing, the equipment needed for mowing is either:

- a tractor-mounted flail mower (ideal for in situ mulching);
- a pasture topper (acceptable for in situ mulching);
- a sit on mower;
- a general garden mower;
- a strimmer;
- a scythe or
- a pair of shears.

The principles of mowing are the same for all scales.

- Make sure that the ground conditions are dry, so that wheels / your feet do not compact the soil.
- Mow several times a year, making the last cut of the year in late September or early October.
- Do not allow the green manure to go to seed.
- Mow tightly - as close as possible to the base of the green manure stems to ensure that the annual weeds are also killed but do not skim the surface.
- If large quantities of material are deposited by the mower, this suggests that the green manure was too long before mowing. Spread the piles of material evenly with a rake so that the clumps do not kill the green manure underneath. Ensure that in future you do not let the ley grow so long.
- Mow from the centre outwards to allow wild mammals and birds to escape (see 9.9).
- Do not mow large areas at once. Insects will migrate to crops when green manure leys are cut and pests like aphids may increase because there is so much raw fertility. Jean Paul Cortens[11] of Roxbury farm suggests leaving areas or strips for the insects to migrate to.

Mowing from April to July can have conservation implications (see 9.8) as ground nesting birds may be sitting on eggs at this time. On a field scale their nests can be marked by bamboo canes and a five-metre mowing exclusion zone can be put around them.

3.5.7 Green manure strips for fertility

Langerhorst method - developed by the Langerhorst family in Austria[12]. This is a technique that involves growing vegetables at fixed row spacings. In early spring, rows of spinach are sown. Between each row of spinach, a different vegetable family is sown or transplanted. When the spinach gets too big, it is cut and left to wilt as mulch. Between every third row there is a green manure strip, which is typically white clover and this also acts as a path. The following season all the rows are moved along by a distance equal to half the row spacing, so that crops are growing where there was either spinach or white clover last year and the green manure is grown where last year's crops were.

Tolhurst technique for onions in the field - Onion sets are planted into a cleared seedbed through black plastic sheeting (which is secured by digging the edges in to the ground) with 30cm strips between the lengths of each plastic sheet. Red clover is sown broadcast into the bare soil left by the tractor wheelings between the onion beds in March / April, where it grows quickly. This has a beneficial effect on the onions, due to the nitrogen transfer between the strips, and also on the subsequent crops in the next year.

Tolhurst technique for courgettes in the market garden - The garden rotation is discussed in detail in section 6.3. In the previous year runner beans on a wide spacing are undersown with red clover. Once the bean haulms have been removed, a stand of red clover remains. The next year several 60cm wide strips are taken out of the red clover, with a pedestrian-operated rotovator, to leave a seedbed. Courgette transplants are planted into the bare earth and regularly hoed to keep down the red clover and the weeds. Once the courgettes are established, the red clover is allowed to grow back, enveloping the crop, with occasional bare patches being undersown with red clover seeds. The red clover is left throughout the following growing season to form a green manure ley, most of which will have been in situ for three years.

Clover strips for mowing - Growing clover in semi-permanent strips next to vegetable beds makes the green manure easier to manage because there is no possibility of root competition with the crops. At the Swedish Agricultural University, Alnarp, and at the Institute of Agricultural Engineering, Vakola, Finland they have developed dedicated mowing and spreading equipment. A strip of clover is mown by an adapted flail mower and then the remnants of the clover are spread onto the vegetable bed to provide mulch around the vegetables.

3.5.8 Planting mature transplants into permanent swards of clover

The Japanese farmers Masanobu Fukuoka (author of The One Straw Revolution) and Yoshikazu Kawaguchi are credited with developing systems of growing crops through established green manures. Their success with the technique might not be applicable to the UK, as flooding in the rainy season in Japan weakens and kills the clover. To apply the clover sward opening technique in the UK needs further research and, therefore, is at present not recommended in this book. At least two small UK on-farm trials have been disappointing, as the roots of the vigorous clovers restricted the tender young transplants. Therefore undersowing is a more reliable technique (see 3.5.10).

3.5.9 Overwinter green manures for fertility

It must be remembered that the *greatest loss of nutrients is due to leaching and not crop off-take*. As seen in Table 3.1 vegetable growing makes heavy demands on the soil and there is no point in building fertility and then allowing it to wash away with the winter rains. Green manures will 'fix nutrients in carbon' in the aerial parts of the plants and, even if the green manure dies over the winter, the nutrients are stored until the soil micro-organisms break them down and are unlikely to be leached.

- The autumn-lifted crops which are not suitable for undersowing (see table 3.6) can be followed by a green manure once the soil is cleared. In field-scale growing this will typically be potatoes and onions.
- Depending on the month it may be possible to sow:
  - clover before early September;
  - cereals from mid September to early November.

Legumes do not fix nitrogen during the winter months. Therefore, non-legumes like cereals are more suited to the role of overwinter cover, as their early growth is vigorous and they can establish themselves quickly.

3.5.10 Undersowing green manures for fertility

Undersowing green manures will, even in a growing crop, add some nitrogen and organic matter to the soil. But its real value comes in ensuring that the soil is covered prior to the winter period, when so many nutrients will be lost from the soil due to leaching. Their use is also likely to favour the following crop.

Preparing for undersowing

Eliot Coleman's[13] tips for successful undersowing include:

• a clean, weed-free seedbed providing the motivation for regular weeding;

Table 3.5 Crops suitable for undersowing[15]

Crop	Height	Green manure	Germination	Optimum
Brassicas	20cm	White clover/ phacelia	April - E Sept	July or later
Leeks	When early leeks are fully grown	Cereals	Sept - Nov	Late Oct
Squashes & courgettes	6 leaves	Red clover	April - E Sept	July
Sweetcorn	25cm	Red clover	April - E Sept	July
Runner beans	50cm	Red clover	April - E Sept	July
Tomatoes	50cm	Yellow trefoil/ Kent Wild White clover	April - E Sept	July
Cucumbers	50cm	Y trefoil/ KWW clover	April - E Sept	July
Melons	6 leaves	Y trefoil/ KWW clover	April - E Sept	July
Aubergine	20cm	Y trefoil/ KWW clover	April - E Sept	July

Table 3.6 Crops not suitable for undersowing	
Potatoes	Too dense foliage
Onions	Cannot tolerate root competition (see 3.5.7 for strip method)
Carrots	Root crops cannot tolerate competition
Parsnips	Too dense foliage
Lettuce	Growing period too short
Winter salads	Cannot tolerate root competition
Spinach etc	Too dense foliage
Celery	Cannot tolerate root competition
Beetroot	Growing period too short – cannot tolerate root competition
Radish/turnips	Growing period too short – cannot tolerate root competition
Swede	Cannot tolerate root competition

- hoeing at least three times before undersowing;
- the last weeding should be the day before undersowing.

Undersowing using a broadcast method

- Field scale – at Tolhurst Organic Produce we grow vegetables on ridges and spring tines are taken between the ridges to aid weeding and to provide a seedbed for the green manures. The crops are then undersown using a seed fiddle.
- Garden scale – crops are hand hoed or cultivated with tines mounted to a two-wheeled tractor to provide the seed bed for the green manure seeds. The crops are then undersown with us holding a container in our hands.

The advantage of broadcasting is speed. The disadvantage is inaccuracy with possible patchy areas of green manure. Also, with crops like cabbages and cauliflowers, green manure seeds may germinate in their hearts.

Undersowing using a drill
Eliot Coleman recommends drilling the green manure, as he does not grow on ridges. He has invented a multi-row pedestrian seed drill which can be

imported through Johnny's Selected Seeds[14]. All five hoppers are filled with either the same seed or a combination of legumes and grasses.

3.6 Recommended - Compost or hay made from green manures grown on the registered holding

The Organic Growers of Durham (OGD) have challenged the traditional practice of supplying nitrogen to crops through rotation, because such systems rely on tillage. Instead of cutting, mulching and incorporating green manures (see 3.5.6) they suggest growers use zero tillage systems where permanent green manure leys are kept separate from the crop growing areas. To maximise the amount of nitrogen fixed, OGD cut the separate green manure ley two or three times during the summer and early autumn and remove the material making it into leguminous-rich hay bales. This material is kept and returned to the separate crop growing areas as mulch. OGD have argued that when green manures are allowed to decay in situ part of the fixed nitrogen passes back into the soil. The consequent increase in available nitrogen in the soil causes the activity of the nitrogen-fixing bacteria in the green manure to slow down, so that the net fixation of nitrogen is less than when the cut material is removed[16].

Old hay fields could be the easiest option for such a system, although it is a restricted practice to use hay from non-organic systems under Stockfree-Organic Standard 3.4 (d). Also, plant-based composts from ungrazed upland meadows are singled out for restriction under Stockfree-Organic Standard 3.4(c) because these are fragile ecosystems prone to erosion and forestry is a more sustainable activity for these areas. The removal of hay is further regulated by the Soil Association Standards where removal is restricted to no more than one year in every four and with permission only being granted if monitored by soil analysis or where the hay is taken from a species-rich meadow that requires low fertility. However, it is not clear whether this Soil Association Standard applies if the hay field has no depletion of fertility because it is being fed e.g. with a plant-based compost treatment.

3.6.1 Organic Growers of Durham technique of separate hay fields for mulching materials

At the Organic Growers of Durham's Low Walworth market garden hay is made from a grass-lucerne hay meadow on the holding and straw is currently being bought in until their zero-tillage wheat production commences. The hay

Stockfree-Organic Standard 3.2(c) – compost or hay made from green manures grown on the registered holding

Wider environmental impact	Closing the system.
	Not transporting bulky organic wastes.
Advantages for the grower	Available source of soil fertility.
	Higher nitrogen fixation.
Disadvantages for the grower	Finding enough material on the holding.
	Possible depletion of the fertility of the hay field.
	Increasing the weed seed bank.

: vegetable crop ratio is about 1:1. A four-course strip mulching rotation (described in section 6.7) has been devised for vegetable growing.

The OGD system involves setting aside an area of land solely for green manure production - a mixture of perennial legume and grass, in this case lucerne with tall fescue. The establishment of the ley needed great care (see 3.5.4). OGD contend that lucerne is perennial and capable of growing for an indefinite period so it is grown as a permanent stand. Whether it will be necessary to plough and re-establish the permanent stand of lucerne is not yet known.

Lucerne is sown with a mixture of non-aggressive grasses, because the grasses:

1. mop up some of the nitrogen fixed by the legume;
2. fill in the gaps between the legume plants and thus helps to suppress weeds and
3. give a much better quality of hay.

Some growers have found ryegrass to be too vigorous[17] as it competes too strongly with the legume. A native English grass like a fescue is, therefore, preferred. The grass should be sown before the legume with a flat rolling in between.

Once established the green manure hay is mown three times a year. The main cut is carried out just as the lucerne is beginning to flower, which gives the maximum yield of nitrogen. In the north of England this occurs at the end of June or beginning of July. However, it may be decided to mow later and sacrifice some fertility for the sake of allowing more time for any ground nesting birds in the meadow to raise their young. This must be decided on the individual case. See 9.8 on how to create mowing exclusion zones.

After the main cut two smaller cuts are carried out as soon as the lucerne has grown back sufficiently to make cutting worthwhile. The second cut could be any time from late July to early September. The last cut is done in early October, so as not to leave too much growth on the green manure crop before the winter. Otherwise the dead vegetation on the ground may retard the development of the crop the following spring. If the weather in early October does not allow for hay-making (equipment needed: mower that puts the material in swaths, machinery that turns the grass to dry and baler), the crop may be silage-wrapped or cut and mulched (see 3.5.6).

In every case the bales are rolled off the meadow as soon as they have been made and are allowed to stand in a convenient place till they are used to mulch the vegetable beds. The mowing and haymaking is repeated year after year without any apparent decrease in yield.

3.6.2 Separate hay fields for compost

Eliot Coleman[18] uses the land on his holding that is either too steep or too rocky or too moist as permanent hay fields to feed his compost heaps. If a stockfree-organic holding does not have these, he recommends renting land in the vicinity. If a hay-made compost is the only source of fertility for the vegetable growing land then a ratio of 1:1 (hay : vegetable crop) should be sufficient, although it is the recommendation of this book that green manures are used in rotation.

3.6.3 Closing the system

As outlined in 3.3.2 the criticisms levelled at animal manures (the shortfall of fertility somewhere) can also be levelled at green manure systems. For example, the hay fields described in 3.6.1 and 3.6.2 could eventually run out of fertility. Green manures bring nitrogen and carbon (captured from the atmosphere) into the growing system, but do not physically create other nutrients, unless their deep roots bring up minerals from the subsoil.

The Khadigher Community in the USA can be seen as an example of good

practice for the non-commercial grower. Will Bonsall[19] writes that the
community has an adjoining forest and uses leaves, small twigs and humanure
(prohibited for commercial crops under Stockfree-Organic Standard 3.5(d))[20]
to make rough compost for the hay fields. Products from the forest are also
used on the vegetable fields.

The problem is that, if you trace backwards, there is a depletion of the
fertility of the forest but this may be an ecosystem that can withstand some
removal. The widespread removal of leafmould is not, however,
recommended. The crops at the Khadigher Community are consumed on the
farm and the return of humanure to the hay fields means that it operates in an
essentially closed system. This has allowed the former dairy farm gradually to
improve its fertility with no brought-in nutrients.

3.7 Plant-based materials for fertility from outside the registered holding

Closing the cycle of fertility is difficult for all organic farmers and growers.
Livestock farmers import feed, arable and vegetable growers import manure.
With the demands of commercial cropping it may be necessary to import
some organic material. Under Stockfree-Organic Standard 3.3 the registered
stockfree-organic grower is permitted to use plant-based composts made from
materials outside the registered holding, providing that they are from another
certified organic system.

However, this will prove difficult. It would be unwise for one organic farm to
part with organic material to enhance the fertility of another farm, whilst
allowing their fertility to disappear. Getting hold of certified organic straw is
very difficult.

Therefore, some level of compromise may be necessary for commercial
stockfree-organic growers to replace fertility lost though cropping. At the
same time this may have a wider environmental benefit by finding a market
for what are essentially waste products currently going to landfill, like
householders' green waste. The workers co-operative Growing with Grace
in Clapham[21], North Yorkshire, are currently running a community
composting scheme in conjunction with Craven District Council, whereby
all the local garden green wastes are being collected and brought to the

---

Stockfree-Organic Standard 3.3 and 3.4 Plant-based materials from outside the registered holding

Wider environmental impact	Working outside a closed system. Transportation. May find a market for waste products that otherwise would go to landfill.
Advantages for the grower in terms of fertility	Save growers time and land. Delivered in a useful form (e.g. baled straw).
Disadvantages for the grower	Cost. Possible pathways for contaminants.

---

market garden by the council collection services. The workers' co-operative are composting the material on site and the finished compost is being applied to the glasshouse soils.

The main soil fertility inputs (i.e. over 51%) should be generated on the registered holding. In the future this is likely to be subject to regulation by the certification bodies. Sections 3.7 and 3.8 describe plant-based materials that can fill a fertility shortfall and are suitable for stockfree-organic systems under restriction. If you are a registered grower, before using any of the following restricted materials it is important to obtain written permission from the approved certification body. Decisions will be made on a case-by-case basis. The following will be taken into account:

Pathways into the stockfree-organic growing system for the following contaminants:

- animal manures and dead animals;
- pathogens;
- heavy metals;
- toxic substances;
- synthetic substances;
- genetically modified organisms (GMOs) and
- radioactive substances.

3.7.1 Plant-based composts made from green waste e.g. garden waste collected by local authorities

These are restricted under Stockfree-Organic Standard 3.4(a) because they cannot be assured to be free from toxic or genetic engineering contaminants or animal residues.

- Most local authorities have sites where garden waste is shredded and composted and the resultant compost is sold as 'soil conditioner'. This is because they cannot guarantee the quality of the compost. The compost is often very woody and several of the heaps that the author has seen have been poorly managed, e.g. weeds are allowed to grow on the surface and plastic is in the windrows.
- However, green waste composts attaining the Soil Association symbol have quality control at the input and management stages and so these composts are preferred. Their heavy metal contamination levels will also be compliant with both the Soil Association and Stockfree-Organic Standards (see 10.3.2).
- If the product does not attain the Soil Association certified product symbol, then certified growers will need their supplier to sign an 'Animal-Free Declaration.'
- The main constituents of green waste composts are hedge and tree removals, woody clippings and grass clippings.
- The cost of haulage can be expensive for what may be an essentially a low quality product.

HDRA Consultants conducted a four-year programme 'The Wyvern Green Waste Compost Trials' researching the performance of three green waste composts (garden wastes) from different local authorities. Generally speaking, green waste composts have half the nitrogen and phosphates and a third of the potassium of farm yard manure but comparable organic matter levels. Larger amounts of the most stable form of carbon lignin tended to be detected in the green waste compost than in manures, suggesting that adding compost will have a long-lasting effect on the recalcitrant organic matter levels.

Even at triple application rates none of the green waste composts exceeded the annual permitted heavy metal levels according to the UK Sludge regulations and none of the composts tested contained significant amounts of metal, glass, plastic, salmonella or E.coli pathogens. Stockfree-organic growers may therefore feel that green waste compost can make up the fertility shortfall. However, they tend to contain a lot of woody materials and therefore it is important to request that they have been through a fine mesh. Even still they may need sieving, especially if you want to use them in a propagation mix.

Community composting in an urban setting has often involved collecting raw vegetable wastes from householders in built-up areas. In the wake of foot and mouth there have been worries about such collections. Householders' kitchen waste, even if this is raw vegetable wastes from a vegan household, is classed as catering waste and is covered by the Animal By-products Order (ABPO), although the legal situation is changing at the time of writing.

ABPO does not prevent community composting to create plant-based compost. It just makes the whole process more difficult, stipulating that the composting has to take place under cover and has to reach 60°C for two days. However, bulk collecting of green wastes from retailers, e.g. greengrocers or garden wastes from householders should not be subject to ABPO and this will prove less onerous for a stockfree-organic holding. There is considerable funding to encourage community composting. For more information contact the Community Composting Network[22].

3.7.2 Leafmould collected by local authorities / parks contractors

- Leafmould is restricted under Stockfree-Organic Standard 3.4 (b) because it cannot be assured to be free from the toxic residues of road traffic or from dog faeces.
- The widespread collection of leafmould from woodlands and forests is not recommended. Trees feed themselves with humus from their own leaves. This is why foresters do not sell leafmould.
- Most local authorities or their contractors collect leaves from the roads and pavements. These are not suitable for stockfree-organic growing because they are likely to be contaminated with heavy metals from traffic fumes.
- Teams from the local authority and contractors will be charged with just clearing the parks of leaves in autumn. This is a better source of leafmould and it may be possible for them to deliver leaves, as it relieves them from the cost of skipping. These leaves will be contaminated with litter and occasional dog faeces, but the pathways for other contaminants are low.

3.7.3 Plant-based composts from ungrazed upland meadows

These are restricted under Stockfree-Organic Standard 3.4(c), because upland meadows are fragile ecosystems prone to erosion. Forestry is a more sustainable activity for these areas. Whilst the pathways for contaminants are very low, the wider environmental reasons make it important that a stockfree-organic grower avoids these materials.

3.7.4 Hay bales from conventional farming systems

Conventional hay is restricted under Stockfree-Organic Standard 3.4(d) because organic systems should not rely on the inputs from conventional farming. See section 3.6.1 and 3.6.2 as to their treatment.

3.7.5 Straw bales from conventional farming systems

Conventional straw is restricted under Stockfree-Organic standard 3.4(d), because organic systems should not rely on conventional farming inputs. Conventional barley straw is the only outside input into the growing system at Tolhurst Organic Produce and conventional wheat straw the only input into the system at Organic Growers of Durham.

- Straw has lower weed content than hay and its hollow stems can help aerate a compost heap.
- Barley straw can bring P and K into the system and is generally grown with little chemical input, although it is important to enquire what chemicals have been used.
- Small square bales are easier to handle for composting and they can also make the composting bays and potato clamps.
- Round bales are easier for mulching, as they can be rolled out, but are very heavy and require at least three people to move them.

3.7.6 Plant wastes and by-products, from food processing industries e.g. spent hops and oil seed cake

Plant wastes and by-products are restricted under Stockfree-Organic Standard 3.4(e), because organic systems should not rely on the inputs from the conventional manufacturing sector. After hops have been used in the brewing process, the later stages of the process are not always stockfree, as many breweries still use fish bladder extract for clarifying the beer. It is important to enquire whether any animal by-products have been used. If plant wastes from food processing industries are not contaminated with animal by-products, they make a suitable material for composting and mulching.

3.7.7 Self-collected seaweed (see also 3.9.3)[23]

Self-collected seaweed is restricted under Stockfree-Organic Standard 3.4(e) as the stockfree-organic growers need to show that it is collected away from a pathogen contamination source e.g. raw sewage outlet, a heavy metal source, e.g. industrial effluent or a radioactive contamination source, e.g. nuclear power station. These are important considerations for the stockfree-organic grower, but once it is established that the contamination levels are low, seaweed is a good source of fertility. Some have argued that, since much sewage ends in marine eco-systems, it can be seen as a way of reclaiming lost fertility from the sea to the land.

It is the brown seaweeds that are most often washed-up on British beaches. The two commonest types are the Laminarias (long, flat fronds) and the bladderwracks (Fucus species). Loose seaweed can be collected from the sea or, if it is newly washed up, from the shore. In this state the salt levels are low and will cause no problems in the soil. Old weed that has lain above the high water mark for some time should not be used as it will be very high in salt. Living seaweed should never be removed from rocks. Seaweed makes excellent mulch, because it is free of contamination from weed seeds and plant pests and diseases. It is not a good idea to make a compost heap purely out of seaweed, as this may turn slimy and smelly (see chapter 4 for best composting practice).

A typical analysis shows nitrogen, phosphate and potassium levels roughly comparable to farm yard manure (slightly lower in phosphate) plus an impressive array of other minerals, trace elements, vitamins, amino acids, plant hormones and carbohydrates. The advantages of using seaweed go beyond the nutrients it adds to the soil, because it is also high in alginates that help make plants healthy, although the mechanism is not fully understood. Trials suggest that crops treated with a root or foliar spray, show increased resistance to red spider mite, aphids, eelworm, grey mould and viruses.

3.8 Chipped branch wood and soil fertility[24]

The usefulness of woodchips and prunings is a subject that is certain to provoke a lively discussion between growers. As mentioned in 3.6.3 the Khadigher community in the USA add woody prunings to their compost heaps and later apply the rough compost to the fertility-building hay pastures. The rough compost is applied to the surface and is not turned in with tillage, as the hay meadows are a permanent stand.

The difficulty is that incorporating sawdust, shavings or bark into the soil will lock up nitrogen for annual organic crops for many years. To be in equilibrium with the soil, organic materials need a C:N ratio of about 10:1 (good quality compost), but trunk wood has a ratio of between 300:1 to 600:1.

However, there is a distinction between trunk wood and chipped branch wood. Chipped branch wood:

- is made from deciduous trees in full leaf whose twigs / stems have a diameter of less than 7cm;
- have a lower C:N ratio (between 30:1 to 150:1) than trunk wood;
- have a higher protein content than trunk wood, with all the amino acids, plus sugar, cellulose, pectin and starch.

The issues with nitrogen immobilisation are not as critical with chipped branch wood because:

1. immobilisation is less than might be expected because the carbon supply in the wood is protected by lignin and the C:N ratio of branch wood is relatively low;
2. in the autumn and winter immobilisation is beneficial, because it mops up excess nitrate that would otherwise be lost through leaching;
3. immobilisation of nitrogen will benefit a leguminous green manure crop by stimulating it to fix more nitrogen from the air;
4. by the following season, when the next crop is grown, the immobilised nitrogen will be being released into the soil again.

Chipped branch wood also adds to the recalcitrant organic matter which takes a long time to degrade and therefore helps provide good soil structure. On the other hand green manures just tend to add to the labile organic matter which is consumed within months by the soil's micro-organisms. Green manuring and chipped branch wood are therefore complementary techniques with the labile part constituting a temporary larder of organic matter, whilst the recalcitrant part is a more permanent store.

The following recommendations for the use of chipped branch wood as a soil amendment are taken from Gilles Lemieux[25], the Canadian forestry scientist who has done most of the research on the subject. A few rows of quick-growing poplars, ash or alders could be reserved for the purpose of providing chipped branched wood, although it is important to observe the following conditions:

- apply in autumn or early winter with a muck spreader or by hand to prevent the worst effects of nitrogen immobilisation and before the soil conditions get too wet;
- apply in rotation before a green manure ley or an overwinter green manure that is followed by a crop that does not require a high level of fertility (e.g. carrots);
- chip the wood to small pieces, no larger than a few millimetres thick and a centimetre or two in length;
- do not compost the chips because much of the useful energy will be lost;
- do not let them heat up in a pile;
- spread immediately after chipping on the soil to a thickness not exceeding 200m³ / ha in the first application and around 50m³ / ha thereafter. This equates with between 20 and 50 cubic metres to the hectare annually. At 50% humidity a cubic metre of chipped wood weighs about 400kg, so on a small scale we are talking about 1 - 2kg per square metre per year or 4 - 8kg per square metre every four years;
- the chips are not a mulch and therefore need to be in very close contact with the soil in order to be decomposed quickly by soil micro-organisms,
- mix the chips with the top 5cm of soil using a spring-tined harrow or a rake;
- do not bury too deeply, because the appropriate organisms are aerobic (they need air) and are most active near the soil surface. For the same reason do not apply to waterlogged or non-aerated soils;
- on soils that have been intensively cultivated the populations of the micro-organisms that decompose wood may be very low, so, at the time of the first application of chipped branch wood, it is recommended to inoculate the soil with these organisms. Leafmould can be used for this purpose and should be applied to the soil at a rate of 10g – 20g per square metre. The

best leafmould is freshly collected from the floor of a deciduous forest at a depth of about 5cm;

- a week or two after the chipped wood application a green manure can be sown.

3.9 Supplementary nutrient fertilisers

Stockfree-Organic Standard 5.1 Permitted soluble fertilisers and alginates for supplementary purposes only

Wider environmental impact	Closed system.
Advantages for the grower in terms of fertility	Home made comfrey juice etc. useful for fruiting crops.
Disadvantages for the grower	Time consuming. Benefits have not been scientifically quantified.

3.9.1 Comfrey and other plant preparations

Comfrey is a perennial plant from the forget-me-not family. It has been promoted by Lawrence D Hills and HDRA - the Organic Association for decades as a foliar feed for fruiting crops and is permitted (not recommended) under Stockfree-Organic Standard 5.1(a). It is feeding the plant directly and therefore is at odds with the requirement in organic systems to feed the soil.

Comfrey is, however, excellent on the compost heap or for surface mulching, as it has a C:N ratio of 9.8 :1, which matches the equilibrium of the soil. Comfrey is a plant food collector, but comfrey liquid does not contribute to humus. Compared to farm yard manure it has double the percentage of potash.

Comfrey beds should be in full sun and, as they will last for twenty years, you need to find a place where they can grow on undisturbed. They can be propagated through root division of established plants. It is recommended that they be grown through weed-suppressing mulch. Growers often use black woven plastic. Plant them at a spacing of 60cm apart.

Comfrey liquid extract can be made
at any time of the year when the
leaves are available.

- Place leaves in a water butt or
  bucket, pressing them well down.
- The comfrey will blacken and
  decay and there will be a brown
  liquid to draw from the bottom.
- Let the concentrate drip out
  by itself.
- This concentrated liquid can be
  diluted 10:1 (10 parts water to 1
  comfrey concentrate).
- Use diluted extract for watering
  / foliar-feeding tomatoes when
  they are setting their first truss.
- Comfrey concentrates store well.

Nettle tonics and herb tonics, e.g.
camomile and tansy, can be prepared in the same way.

3.9.2 Compost tea extracts

Compost tea is the deliberate placing of compost in water to extract beneficial
micro-organisms to add to the soil and has been shown to have an ability to
suppress fungal diseases. It contains soluble nutrients (both organic and
inorganic) and micro-organisms including bacteria, fungi, protozoa and
nematodes and is a probiotic as opposed to an antibiotic.

Poor compost means poor tea. Best composting practice involves (see chapter 4):

- using select ingredients, including crop wastes, grass clippings, legume-
  rich hays and straw;
- mixing plant-based ingredients: 'greens' and 'browns';
- composting plant-based materials and leafmould separately;
- building a heap of sufficient volume - at least one cubic metre;
- turning the heap to assist with aeration;

- monitoring temperature rises;
- covering the heap or windrow to prevent it from becoming waterlogged;
- allowing for the compost to mature (one year).

Using water to extract compost tea can be done in any number of ways. The most common methods include (1) suspending the compost on a screen and running water through it[26] or (2) placing compost in a hessian bag in a water butt. The ratio of water to compost is typically 4 parts water to 1 part compost. The resulting liquid must be used soon after it is made and must not turn anaerobic.

Compost teas are applied to soil or to plant foliage. Those applied to soil will move into the root zone and affect the rhizosphere of the plant. Those applied to leaf surfaces will typically support beneficial organisms on the foliage, both through inoculation and supply of nutrients. The tea can be applied through the irrigation system. This is not yet commonly used in UK organic food production but is likely to become more popular, especially in protected cropping. More information can be gained from www.soilfoodweb.com. Compost tea must not be confused with compost leachate.

3.9.3 Manufacturers of seaweed fertilisers who have signed 'Animal-free declarations'

One excellent treatment for any suspected mineral shortage is feeding the soil with seaweed meal or seaweed foliar preparations. (These should not be confused with calcified seaweed which is a restricted product because it is from the temperate-oceans equivalent of coral reefs). Seaweed contains a wide range of trace elements, including boron, bromine, calcium, copper, iodine, magnesium, manganese, phosphorus, potassium and sodium. Spray and meal forms of seaweed are available from the following suppliers who have signed 'Animal free declarations'.

- Maxicrop (UK) Ltd – contact M Garner, PO Box 6027, Corby, NN17 1ZH. www.maxicrop.co.uk T 01405 762777
- Glenside Organics Ltd – contact J Robertson, Block 2, Unit 4, Bandeath Industrial Estate, Throsk, FK7 7XY. T 01786 816655
- Seagreens Ltd – contact S Ranger, 1 The Warren, Handcross, West Sussex, RH17 6DX.

Table 3.7 Seaweed fertilisers

Name of Product (Supplier)	Product descriptions	Use	Category in the Stock-free-Organic Standards
Maxicrop	Maxicrop original Maxicrop concentrate Maxicrop Viva Maxicrop Meal	Liquids are foliar spray and root drench Meal - soil conditioning	Permitted under Stockfree-Organic Standards 5.1(c) and (d) but Restricted by Soil Association Standards
Marinure & maerit (Glenside)	Marinure - liquid seaweed extract Maerit – concentrated seaweed extract	Foliar spray and root drench	Permitted under Stockfree-Organic Standards 5.1(c) and (d) but Restricted by Soil Association Standards
Seagreens	Seagreens agricultural puree Seagreens agricultural granules	Foliar spray / seed soak Granules – soil conditioning, compost activator	Permitted under Stockfree-Organic Standards 5.1(c) and (d) but Restricted by Soil Association Standards

Stockfree-Organic standard 5.3 and 5.4 Permitted and restricted mineral amendments

Wider environmental impact	Non-renewable resource. Fossil fuel intensive. Mining damages local environments. Transportation.
Advantages for the grower in terms of fertility	May be necessary to grow crops.
Disadvantages for the grower	Cost.

3.10 Mineral amendments

Organic Growers of Durham have argued that the use of mineral amendments is not sustainable because open cast mining destroys local environments and their transportation is fossil-fuel intensive. At the same time, they recognise that occasionally growers have to make compromises to avoid crop failures, which may justify one-off applications. However, if other recommended practices are followed, stockfree-organic systems should not rely on mineral amendments.

3.10.1 Permitted and restricted amendments

Table 3.8 Mineral amendments and their classification

Deficiency	Indicator	Permitted remedies under standard 5.3	Restricted remedies under standard 5.4 – apply to certification body
Phosphorus	Very dark green leaves with a tendency to develop purple colours, stunted.	Tunisian rock phosphate Calcined aluminium phosphate rock (Redzlaag).	

Deficiency	Indicator	Permitted	Restricted
Potassium	Yellow streaks in the leaves	Wood ashes in the compost heap.	Sulphate of potash - exchangeable K levels must be below index 2 (100mg / litre) and clay content less than 20%.
Magnesium – calcium	Yellow drying and reddening of older leaves while veins remain green	Limestone. Dolomite limestone. Gypsum / calcium sulphate. Foliar feed epsom salts (for acute deficiency). Magnesium rock (including Kierite).	Calcium chloride. Industrial lime from sugar production. Calcified seaweed.
Sulphur	Younger leaves turn yellow and then all the leaves turn yellow	Gypsum	Sulphur.
Boron	Soil test - canker / curd browning	More compost / less lime.	Direct application for extreme cases only.
Copper	Top leaves wilt and do not recover		Direct application for extreme cases only.
Iron & Manganese	Pale green leaves	More compost less lime.	Direct application for extreme cases only.
Molybdenum	Soil test		Direct application for extreme cases only.
Cobalt	Soil test		Direct application for extreme cases only.
Selenium	Soil test		Direct application for extreme cases only.
Zinc	Same as copper may have a bitter after taste		Direct application for extreme cases only.

N.B. mineral deficiencies can be confused with plant diseases (see 8.17 and chapter 11 for individual crop problems.)

3.10.2 Phosphate application rates every four years.
- Low fertility soil - 5 tonne per hectare / 2 tonne per acre
- Maintenance application 2.5 tonne per hectare / 1 tonne per acre

3.10.3 Manufacturers of potash fertilisers who have signed 'Animal-free declarations'
- WL Dingley – contact B Urbanski, Buckle St, Honeybourne, Evesham, Worc. WR11 7QE. T / F 01386 830242.

Table 3.9 Potash fertilisers

Company	Product	Description	Category
Cumulus (W.L. Dingley)	Cumulus K	Kali vinasse, sugar beet industry by-product	Permitted under SOS 5.1(e) and Permitted by Soil Association Standards
Vitax	Pelleted fertilisers Vitax natural high K	Based on kali vinasse, Keiserite and calcified seaweed	Restricted under SOS 5.4(a) and restricted by Soil Association Standards
Seagreen K (Glenside)	Calcified seaweed and rock phosphate		Restricted under SOS 5.4(a) and restricted by the Soil Association standards

- Vitax Ltd – contact C Platt, Owen street, Coalville, Leics. LE19 3DE. www.vitax.co.uk T 01530 510060
- Glenside Organics Ltd – contact J Robertson, Block 2, Unit 4, Bandeath Industrial Estate, Throsk, FK7 7XY. T 01786 816655

3.10.4 Liming

Lime has two functions - supplying calcium and correcting an over-acid soil. It is necessary to correct an over acid soil because:

- the majority of plant nutrients are only available within a pH range of 6.2 to 6.8;
- the soil micro-organisms are most effective within a pH range of 6.2 to 6.8;
- pH below 6.0 is not suitable for earthworms or soil micro-organisms;
- legumes will not establish below 6.0 and
- nitrogen fixation by legumes and bacteria is most effective within a pH range of 6.2 and 6.8.

Liming application should aim to bring the soil to a pH of 6.7 and it will be necessary to take advice as to how much lime you will need. Dolomite limestone has the added advantage of containing magnesium.

3.11 Prohibited materials for fertility

Stockfree-Organic Standard 3.5 Prohibited as sources of fertility	
Wider environmental impact	Non-renewable.
	Fossil fuel intensive.
	Pathways for contaminants.
Advantages for the grower	Higher status of stockfree-organic food.
Disadvantages for the grower	Cost

3.11.1 Prohibited materials

Under Stockfree-Organic Standard 3.5 the following sources of fertility are prohibited from stockfree-organic systems:

(a) Products of animal or fish origin
(b) Manures, slurry or urine from any animals including livestock, sanctuary animals or domestic animals
(c) Worm compost
(d) Human faeces and urine
(e) Human tissues
(f) Sewage sludge
(g) Extracted peat (as a general soil amendment)
(h) Materials containing GMOs or their derivatives
(i) Radioactive materials
(j) Synthetic fertilisers
(k) Soluble fertilisers as the main source of fertility

In the wake of BSE, the reason for prohibiting slaughterhouse by-products has tended to strike a chord with the British public. However, prohibiting manures seems to challenge millennia of conventional agricultural practice. The problem is that, even if manure from organic animals is superior to manure from conventional animals, there is just not enough organic manure to go around. Traditional organic systems have long been propped up with conventional manures, providing pathways for contaminants.

Under EC regulation 2092/91, which regulates the use of the word 'organic', the use of humanure and urine is prohibited. It was the general view of the Standards Working Group that carefully treated humanure and urine, especially from vegans, should be permitted as an input into certified stockfree-organic systems and this is an area in which to lobby for a change in the law.

70 Growing Green

1 Information adapted from HILLS L (1977) Organic Gardening. Penguin Books.
2 The Organic Advisory Service, Elm Farm Research Centre, Hamstead Marshall, Newbury, Berkshire, RG20 0HR. 01488 657600
3 Taken from BLAKE F (1987) Organic Farming and Growing. Crowood Press.
4 Information adapted from LAMPKIN, NH (1990) Organic Farming. Farming Press and KING, J (1997) Reaching for the Sun: How Plants Work. Cambridge University Press.
5 HUNT H (1987) Biology and Fertility of Soils 5: 57-68.
6 REGUNWURM (2000) reprinted in Growing Green International. No 6 page 9.
7 Information about green manures also from: Eliot Coleman – New Organic Grower; Organic Growers of Durham; Alan Schofield – Growing with Nature; Cotswold Seeds; Johnny's Selected Seeds, a US-based seed company; University of California SAREP cover crop database (www.sarep.ucdavis.edu).
8 TOLHURST I (2002) reprinted in Growing Green International. No 9 page 22 with permission from the Soil Association.
9 KING, J (1997) Reaching for the Sun: How Plants Work. Cambridge University Press.
10 KAHNT, G (1983) Gründüngung. DLG Verlag, Frankfurt taken from Blake (1999).
11 CORTENS J (2004) Fertility Management at Roxbury Farm - a case study. SAC Blackboard.
12 MARGARETE LANGERHORST INTERVIEW (2001) Growing Green International. No.8 page 13.
13 COLEMAN, E (1995) New Organic Grower. A Master's Manual of Tools and Techniques for the Home and Market Gardener. Chelsea Green publishing.
14 Johnny's Selected Seeds, 955 Benton Avenue, Winslow, Maine 04901-2601 USA. www.johnnyseeds.com
15 TOLHURST I (2002) Undersowing Green Manures in Vegetable Crops. In Growing Green International no.9 page 23 reprinted with kind permission of the Soil Association.
16 HAGMEIER, H.U. Uber die Stickstoffversorgung von Winter-weizen and Winterroggen durch Leguminosenvorfruchte auf einem viehlos Betrieb.

Doctoral thesis at Hohenheim University. LOGES, R and TAUBE, F. (1999). Ertrag and N-Fixierungsleistung unterschiedlich bewirtschafteter Futterleguminosenbestande, in: HOFMANN, H. and MULLER, S. (eds.), Vom Rand zur Mitte: Beitrage zur 5. Wissenschaftstagung zum okologischen Landbau, Berlin.
17 Personal communication with Organic Growers of Durham.
18 COLEMAN, E (1995) New Organic Grower. A Master's Manual of Tools and Techniques for the Home and Market Gardener. Chelsea Green publishing.
19 BONSALL W (1997) The Khadigher Community. Ethical Farming in Action. VOHAN News Vol 1 page 6, Khadigher. Towards Self-sufficiency and Biodiversity VOHAN News Vol 2 , page 5.
20 Under EC regulation 2092/91, which regulates the use of the word 'organic', the use of humanure in any form of commercial organic growing (that is growing out of the site of the consumer) is prohibited. It was the general consensus of the standards working group that carefully treated humanure, especially from vegans, should be permitted as an input into certified stockfree-organic systems and is an area that should change.
21 HALL J (2003) Growing with Grace – Friends with the Earth the Quaker Ethic in Action. Growing Green International. Vol 11, page 24.
22 Community Composting Network, 67 Alexandra Road, Sheffield, S2 3EE Tel/Fax: 0114 2580483, E-Mail: ccn@gn.apc.org.
23 The following information about seaweed is taken from HDRA - the Organic Association fact sheets and is reprinted with their kind permission.
24 VEGAN ORGANIC NETWORK Info sheet 9 Chipped Branch Wood by Dave of Darlington.
25 LEMIEUX, G. (1997). Fundamentals of Forest Ecosystem Pedogenetics: an Approach to Metastability through Tellurian Biology. On website www.forestgeomat.for.ulaval.ca/brf. This information was summarised by the Organic Growers of Durham (2005) Chipped branch wood information sheet for the Vegan Organic Network.
26 INGHAM, E. (1999) What is Compost Tea? Biocycle 3: 74-75.

Chapter Four

Composting Procedures

4.1 Introduction

This chapter explains the process of making well-made compost. Composting is a natural biochemical process of decomposition. It is possible for every stockfree-organic grower to produce the darkest, nutrient-rich, earth-smelling compost. Adding well-made compost to the soil will ensure a healthy soil.

4.1.1 Why compost?

Before incorporating plant materials into the soil, it is better to compost for the following reasons.

Fresh materials:

- can act as a breeding ground for diseases, molluscs and competing animals;
- can induce nitrogen lock-up (see 3.3.1) once incorporated;
- can produce short-term leachate, which can inhibit plant growth especially with young seedlings.

Composting on the other hand:

- converts the soluble nutrients in fresh materials into a more stable form, preventing nutrient leaching;
- mixes materials giving a more balanced end-product;
- can kill weed seeds, pests and diseases, if carried out properly;

- reduces the bulk of the materials, making it easier to handle;
- plant nutrients can be stored until they are required.

By applying compost to your soil, your crops will grow better. The compost:

- feeds the soil life;
- helps the soil retain nutrients;
- increases earthworm populations;
- suppresses disease and inoculates the soil;
- produces beneficial hormones for plant growth;
- improves drainage and provides air pockets for the crop roots to grow in.

- See section 2.3 for applying compost to maintain soil structure and recommended levels.
- See section 3.3 for compost application rates to maintain soil fertility and recommended levels.

There are also disadvantages to composting:

- consumes time and energy;
- results in the loss of nutrients in the materials;
- adds to carbon releases into the atmosphere.

There are also situations where composting is impractical, for example 'trimmings' during harvesting should be left on the soil surface as a mulch, providing a good habitat for earthworms. Also there are cases where the post-harvest residues of crops are better:

- left on to grow on (e.g. allowing purple sprouting broccoli to flower) as they will attract beneficial insects or
- left in situ over winter (e.g. sweetcorn) as they will harbour predatory insects like beetles.

Ultimately they will be mown off with a flail mower prior to incorporation.

4.1.2 Support organisations to promote on-farm composting

The Composting Association[1] was formed in 1995 and is the UK's membership organisation that researches and promotes best practice in composting and the uses of composts.

The On-Farm Composting Network[2], based at Harper Adams University, provides training and technical advice on all aspects of composting.

The Community Composting Network[3] – provide advice and support to the community composting sector. They help on the practical side getting people involved, publicity, fundraising and Health and Safety issues.

HDRA – the Organic Association[4] - conducted a four-year research programme 'The Wyvern Green Waste Compost Trials' investigating the performance of three green waste composts from different local authorities with favourable results.

The Organic Resource Agency (ORA)[5] collaborated with Sainsbury's and Waitrose to develop a 'zero waste' disposal system for biodegradable waste from stores.

4.2 Recommended – composting plant-based materials and leafmould separately

Autumn fallen leaves do not contain the right type of carbohydrates to heat a heap. The carbohydrates in the summer leaves return to the tree in the autumn and are stored in the twigs for next year's leaves. The autumn leaves consist mainly of hemi-celluloses and lignins, which break down through a fungal as opposed to the largely bacterial process of the compost heap. The compost heap is covered to provide the ideal aeration and moisture conditions for the bacteria, but the leafmould bin is left open to the elements. Leafmould takes about three years to break down and when added to the soil provides lasting humus. It is also an excellent replacement for peat in propagation composts.

4.2.1 Planning a composting operation for plant-based materials

Successful composting of plant-based materials requires planning. The compost windrow or heap needs to be sited conveniently, especially for vehicle access or a wheelbarrow. Hard standing is essential for generating large quantities of compost to avoid making a quagmire. For the ultimate in housing and convenience a pole-barn structure should be erected. Shelter

FIGURE 4.1 LEAFMOULD BIN

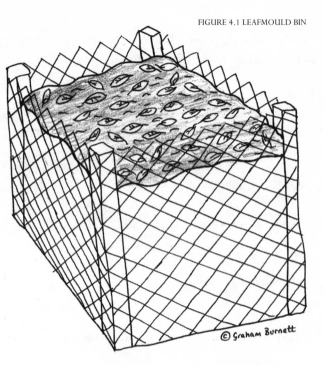

from the wind avoids heaps cooling down too fast, particularly those made later in the year.

Apart from the space needed for the compost heaps themselves you must allow the same area again for turning the heaps and room for tipping trailers and wheelbarrows. The grower managing up to twenty tonnes a year can cope with a fork, but beyond that serious consideration must be given to a tractor and loader or specialist windrow-making equipment.

Stockfree-Organic Standard 4.2(a) – composting plant-based materials and leafmould separately

Wider environmental impact	Soil rendered inert without organic matter. Organic matter (carbon) locked in the soil and not in the atmosphere where it would be adding to greenhouse gases. Organic matter returned to soil and not ending up in landfill.
Advantages for the grower in terms of fertility	Two quality products.
Disadvantages for the grower	Finding enough. Managing a heap and bin can be time consuming.

4.2.2 Windrow composting – above twenty tonnes per annum

Windrow composting consists of placing a mixture of shredded raw materials in long narrow piles which are turned regularly by tractor-pulled or self-propelled windrow turners. The turning operation mixes the plant-based materials and aerates the windrow. This highly managed system ensures high quality plant-based compost. The active composting stage generally lasts three to nine weeks, depending upon the nature of the materials and the frequency of turning.

4.2.3 Straw bale compost heaps – up to twenty tonnes per annum

The following composting system is managed by hand at Tolhurst Organic Produce:

- Line two parallel rows of rectangular straw bales, three bales high, no more than 3m apart.
- Stagger the joins of the bales to make a stronger structure, with one end closed in with bales, thus forming a bin.
- The structure can be any length desired, with more bales being added as space is required.
- The composting materials are piled half a metre above the bales and this soon sinks down to about half.

Drainage pipes placed under the bales and along the floor every metre will allow air in. Alternatively woody prunings can be laid at the base.

4.3 Recommended - mixing plant-based ingredients

Stockfree-Organic Standard 4.2(b) – mixing plant-based ingredients	
Wider environmental impact	Regulate quality and ensure no contaminants enter the heap.
Advantages for the grower in terms of fertility	Quality product.
Disadvantages for the grower	Finding enough browns. Managing a heap can be time consuming.

FIGURE 4.2 STRAW BALE COMPOST HEAP

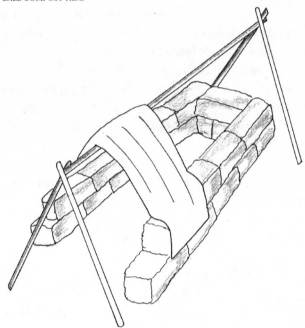

4.3.1 'Greens' and 'Browns'

Choosing compost materials is of major importance. The golden rule of composting is:

> ingredients of - two parts 'greens'
> - one part 'browns'
> in the presence of air and moisture.

4.3.2 Carbon : nitrogen ratios

Compost is ideally prepared from plant-based materials with an initial C:N ratio of 30:1. During the composting process the nitrogen percentage increases, whilst the carbon bulk is lost to the atmosphere as carbon dioxide. It will reduce its carbon content to have a ratio of about 10:1.

When starting composting:
- if the C:N ratio is too narrow, then there will be insufficient carbon to provide the energy for the micro-organisms to degrade the organic wastes and losses of nitrogen will increase;

Table 4.1 Compost ingredients suitable for stockfree-organic systems

Greens Nitrogen rich Lush and fresh	Browns Carbon rich Dry and stemmy	Not recommended	Prohibited Under the Stockfree-Organic Standards
Vegetables (peelings, cores, grade outs)	Straw	Autumn leaves (better for leafmould see 4.2)	Meat
Crop residues / foliage	Bean haulm Tomato vine	Perennial weeds unless heap reaches 50°C / for one week	Dairy products
Grass cuttings	Hay	Annual weeds in seed	Fish
Fresh green manure plants	Bracken	Cooked food. unless it is entirely vegan. May still attract rodents.	Animal manures
Annual weeds not in seed	Any other older plant foliage	Twigs and sawdust (carbon ratio too high)	Synthetic materials

- if the C:N ratio is too high, then breakdown will take a long time and will lock up the nitrogen.

The difficulty the stockfree-organic grower will often encounter is finding enough 'browns'. Do not rely on twigs or perennial weed roots to make up this element, as they take a longer time to break down and can ruin the quality of the compost. If you are trying to make fine grade compost suitable for vegetable growing, it is better to chip branches separately (see 3.8) or use them for wildlife habitats (see 8.5.5).

Buying in straw will prove the easiest way to find sufficient 'browns'. Straw has hollow stems and can improve aeration of the heap. It is a restricted practice under Stockfree-Organic Standard 3.4(d) to use hay or straw from non-organic systems. Apart from aeration, the advantage of straw (dried cereal stems) over hay (dried grass) is the lower weed seed content. For other bought-in materials for the compost heap see 3.7.

Table 4.2 Nitrogen percentages and C:N ratios[6]		
Material	**Nitrogen** (% dry-weight basis)	**C:N ratio (x:1)**
Grass	4	20
Brewer's waste	3-5	14
Wheat, barley, rice straw	0.4-0.6	14
Fallen leaves	0.4	45
Rotted sawdust	0.2	200
Fresh sawdust	0.1	500

4.3.3 Layering and chopping materials

Plant-based materials will compost best if they are between 2cm and 5cm in size, although growers will not have the time to go around cutting all materials to this size. Of more importance is correct layering. Ensure that the different types of 'greens' and 'browns' are well mixed by adding layers no thicker than 10cm. Waste vegetables such as root crops and onions should be kept in individual layers.

Shredding materials may seem a sensible option if processing a lot of material, although at Tolhurst Organic Produce we are managing a twenty-tonne heaps without a shredder. Soft, succulent 'greens' decompose rapidly and do not need shredding. The harder more woody tissues, like brassica stems, need to be made smaller to decompose rapidly in smaller heaps. This woody material can be put through a shredder, although petrol-powered shredders are expensive. Therefore, it may be cost effective to hire a machine for occasional use and chip stockpiled woody material in one session. Electric-powered shredders available from garden centres are not powerful enough for this type of work. Brassica stems and prunings can easily be chopped with a sharp shovel or pulverised by a hammer.

R Dalziel O'Brien[7] describes a process of keeping two heaps a 'fine' heap and a 'rough' heap. The rough heap has the tough materials like brassica stems thrown on to it which are allowed to decompose slowly in their own time. The materials of the rough heap are added to the fine heap once they are fine enough. For small heaps, this may be a worthwhile process, because it may mean not having to sieve.

4.4 Recommended – building a heap of sufficient volume – at least one cubic metre

Stockfree-Organic Standard (c) – building a heap of sufficient volume – at least one cubic metre	
Wider environmental impact	Reducing pathogens.
Advantages for the grower in terms of fertility	Quality product.
Disadvantages for the grower	Finding sufficient materials. Time consuming.

To get a good heat you need to create at least a one-metre-cubed compost heap. Materials should be stockpiled until there are enough 'greens' and 'browns'.

If done correctly, a pile will heat to high temperatures within three days. If it doesn't, the heap either:

- is not large enough – add more materials;
- is too wet and you will need to spread the materials out to dry;
- is too dry and you will need irrigate the heap with a hose or watering can; or
- has not enough nitrogen – add grass cuttings from the holding or brewers hops (restricted practice see 3.7.6).

4.5 Recommended - turning the heap to assist with aeration
It is very important to maintain a schedule of turning. The turning operation mixes the plant-based materials, improving aeration and assisting aerobic decomposition. The frequency of turning depends on the rate of

decomposition, the moisture content, the porosity of the materials and the desired composting time. Because the decomposition rate is greatest at the start of the process, the frequency of turning decreases as the heap ages. If a heap is too large, above four metres cubed, anaerobic zones will occur near its centre which release odours when it is turned. On the other hand, a small heap will lose heat quickly and may not achieve temperatures high enough to kill pathogens and weed seeds.

Stockfree-Organic Standard 4.2(d) – turning the heap to assist with aeration

Wider environmental impact	Reducing pathogens.
Advantages for the grower	Quality product. Faster composting process.
Disadvantages for the grower	May require machinery / physically demanding. Time consuming.

4.5.1 Turning windrows

A number of specialised machines have been developed for turning windrows. These machines greatly reduce the time and labour involved, mixing the materials thoroughly and producing more uniform compost. Some of these machines are designed to attach to a tractor or a loader whilst others are self-propelled.

For small to moderate scale operations, turning can be accomplished with a bucket loader on a tractor. The loader simply lifts the materials from the windrow and spills them down again, mixing the materials and reforming the mixture into a loose windrow. The loader can exchange material from the bottom of the windrow with material on the top by forming a new windrow next to the old one. This needs to be done without driving onto the windrow. If additional mixing of the materials is desired, a loader can also be used in combination with a muck spreader.

4.5.2 Turning a heap within the straw bale compost bin

The easiest way to turn a heap is to extend the side bales by about two bales long and turn the heap into the new area with a fork, adding more greens or browns as required. It should be recovered with the tarpaulin.

4.6 Recommended – monitoring temperature rises

Stockfree-Organic Standard 4.2(e) – monitoring temperature rises

Wider environmental impact	Reducing pathogens.
Advantages for the grower in terms of fertility	Quality product.
Disadvantages for the grower	Time consuming.

Stockfree-Organic standard 4.1 states

During composting, which is a process of aerobic fermentation, a minimum maintained temperature of 60°C is strongly advised to kill weed seeds and pathogens.

A heap that does not heat to at least 60°C for a week is likely to contain weed seed and disease organisms. Under optimal conditions, composting proceeds through three stages[8]:

1) the mesophilic, or moderate-temperature phase, which lasts for a couple of days;
2) the thermophilic, or high-temperature phase, which can last from a few days to several months, and finally;
3) a several-month cooling and maturation phase.

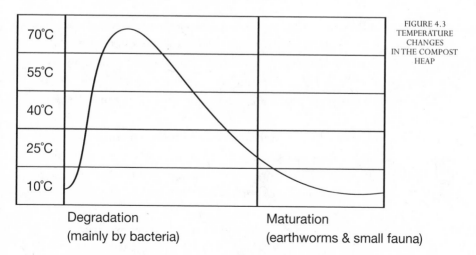

FIGURE 4.3
TEMPERATURE
CHANGES
IN THE COMPOST
HEAP

Different communities of micro-organisms are active during the various composting phases.

Stage 1
Initial decomposition is carried out by mesophilic micro-organisms, which are common in topsoil. They rapidly break down the soluble, readily-degradable compounds. The heat they produce causes the compost temperature to rapidly rise.

Stage 2
As the temperature rises above about 40°C, the mesophilic micro-organisms become less competitive and are replaced by others that are thermophilic (heat-loving) micro-organisms, which are ever-present in nature and become active whenever environmental conditions are favourable. At temperatures of 55°C and above, many micro-organisms that are pathogens are destroyed. During the thermophilic phase high temperatures accelerate the breakdown of proteins, fats and complex carbohydrates like cellulose and hemicellulose - the major structural molecules in plants. Because temperatures above 65°C will kill even the thermophilic bacteria and limit the rate of decomposition, the stockfree-organic grower must use aeration and moisture to keep the temperature below this point. This is why regular turning will encourage faster composting as the temperature will remain nearer to the ideal.

Stage 3
As the supply of these high-energy compounds becomes exhausted, the compost temperature gradually decreases and mesophilic micro-organisms once again take over for the final phase of maturation of the remaining organic matter. In general, the longer the curing phase, the more diverse the microbial community it supports. Stage 2 temperature rises and Stage 3 'hygieniser' micro-organisms serve to remove pathogens. The 'hygienisers' produce antibiotics and provide microbial competition and antagonism. It is important to manage the processes as pathogens will only grow on soluble organic compounds (short-chain organic molecules), and not humified organic matter (long-chain ligno-cellulose) compounds.

Bacteria are the primary decomposing organism, but there are many others that enter at Stage 3 and improve the biodiversity of the compost. These include fungi, actinomycetes, brandling worms, ants, millipedes, snails and slugs, nematodes, fermentation mites, beetles, spring tails, spiders, centipedes, flies, white worms, small mammals, amphibians and slow worms.

Once humified, plant-based composts should be free from weed seeds, pathogens and nematodes. They should also be disease suppressive with large numbers of beneficial micro-organisms and a high humus fraction. After the composting process is complete, the top 10cm of the heap should be taken off before use and added to new heaps, as this material may only be partially compost and contain weed seeds. This problem can be avoided by covering the heap with a heat insulating material.

4.7 Recommended - covering the heap or windrow to prevent it from becoming waterlogged

Stockfree-Organic Standard 4.2(e) – covering the heap or windrow to prevent it from becoming waterlogged	
Wider environmental impact	Reducing pollution from compost leachate.
Advantages for the grower in terms of fertility	Quality product.
Disadvantages for the grower	Ensuring rain water does not enter the heap or windrow.

Excess moisture will drown the beneficial micro-organisms. The moisture level should be the equivalent of a wrung-out sponge. Therefore, rain should not be allowed to enter and wash through the heap. There is no point in going to all the other effort with the composting process, only to allow the goodness in the heap to be washed away.

Covering windrows - This may prove difficult with the windrows, although Eliot Coleman suggests covering them with woven plastic matting which helps shed the rain but still allows for aeration. Growing with Grace carry out their windrow composting operation in a polytunnel.

Covering the straw bale heap - a simple way is with a tarpaulin draped over a ridge pole erected on posts. The tarpaulin should be tied down by bales on the sides, but be careful not to cover the sides of the bales, as this will prevent air entry (see fig 4.2).

4.8 Risk assessments

Nowadays, assessing the risk of any activity that poses significant hazards is standard practice. Fortunately, serious and immediate threats from on-farm composting have not been experienced by composters. Specific hazards to workers are recognised, as well as possible unresolved issues of long-term, chronic exposures. Those responsible for risk management must be proactive to safeguard the health of workers, public health and the environment.

The risk assessment process involves the structured gathering of information in order to form a judgement about the associated risks.

FIGURE 4.4 STEPS IN RISK ASSESSMENT

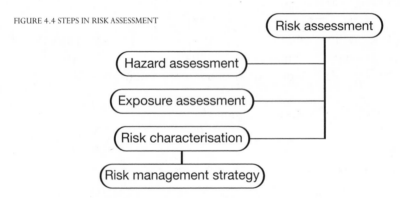

4.8.1 Hazard assessment

People	Environment
identify exposed individuals:	identify possible risks:
• pathways for pathogens and fungi spores to affect handlers;	• concentrated leachate pollution
• heavy lifting;	• rodent nuisance;
• using machinery.	• odour nuisance to nearby residents

4.8.2 Exposure assessment

People	Environment
People	**Environment**
• frequency;	• frequency;
• duration;	• duration;
• intensity with which an agent or activity is presented to an individual;	• intensity with which an agent or activity is presented to the environment;
• pathways by inhalation, ingestion, skin contact.	• pathways – site waterlogged, slopes and drainage present for leaching to water courses;
	• proximity of composting operation to dwellings.

4.8.3 Risk characterisation – Low, Medium or High

Most of the risks associated with composting should be low. The greater risks are described below.

People

While a variety of primary pathogens are present in composting, the actual composting process kills most of them. There have not been documented cases of exposure-related infectious disease from primary pathogens among compost workers. On the other hand, secondary pathogens, which are fungi and other micro-organisms produced during the composting process are of greater concern. A variety of symptoms, ranging from red and irritated eyes to runny nose and nausea, have been reported and may be attributed to dust-borne bacterial and fungal spores and endotoxins from organisms present in the compost.

The most serious health threat seems to come from a secondary pathogen, the heat tolerant fungus Aspergillus fumigatus, and several related fungi, which cause 'aspergillosis' (also known as 'farmer's lung' or 'brown lung' disease). This fungus, a well known product of silage, manure, compost and wastewater sludge compost, grows on decaying vegetable matter at temperatures above 45°C and thus survives most of the composting process. Infection of susceptible individuals (including those on immunosuppressant drugs, antibiotics, adrenal corticosteroids or with pulmonary disease, asthma and certain other infections) may cause debilitating symptoms.

Environment
Compost leachate entering watercourses will cause nutrient enrichment (eutrophication), leading to algal blooms, lack of oxygen and a decline in aquatic life.

4.8.4 Risk management strategy
Proper design of the composting operation and good management practices can prevent the risks associated with composting.

People
To avoid pathways for pathogens and fungi spores

- Wear face masks.
- Wear gloves.
- Wear protective clothing.
- Consult Health and Safety Executive advice about heavy lifting (see www.hse.gov.uk).
- Do not work alone.

Environment
To avoid windrows or heaps becoming saturated, do not place them on a slope or near water courses.

4.9 Prohibited practices for composting
Under Stockfree-Organic Standard 4.3 the following are prohibited:

(a) Placing heaps or windrows on a slope.
(b) Placing heaps or windrows adjacent to water bodies e.g. ponds and streams.

If a heap or windrow is placed on an incline or at the bottom of a hill, rain water will run into it and percolate through the heap or windrow. Especially with slopes above 10%, erosion, vehicular access and equipment operation problems will prove severe. Therefore it was the general consensus of the

Standards Working Group that siting on a slope should be prohibited. Even with the best intentions, compost leaching may occur. It is therefore prohibited under Stockfree-Organic Standard 4.4(b) to place a heap or windrow adjacent to water bodies, e.g. ponds and streams, to remove this risk entirely.

1 The Composting Association, Avon House, Tithe Barn Road, Wellingborough, Northamptonshire, NN8 1DH. www.compost.org.uk Email: membership@compost.org.uk Tel: 01933 227777.

2 The On-Farm Composting Network, Harper Adams University College, Edgmond, Newport, Shropshire, TF10 8NB. www.farmcompost.com. Email: info@farmcompost.com Tel: 01952 815335.

3 Community Composting Network, 67 Alexandra Road, Sheffield, S2 3EE Tel/Fax: 0114 2580483, E-Mail: ccn@gn.apc.org.

4 HDRA, Ryton Organic Gardens, Coventry, CV8 3LG. 024 7630 3517 www.hdra.org.uk

5 Organic Resource Agency Ltd., Malvern Hills Science Park, Geraldine Road, Malvern, WR14 3SZ www.o-r-a.co.uk Tel: 01684 585423

6 GRAY & BIDDLESTONE (1981) in STONEHOUSE, B (ed) Biological Husbandry - a Scientific Approach to Organic Farming. Butterworth.

7 DALZIEL OBRIEN R (1956) Intensive Gardening. Faber.

8 The information about composting processes is adapted from the Cornell University website www.cfe.cornell.edu

Chapter Five

Propagation

5.1 Introduction

Propagation is about giving seeds and vegetative propagating material their best start. A well grown crop is the result of paying attention to the many small details that make for successful propagation. As can be seen from this chapter, stockfree-organic propagation is very much in its infancy. This newly developing field is attracting attention from growers and researchers alike because of increasing EU demand for organic transplants to be free from slaughterhouse by-products.

5.2 Recommended practice - Stockfree-organic seed grown on the registered holding

---

Stockfree-Organic Standard 6.1(a) Recommended Stockfree-organic seed grown on the registered holding

Wider environmental impact	Working within a closed system. Preserving localised genetic diversity.
Advantages for the grower	Saves seed costs.
Disadvantages for the grower	Skilled job that is time consuming. Unreliable results. Difficult to reproduce the benefits of F1 Hybrids.

The ideal should be that every grower saves their own seed. This is perfectly feasible for an amateur grower. As part of their services HDRA[1] have the Heritage Seed Library (HSL) (visit www.hdra.org.uk/hsl) where they produce comprehensive guidelines on seed-saving for all vegetable species.

However, there are problems for commercial growers saving their own seed. This was the subject of a research study by the Horticultural Research Institute[2]. Results to date have been mixed. Brassica seed of sufficient quality has proved difficult to produce following organic guidelines. Major plant losses have occurred due to neck rot in the onion crop. On testing, epidemiologically significant levels of Botrytis allii have been detected on organically-produced onion seed. On the brighter side, organic parsnip seed production has so far been satisfactory, with promising yields of Itersonilia-free seed.

More research is needed to produce an entire range of quality stockfree-organic vegetable seed from the registered holding. At this point in time seed saving may be seen by commercial growers as a specialist art best left to plant breeders, who have the time, the resources and the necessary hygienic conditions to develop varieties that are suitable for organic growing systems.

5.3 Recommended practice - Stockfree-organic propagating composts made on the registered holding

Stockfree-Organic Standard 6.1(b) Recommended Stockfree-organic propagating composts made on the registered holding	
Wider environmental impact	Working within a closed system.
Advantages for the grower	Traceability. Reliability once you have perfected the right media.
Disadvantages for the grower	Making your own mix is time consuming. May need to buy in materials.

5.3.1 Traditional growing media mixes[3]

- Seed mixtures need to drain freely, allow for aeration so that they can warm up quickly and have the ability to retain moisture. They need to be free from weed seeds, pests and diseases. A fine texture ensures that they make good contact with the seeds. They do not need high levels of nutrients, just enough to sustain the seedlings for four to seven weeks.
- Potting mixtures are generally for plants growing for a longer period (several months before transplanting) or permanently in pots[4]. They can have a coarser texture and need short-term and long-term nutrient supplies. They are generally not used in annual vegetable production.

The following mixes should be suitable for raising transplants but have not been rigorously tested:

1. Tolhurst Organic Produce mix for module trays

- Two units sieved green waste compost (at least 12 months old).
- One unit perlite.
- We experimented with adding bark as a peat alternative but found that it diluted the mix.

2. Standard soil-free mix for module trays

- Two units sieved plant-based compost.
- Two units peat[5].
- One unit sharp sand or vermiculite or perlite.

3. Standard blocking mix (free-standing blocks)

- Two units plant-based compost.
- Three units peat[6].
- Two units coarse sand or perlite.

To the above three mixes you can add the supplements of:

- ⅛ unit base fertiliser (see 5.3.2 and 5.3.3).
- ⅛ unit seaweed meal (see 3.9.3 restricted practice).

- ⅛ unit lime (permitted practice).
- ⅛ unit soft rock (colloidal) phosphate (permitted practice).

The ingredients must be mixed well to form a uniform end product. First measure the units in buckets. It will be necessary to sieve coarse materials. Spread the contents on a clean hard surface and mix in the same way that you would with cement using a spade or shovel, piling them up in a heap and turning it in. For larger quantities, it is worth using a cement mixer. Seed mixtures are better if they are six months old.

5.3.2 Alternative base fertilisers to blood, fish and bone (BF&B)

Base fertilisers are very different from supplementary fertilisers (see 3.9), in that the nutrients need to be released slowly so that they are available to the plant throughout its development. Supplementary fertilisers provide more readily available nutrients e.g. potash boost from comfrey extract.

The following information is taken from the US Appropriate Technology Transfer for Rural Areas (ATTRA)[7] and the desktop research study of HDRA and Elm Farm[8] who have examined non-animal based ingredients suitable for organic transplant mixes. The use of blood, fish and bone is prohibited under the Stockfree-Organic Standards and is included in the following table for comparison purposes only, to allow growers to assess the effectiveness of their own animal-free mix of ingredients. This is still a matter of experimentation because at the time of writing alternatives to BF&B have not been tested on any widespread scale or by the authors.

The Elm Farm Bulletin 71[9] reports a favourable comparison in trails between the standard organic supplementary feed Nu-Gro (a feed based on fish by-products) and the animal-free commercially available alternatives AmegA + P[10] and Westland Organic Tomato and Vegetable liquid feed[11] for cabbage and leek transplant raising. At the time of writing, these manufacturers have not signed 'Animal Free Declarations'.

Table 5.1 Animal-free base fertilisers

Material	N	P	K	Nutrient release	UK Suppliers
Blood	12.5	1.5	0.6	Medium	Prohibited SOS
Fish	10.0	5.0	0.0	Medium	Prohibited SOS
Bone	4.0	21.0	0.2	Slow	Prohibited SOS
Alfalfa (lucerne) meal	2.5	0.5	2.0	Slow	US import or self production see 5.3.5.
Soya bean meal	6.5	1.5	2.4	Slow to medium	Self production
Lupin seed meal	2.8	NT	NT	NT	Self production
Castor bean meal	3.0	NT	NT	NT	Maltaflor in Germany.
Faba bean meal	1.7	NT	NT	NT	Self production
Field peas meal	1.0	NT	NT	NT	Self production
Wood ash	0.0	1.5	5.0	Fast	Self production
Sugar beet	5.0	2.5	NT	NT	Various see 3.9.3
Seaweed meal	1.0	0.5	8.0	Slow	
Soft rock (colloidal) phosphate	0.0	6.0	0.0	Slow	Various
Rock phosphate	0.0	8.0	0.0	Very slow	Various

NT = not tested

5.3.3 Manufacturers of fertilisers suitable for propagation who have signed 'Animal-free declarations'

Table 5.2 Compound fertiliser products

Name of Product (Supplier)	Product descriptions	Category in the standards
Cumulus **W.L. Dingley**	Cumulus 5-5-5 Cumulus 5-1-10 Cumulus 5–1-4	Permitted under Stockfree-Organic standard 5.1(e) but restricted by Soil Association Standards
Vitax	Pelleted fertilisers Vitax natural 2-1-4 Vitax natural 1-1-1	Restricted under Stockfree-Organic standard 5.4(a) and restricted by Soil Association Standards.
5F's **Fertiliser** **Fertile Fibre**	Pelleted fertiliser 5-5-5	Permitted under Stockfree-Organic standard 5.1(e) but restricted by Soil Association Standards

- WL Dingley – contact B Urbanski, Buckle St, Honeybourne, Evesham, Worc. WR11 7QE. T / F 01386 830242.
- Vitax Ltd – contact C Platt, Owen street, Coalville, Leics. LE19 3DE. www.vitax.co.uk T 01530 510060.
- Fertile Fibre- contact Matthew Dent, Fertile Fibre Ltd, Withington Court, Withington, Hereford, HR1 3RJ. T / 01432 853111 www.fertilefibre.co.uk

5.3.4 Alternatives to peat

Instead of using peat in propagation mixes for module trays as discussed in 5.3.1, the Stockfree-Organic grower can substitute the following ingredients for peat.

5.3.4.1 Plant-based compost (with certain additives)

Plant-based compost is rarely used as the sole potting medium since it is too porous and has levels of soluble salts that are considered to be too high. Experiments by Ozores-Hampton et al[12] in Florida compared three tomato propagating mixes:

- green waste compost (sieved to < 2.4 mm) / vermiculite mix;
- green waste / peat / vermiculite mix;
- sphagnum peat / vermiculite mix.

and found that, whilst the mix including all three ingredients was the best, once transplanted the former seedlings caught up and there was generally no differences in yields. However, the researchers did note that generally a lack of physical and chemical consistency in the green waste compost could compromise vegetable transplant production.

Experienced compost makers know that compost quality is directly affected by the raw ingredients. To produce media-grade compost it is advisable to make it according to a recipe (see 5.3.1), using a specific blend of balanced ingredients, rather than from a cool compost heap which has had materials added in a random manner. The end product will be more consistent.

- Use crop wastes, grass clippings, legume-rich hays and straw.
- Ensure that the compost heap heats up (see 4.4, 4.5 and 4.6).

Plant-based compost made on the registered holding is a recommended input under Stockfree-Organic Standard 6.1(b). Bought in green waste composts for propagating purposes would be a permitted input under Stockfree-Organic Standard 6.2(c) and provided that it carries the Soil Association symbol an 'Animal Free Declaration' will not be needed. In general the quality of green waste compost is quite good although there will inevitably be seasonal variations in the ingredients and hence the supply of plant nutrients will not be consistent.

5.3.4.2 Composted pine bark[13]

Composted pine bark has high lignin content, making it slow to degrade. Bark lightens the mix, increases bulk density, increases air space, and decreases the water-holding capacity of a mix making it a suitable alternative to peat. Its pH is generally 5.0 to 6.5, it is low in soluble salts, and it will probably require more nitrogen base fertilisers if used in a mix. The product Sylvamix Natural for commercial growers is currently available from Melcourt[14] again its performance was rated in the Elm Farm Bulletin report[15] and this input would be permitted under Stockfree-Organic Standard 6.2(c).

5.3.4.3 Alfalfa (lucerne) meal

Alfalfa meal provides nutrients which are released slowly. Alfalfa must be processed before being used in growing media. Dried alfalfa hay is ground and passed through a 2cm screen. Water is added and the alfalfa is allowed to decompose for twenty days. It is then air-dried for another twenty days before use. Plant-based compost made on the registered holding is a recommended input under Stockfree-Organic Standard 6.1(b).

5.3.4.4 Comfrey leafmould

Leafmould contains little in the way of nutrients, but fine grade leafmould that has decomposed for three years can be mixed to make comfrey leafmould, which is a useful ingredient in seed composts. Fill a dustbin with alternative layers of 10cm of leafmould and chopped comfrey leaves. Leave until the comfrey leaves have disappeared, which can take up to five months. If the mixture turns soggy, turn out the mix and build it up again, adding further dry leafmould. If it is too dry, add water. Plant-based compost made on the registered holding is a recommended input under Stockfree-Organic Standard 6.1(b).

5.3.5 Raising transplants

Transplanting is the practice of starting seedlings in one place and setting them out in another. It is the most reliable method for obtaining a uniform stand of plants.

- It is easier to lavish care on thousands of tiny seedlings in the greenhouse rather than letting them take their chances in the open field.
- It allows for a more productive use of green manures. Directly sown seeds

will germinate poorly in newly turned-in green manures because of phytotoxic effects (toxins that are produced during the early stages of decay), requiring a four week delay between incorporating and sowing. Larger transplant seedlings can withstand this. Therefore, green manures can be left to grow longer and turned in two weeks before setting out transplants.

• It gives crops a greater chance of competing with the weeds.

It is possible to scatter seeds into a seed tray and later prick out the plants[16] (either into plugs or the soil), but the preferred method for commercial growing is sowing directly into module trays (plugs) or free standing 'blocks'. The advantage is no fiddly pricking out or root disturbance when transplanting. The disadvantages are that the modules take up space in the greenhouse and for large commercial quantities you need a seed sowing machine, which is expensive and at best you will get a 90% stand. Therefore, it is a good idea to allow for extra trays to make up the difference.

FIGURE 5.1 SOIL BLOCKER, MODULE TRAY, FREE-STANDING BLOCKS AND SEEDER

Transplant seedlings are raised in modules of firm (not jam packed) seed compost, which is either placed in trays or pressed in a 'block maker'. Seeds need:

- air to germinate, so ramming the seed compost as hard as you can into a module will result in poor germination;
- moisture to germinate, but water logging will lead to fungal problems and again drives out of air.

Choosing the size of your module depends on the type of seedling that will emerge.

- Most crops will grow well in a small 4cm module.
- Brassicas, with their larger rooting system, prefer an intermediate size but are better raised as bare root transplants (see 5.4).
- Courgettes, pumpkins, squashes and cucumbers can be grown in 9cm modules.

Make an indentation in the compost in the centre of the module and place into this one seed. The following crops can support several seeds per module:

- Spring onions: twelve seeds[17] to a module so that they are pre-bunched before lifting.
- Beetroot: three seeds to a module so that they can be pre-bunched before lifting.
- Maincrop onions: five seeds[18] to a module.

Plants sown inside must be acclimatised to the outside conditions in a process known as hardening off. Put them outside 7 days before they are due to be transplanted into their final position. The following can be used as a checklist for best transplant practice[19].

1. Greenhouse environment

- Aim for good hygiene: regularly sweep and wipe down surfaces.
- Remove weeds from under tables etc.
- Remove plant debris, which may attract slugs.
- Remove discarded transplants.

Table 5.3 Crops suitable for transplanting
DSR = double staggered rows with paths in between.
Bold text = higher germination temperature.
Normal text = middle range temperatures.
Italics = lower germination temperature.

Vegetable	Temperature range °C	Age weeks	Average spacing apart cm	Average spacing between rows cm
Tomato (see 11.2)	**24 - 27**	**8**	**60cm**	**75cm DSR**
Aubergine	**24 - 27**	**8**	**45cm**	**75cm DSR**
Pepper	**24 - 27**	**8**	**45cm**	**75cm DSR**
Cauliflower (see 11.3)	*15 - 21*	*4 – 6*	*60cm*	*60cm*
Spring greens	*15 - 21*	*4 – 6*	*10cm*	*35cm*
Spring cabbage	*15 - 21*	*4 – 6*	*30cm*	*35cm*
Cabbages	*15 - 21*	*4 – 6*	*40cm*	*55cm*
Single head calabrese broccoli	*15 - 21*	*4 – 6*	*40cm*	*55cm*
Brussel sprouts	*15 - 21*	*4 – 6*	*45cm*	*70 cm*
Kale	*15 - 21*	*4 – 6*	*45cm*	*45cm*
Chinese cabbage (loose) (11.4)	*15 - 21*	*3*	*60cm*	*60cm*
Chinese cabbage (headed)	*15 - 21*	*3*	*40cm*	*40cm*
Pak choi (headed)	*15 - 21*	*3*	*40cm*	*40cm*
Pak choi	*15 - 21*	*3*	*30cm*	*30cm*
Giant leaved mustard	*15 - 21*	*3*	*60cm*	*60cm*
Green-in-the-snow	*15 - 21*	*3*	*40cm*	*40cm*
Mustard leaf	*15 - 21*	*3*	*30cm*	*30cm*
Mizuna greens	*15 - 21*	*3*	*30cm*	*30cm*
Komatsuna	*15 - 21*	*3*	*30cm*	*30cm*
Rocket	*15 - 21*	*3*	*30cm*	*30cm*
Watercress / landcress	*15 - 21*	*3*	*40cm*	*40cm*
Swede (11.5) usually direct	21 - 24	4 – 6	50cm	50cm
Kohl rabi	21 - 24	4 – 6	40cm	40cm

Vegetable	Temperature range °C	Age weeks	Average spacing apart cm	Average spacing between rows cm
Onions / bulb (11.6)	21 - 24	5 – 8	15cm	15cm
Leeks (bed system)	*15 - 21*	*5 – 8*	*20cm*	*30cm*
Leeks (ridge system)	*15 - 21*	*5 - 8*	*15cm*	*Ridge*
Spring onions	*15 - 21*	*5 – 8*	*15cm*	*15cm*
12 seeds per module				
Celery (11.9)	*15 - 21*	*8*	*25cm*	*30cm*
Celeriac	*15 - 21*	*8*	*30cm*	*35cm*
Fennel	*15 - 21*	*4 – 6*	*25cm*	*50cm*
Courgette (11.10)	**24 - 27**	**3**	**75cm**	**Path**
Summer squash	**24 - 27**	**3**	**75cm**	**Path**
Winter squash (trailing)	**24 - 27**	**3**	**90cm**	**Path**
Pumpkin	**24 - 27**	**3**	**90cm**	**Path**
Cucumber (11.11)	**24 - 27**	**3**	**75cm**	**75cm DSR**
Melon	**24 - 27**	**3**	**75cm**	**75cm DSR**
Sweetcorn (11.12)	21 - 24	3	25cm	75cm
Runner beans	21 - 24	4	30cm	60cm DSR
French beans	21 - 24	4	15cm	Path
Bunch beetroot (11.14)	21 - 24	4	20cm	35cm
Main crop beetroot	21 - 24	4	10cm	35cm
Annual spinach	21 - 24	4	15cm	35cm
Leaf beet	21 - 24	4	30cm	35cm
Swiss chard	21 - 24	4	30cm	35cm
Little gem lettuce (11.15)	*15 - 21*	*3*	*20cm*	*25cm*
Cos, butterhead	*15 - 21*	*3*	*30cm*	*30cm*
& continental				
Crisp & iceberg lettuce	*15 - 21*	*3*	*35cm*	*25cm*
Chicories and endives (11.16)	*15 - 21*	*3*	*30cm*	*30cm*
Corn salad	21 - 24	3	10cm	15cm
Claytonia	21 - 24	3	10cm	30cm
Sorrel	21 - 24	3	10cm	30cm
Leaf amaranth	21 - 24	3	10cm	30cm

2. Trays and equipment

- Let the frost get at module trays and other equipment.

3. Propagating media

- If mixing your own, aim for a uniform propagating media.
- Keep mixing equipment and surfaces clean.

4. Seeds and planting material

- Buy only disease resistant seed.
- Do not bring diseased cuttings into the greenhouse.

5. Watering

- Avoid moisture stress in transplants by regular watering.
- Do not over water.
- Be aware that transplants at the edges can dry out faster than those in the middle of trays.

6. Air conditions

- Avoid free moisture from sprinkler irrigation or condensation.
- Ventilate if too hot.
- Use fans if venting is still not bringing about air movement.

7. Light intensity

- Be aware that transplants grown under reduced light will stretch.
- Clean greenhouse glass / replace ageing polythene.
- Use supplementary lighting for season extension in early spring.
- Use shading if the light is too bright.

8. Temperature

- Low temperatures can have adverse effects.

- Consider frost protection through fleecing, bubble wrap and heaters.

9. Hardening off

- Put plants outside 7 – 10 days before transplanting.
- Do not impose conditions so severe that plants will be over-hardened.

10. Transportation

- Ensure that the transplants can be transported without damage to their final destination.

Chapter 12 discusses season extension, with section 12.3 looking specifically at raising early season transplants from January to March.

5.3.6 Blocking transplants

Eliot Coleman[21] is a great exponent of blocks and has devoted a chapter to them in the New Organic Grower. The blocks are composed entirely out of blocking compost made in a press and have no walls as such. At the time of writing, peat substitutes seem unlikely to satisfactorily bind the propagation mix together and therefore peat is needed.

Air spaces provide the walls ensuring that the seedlings cannot become pot bound if left too long. They have the other advantage that the person doing the transplanting can grab the block rather than the plant. (It can sometimes be difficult to get delicate young seedlings out of modules, particularly polystyrene trays, without damage.) Also the blocks can sit slightly proud of the soil and can be slotted straight into a dibbed hole without having to worry about newly exposed roots, thus reducing transplant shock.

5.3.7 Planting out by machine

Once the transplant roots have filled the module, they needed to be planted out. Blocks and bare root transplants can be planted out with a tractor-mounted vegetable transplanter. One to five operatives sit behind coulters that open up the soil. Trays of seedlings are suspended in front of the operatives and they remove the transplants and place them onto a conveyor which takes them to the soil and then the soil is moved back around the plants. Even basic machines can plant up to 8,000 per day.

Table 5.4 Diagnosis and correction of transplant disorders[20]

Symptoms	Possible causes	Preventative practice
1. Spindly growth	Shade, cloudy weather, excessive watering, excessive temperature.	Provide full sun, reduce temperature, restrict watering, ventilate.
2. Stunted plants		
Purple leaves	Phosphorous deficiency.	Add soft rock (colloidal phosphate) to the propagating media.
Yellow leaves	Nitrogen deficiency.	Ensure that the compost element of the propagating mix has been prepared well.
Wilted shoots	Root rot, waterlogging,. soluble salt damage	Do not over water, add other materials aside from plant-based compost.
Discoloured roots	High soluble salt damage.	Add other materials aside from plant-based compost.
Normal roots	Low temperature.	Maintain suitable day and night temperature.
3. Tough woody plants	Over hardening.	Consider fleecing and heating at night.
4. Water soaked and decayed stems	Damping off.	Use a well drained medium. Do not over water and ventilate to provide a less moist environment.
5. Poor root growth	Poor media aeration. Poor drainage. Low fertility. Low temperature.	Determine the cause and take corrective measures
6. Mosses and algae on the surface	High soil moisture, especially in shade or during cloudy periods.	Adjust watering and ventilating practice to provide a less moist environment. Use better drained media.

5.3.8 Heeling in bare root transplants
It is possible to 'heel in' bare root brassica transplants (see 5.4) using your foot. The seedbed needs to have received a secondary cultivation (see 2.7.3 and 2.7.5).

- Gently throw the plant onto the ground and simply push the roots into a bed using the heel of your foot.
- This avoids bending down and is very efficient for planting large quantities of bare root transplants by hand.

5.3.9 Planting out by hand
- Take out the seedlings from the trays by pushing from underneath and transplant them into the soil.
- Unlike plugs, soil blocks don't need to be tucked all the way into the soil. They can be quickly set into the soil and barely tamped in.
- Always plant vegetables to a line and measure the row spacings. This is to assist hoeing and weeding (see 7.4.1).

Block transplants can be dropped into holes without having to pull extra soil around the plants. The holes can be made with a:

- 'dagger style' trowel adapted from a bricklayers trowel[22] or
- studded roller that not only firms the soil but makes the dibbed holes at a pre-set spacing to facilitate weeding with a wheel hoe. This system only works on sandy loams.

For plug plants holes can be made either with a dibber or trowel. The advantage of trowels is that they are less likely to compress the soil at the sides of the hole, which can inhibit the spread of roots. It is important to achieve the correct planting depth and the soil must be firmed around the plant roots of transplants.

5.4 Recommended practice – Bare root transplants raised on the holding

Stockfree-Organic Standard 6.1(c) Recommended
Bare root transplants raised on the holding

Wider environmental impact	Working within a closed system. Saves transportation of growing materials. Saves energy.
Advantages for the grower	Saving on costs of propagating media. Saves space in the greenhouse.
Disadvantages for the grower	Only works with certain crops.

Most brassicas (except kales and oriental salad leaves) and leeks can be raised in nursery seedbeds and then bare root transplanted to their permanent position between 6 to 8 weeks later for brassicas and 12 weeks later for leeks[23]. This saves space in the greenhouse, saves propagation media and helps with weeding strategies. The nursery seed bed should be in an open sunny but sheltered position.

- Ideally make a seedbed on soil that does not have high levels of fertility as such soil will tend to produce weak plants that succumb to pest and diseases.
- Observe a stale seedbed (see 7.3).
- Use secondary cultivations or use a rake to produce a fine but firm tilth.
- Make shallow drills (see 5.5.3) 30cm apart and 1.5cm deep.
- Use a precision seed drill to drop one seed every 2cm apart for brassicas and leeks can be three to four times denser than this.
- Fleece covers will be needed for brassicas and must be placed after drilling to control flea beetle.
- Mark each row carefully and ensure that the leeks are finger-weeded so that the young seedlings experience no competition.

5.5 Permitted practice - Organically grown seed

Stockfree-Organic Standard 6.2(a) Permitted	
Organically grown seed	
Wider environmental impact	Working outside a closed system. Transportation.
Advantages for the grower	Reliable seeds with the characteristics required by the grower.
Disadvantages for the grower	Cost.

5.5.1 www.cosi.org.uk and www.organicXseeds.com

To find stockists of organically grown seed visit www.cosi.org.uk and www.organicXseeds.com on the internet. COSI stands for the Centre for Organic Seed Information. The databases will give you fully up-to-date information on the availability of organic seeds for the UK.

5.5.2 Storing seed

The lifetime of seed can be up to four years, but they must be stored in a sealed packet in a cool, dry place. It is essential that all the seeds germinate at the same time and that each of the seedlings have the same form and vigour. Therefore, it is sensible to work out how much seed you will need in one growing season and not order excessive amounts, so that you can order new seeds each year. Any seed left from previous years can be thoroughly mixed with fresh seed providing that you have carried out a germination test and found them to still be viable.

5.5.3 Direct sowing

It is important that you do not sow seeds until the soil has warmed up in spring. A well-drained soil heats up more quickly than a heavy soil. However, you can increase the warmth by covering with plastic, either cloches or sheets, two weeks prior to sowing.

Before sowing the soil should be just moist. The seeds need to make good contact with the soil particles so:

- if using machinery, make a secondary cultivation (see 2.7.3 and 2.7.5) and roll the seedbed (see 2.7.4);
- if sowing by hand, rake the seedbed;
- if using zero tillage mulching systems take back the mulch and then rake the soil underneath (see 2.9.3).

The finer the seed the finer the tilth needed. To sow the seed using machinery either utilise:

- a precision tractor-mounted seed drill or
- a pedestrian-pushed seed drill like the Earthway™ seed drill.

For direct sowing by hand:

- Peg a taut line where the seeds are to be sown.
- Draw the corner of a hoe tightly against the line to make a shallow V-shaped furrow known as a drill.
- Water the bottom of the drill.
- Carefully sow the seeds using a hand-held precision seed drill or sow through the finger tips. Thinning i.e. removing unwanted seedlings is essentially a gardener's technique and precision drilling should be opted for in commercial situations.
- Cover the seed drill with soil or mark it with compost.
- It is important that the drill is marked, either:
  - with compost;
  - by pegs at either end of the drill or
  - by leaving the line up
  so that it can be weeded before the seedlings germinate. This is particularly important with seeds that are slow to germinate.

- Be careful how you water because it is very easy to flood the seed drill and scatter the seeds. Also overwatering can cause capping at the soil surface (particularly with clay and silt soils) and prevent the seedlings from emerging.

5.6 Permitted practice – Organically grown vegetative reproductive material such as potato tubers, onion sets, strawberry runners and fruit tree root stock and bud material

Stockfree-Organic Standard 6.2(d) Permitted
Organically grown vegetative reproductive material such as potato tubers, onion sets, strawberry runners and fruit tree root stock and bud material

Wider environmental impact	Working outside a closed system. Transportation.
Advantages for the grower	Reliable reproductive material with the characteristics required by the grower.
Disadvantages for the grower	Cost.

Most commercial stockfree-organic growers will buy in vegetative reproductive materials from breeders, as these can be certified to be virus-free and disease-free. However, a few techniques are described below where the stockfree-organic grower can propagate herbs and plants for wildlife.

5.6.1 Propagation by cuttings
Taking herb cutting from woody herbs e.g. sage, rosemary, thyme.

* Take cuttings before the herb flowers.
* Clip 7cm / 12cm growth from the top of the herb plant just below a leaf.
* Strip the stem of its bottom leaves leaving up to 4cm bare stem and the rest as leaf.
* Pinch out the growing point.
* Hormone rooting solutions are prohibited under Stockfree-Organic Standard 6.4(d). Commercial organic herb growers have found that cuttings will still root without them.
* Place one cutting in each module up to its leaves.
* Water with a fine mist and keep covered with a transparent plastic lid or under cloches (in a greenhouse) to keep the humidity high.
* After five weeks pot onto 9cm pots.
* Harden off before planting in their final position.

5.6.2 Propagation by root division
Herbs like chives can be propagated through division.

- Divide the clumps in spring and autumn.
- Leave at least six little bulbs together in a small clump, which can spread in the course of a year.
- The divided plants can be subdivided into 9cm pots filled with stockfree-organic potting mix or planted outdoors in their final planting space.

5.7 Permitted practice - Commercially available stockfree-organic composts that are free from animal inputs
Under Stockfree-Organic standard 6.2(c) it is a permitted practice to use commercially available stockfree-organic composts that are free from animal inputs. At the time of writing there are no well researched and reliable animal-free propagating mixes for commercial growers and so it is recommended that stockfree-organic growers mix their own (see 5.3.1). This is set to change, with public and EU interest in the avoidance of slaughterhouse by-products for transplant raising and the re-structuring of the waste management sector in the UK.

5.8 Restricted materials
Under Stockfree-Organic Standard 6.3 before using any restricted materials in seed composts it is important to obtain written permission from the approved certification body.

5.8.1 Coir
Coir dust, a mixture of short and powder fibres, is a by-product of the coconut fibre industry. Most coir (sold usually as blocks) comes from India, Sri Lanka, the Philippines, Indonesia and Central America[24] and is restricted, because it is felt that this valuable source of organic material should stay within these countries. It looks like sphagnum peat but is more granular, with a pH of 5.5 to 6.8, and usually contains higher levels of potassium, sodium and chlorine. It lasts two to four times longer than peat and is more expensive, mainly because of shipping costs[25].

5.8.2 Peat
Peat is restricted as a material for stockfree-organic seed composts only (and

is prohibited as a general soil conditioner). The journal New Scientist reports that 455 billion tons of carbon is sequestered in peat bogs worldwide. That is equivalent to about 70 - 75 years of industrial emissions, making conservation of peat bogs as important an issue as saving the rainforests[26].

5.8.3 Non-organic seeds
These are currently restricted but are set to move to the prohibited category at the discretion of the regulatory authorities.

5.8.4 Non-organic vegetative reproductive material
These are currently restricted but are set to move to the prohibited category at the discretion of the regulatory authorities.

5.8.5 Commercially available organic propagating composts containing animal inputs
At the time of writing these are restricted and are set to become prohibited on the 31st December 2007. This is to allow registered growers the opportunity to find a suitable alternative to the composts they have been using and to stimulate a market for such products.

5.9 Prohibited materials
It was the unanimous view of the Standards Working Group that the following are not acceptable in stockfree-organic systems. Under Stockfree-Organic Standard 6.4 the following are prohibited:

(a) Propagating composts containing synthetic inputs.
(b) Seed dressings.
(c) Varieties of seeds or plants that have been produced using genetic engineering.
(d) Hormone rooting powders and solutions.

1 HDRA the Organic Association, Ryton Organic Gardens, Coventry, CV8 3LG. 024 7630 3517

2 WOOD R & SMITH B (2001) Economic and Agronomic Feasibility of Organic Vegetable Seed Production in the UK and the Subsequent Seed Quality. MAFF funded project OFO166.

3 Adapted from KUEPPER G & ADAM K (2002) Organic Potting Mixes for Certified Production. Horticulture Technical Note of ATTRA.

4 Permanently growing plants in pots is not 'organic' in the terms of the Stockfree-Organic Standards, which require that plants are grown at some point in the soil.

5 Restricted practice under Stockfree-Organic standard 6.3(b) see section 5.8.2

6 Restricted practice under Stockfree-Organic Standard 6.3(b) see section 5.8.2

7 KUEPPER G & ADAM K (2002) Organic Potting Mixes for Certified Production. Horticulture Technical Note of ATTRA.

8 DEFRA funded research 0F0308 (2002) Alternative, Non-Animal Based Nutrient Sources for Organic Plant Raising.

9 PEARCE B et al (2004) Alternative Non-Animal Based Nutrient Sources, for Organic Plant Raising. Elm Farm Bulletin 71: 7-10

10 AmegA Sciences, A division of Service Chemicals Plc, Lanchester way, Royal Oak Industrial Estate, Daventry, Northants NN11 5PH

11 Westland Horticulture, 14 Granville Industrial Estate, Granville Road, Dungannon, Co Tyrone, Northern Ireland BT70 1NJ

12 OZORES-HAMPTON M et al (1999) Yard Trimming - Bio Solids Compost: Possible Alternative to Sphagnum Peat Moss in Tomato Transplant Production. Compost Science and Utilization. 1999, 7: 4, 42-49

13 Information adapted from RYNK, R (ed.) 1992. On-Farm Composting Handbook. Publication NRAES-54. Northeast Regional Agricultural Engineering Service, Cornell Cooperative Extension, Ithaca, NY. p. 81.

14 Melcourt industries, Boldbridge Brake, Long Newnton, Tetbury, Glos,GL8 8RT.

15 PEARCE B et al (2004) Alternative Non-Animal Based Nutrient Sources for Organic Plant Raising. Elm Farm Bulletin 71: 7-10

16 This is however, a recommended technique for very small seeds like celery and celeriac.

17 COLEMAN, E (1995) New Organic Grower. A Master's Manual of Tools and Techniques for the Home and Market Gardener. Chelsea Green publishing.

18 SCHOFIELD A (2004) of Growing with Nature technique. Personal communication.

19 Adapted from MAYNARD DN & HOCHMUTH GJ (1997) Knott's Handbook for Vegetable Growers. Fourth Edition. John Wiley and Sons Inc.

20 Adapted from MAYNARD DN & HOCHMUTH GJ (1997) Knott's Handbook for Vegetable Growers. Fourth Edition. John Wiley and Sons Inc.

21 COLEMAN, E (1995) New Organic Grower. A Master's Manual of Tools and Techniques for the Home and Market Gardener. Chelsea Green publishing.

22 Available from Johnny's Selected Seeds, 955 Benton Avenue, Winslow, Maine 04901-2601 USA. www.johnnyseeds.com

23 DEANE, T (2005) Peg Tales – Benefits of Bare Root Transplants. Organic Farming 86: 21-22

24 NELSON, J. (1998) Coconuts to the Rescue. Organic Farms, Folks & Foods. (Published by NOFA-NY). July-August. p. 8-9.

25 Anon. 1999. Going coconuts. Ecological Landscaper. Winter. p. 12.

26 SADOWSKI, I.E. 2001. Doing the Peat Bog Two-Step. Mother Earth News. June-July. p. 18

Chapter Six

Rotations

6.1 Defining rotations

The basic principle of rotations is to keep closely related crops together and grow them on a different piece of land each year.

The crops are moved around in a regular sequence so that they do not return to the same piece of land for at least four years.

Rotations:

- avoid the build up of soil borne diseases;
- spread the risk of pest attack;
- help with weed suppression strategies.

Rotations are based on the principle that diversity and complexity provide stability. There is always diversity in 'natural' ecosystems with harmony depending on the balance between competition and co-operation among component parts. Rotations have wider benefits for the stockfree-organic grower.

They allow for a soil fertility management programme:

- some crops are heavy feeders, others prefer low fertility conditions;
- some crops prefer slightly acid, others prefer slightly alkaline conditions;
- green manuring;

- additions of compost, lime and other mineral amendments;

a soil structure improvement programme:

- potatoes have a cleaning effect, making the soil more friable;
- deep rooting crops should follow shallow rooting crops, helping to keep the soil structure open and assisting with drainage e.g. carrots and parsnips following onions and leeks;

and a weed management programme:

- different crops have differing weed problems, some will discourage weeds e.g. potatoes and parsnips whilst others may encourage certain weeds e.g. onions.

Setting up a rotation requires planning and keeping records is essential. Divide the growing area into the number of courses for the rotation. Plan the rotation for each course year by year but also keep records of what was actually grown. There are many examples of rotations: a few are given in this chapter. There is often a need for specific rotations and their form will depend on many factors:

Table 6.1 Families of different annual crops

Cabbage family	Brassicae	Brussel sprouts, broccoli, kale, cabbage, swede, kohl rabi, cauliflower, calabrese, radish, oriental brassicas, turnip, mustard.
Pea and bean family	Leguminosae	French bean, runner bean, broad bean, clover, lucerne, lupin, trefoil, vetch.
Carrot family	Umbelliferae	Carrot, celeriac, celery, fennel, parsley, parsnip.
Onion family	Allaceae	Chives, garlic, leek, onion, shallot.
Potato family	Solanaceae	Aubergine, pepper, potato, tomato.
Beetroot family	Chenopodiaceae	Beetroot, spinach, chard, spinach beet.
Cucumber family	Cucurbitaceae	Cucumber, squash, courgette, pumpkin, marrow.
Lettuce family	Compositae	Chicory, endive, lettuce, salsify.
Grass family	Gramineae	Sweetcorn, grazing rye, all grasses.

- soil type;
- geographical location and climate;
- inherent pest or weed problems;
- crop preferences of the grower;
- ability of the grower;
- access to labour and equipment;
- the available markets for produce;
- facilities available on the farm e.g. for storage.

Rotations will sometimes change as the registered holding and grower develops or in light of new technologies. A plan needs to be drawn up taking many factors into account and this plan will inevitably develop in future years.

The Stockfree-Organic Standards

7.1 Standard Requirement
Central to stockfree-organic systems is a well-designed crop rotation. It is advised that a grower achieves a balance between exploitative cropping (vegetables, pulses or cereals) and nitrogen-fixing green manures.

7.2 Recommended
(a) Nitrogen-fixing green manure leys e.g. clovers and lucerne.
(b) Using crops and green manures with different rooting systems.
(c) Avoiding plant families with similar pest and disease susceptibility on the same plot in the same course of the rotation.
(d) Separating crop families by a four-year interval (from harvesting to planting).
(e) Carrying out a soil analysis every rotation to monitor nutrient levels.

7.3 Restricted
(a) Greenhouse and polytunnel monocropping of annual crops.

7.4 Prohibited
(a) Alliums, brassicas and potatoes returning to the same land before a period of 48 months has elapsed.
(b) Continuous cereal crops.

Several examples of rotations that fulfil the desirable features and avoid other practices are discussed. These rotations tend to be above seven courses and there is good reason for this. Providing an all-year-round harvest is not the easiest of tasks and will take the individual stockfree-organic grower years to perfect. Other organic growing publications often discuss a simplified four-course rotation for vegetables. This type of rotation has proved inadequate for the crop production for box schemes that utilise green manures.

6.2 Field-scale rotations for staple and bulky crops

At Tolhurst Organic Produce we have devised a complex but highly successful cropping rotation. Three different rotations for the different scales are combined to supply an organic vegetable box scheme to 350 customers all year round. The rotations have taken over two decades to develop.

1. Field-scale rotation – covering fourteen acres (all fertility comes from green manures).
2. Walled garden rotation – covering two acres (fertility largely comes from green manures).
3. Polytunnel rotation – covering half an acre (fertility comes from a mixture of green manures and plant-based composts).

The field is divided into 7 two-acre plots. Each plot is planted with one family group with a fertility building ley at the beginning.

Plot 1 – Red clover or lucerne or sweet clover (pure stand).
Plot 2 – Red clover or lucerne or sweet clover (pure stand).
Plot 3 – Potatoes.
Plot 4 – Brassicas: cabbages, cauliflower, brussel sprouts, purple sprouting broccoli.
Plot 5 – Alliums: onions and leeks (one acre block each).
Plot 6 – Umbellifers: carrots and parsnips (one acre block each).
Plot 7 – Squash and sweetcorn (½ acre block each).

After a thirty-month red clover ley (which begins by undersowing the squash and sweetcorn in the seventh course of the rotation) the land in plot three is ploughed in the February or March and potatoes are planted. Potatoes require more nutrients than any other vegetable. After the potatoes are lifted (in a good year in September) red clover is planted after the earlies and also the maincrop. In a wet year when the potatoes are lifted late, the green manure after the maincrop is likely to be a cereal like oats, which will have a mopping up effect, preventing nitrate leaching.

The red clover or cereal green manure is ploughed in during early June and then there is a two-week delay before the overwinter brassicas are planted into Plot 4. The brassicas are planted as bare root transplants raised in the walled garden (see 6.3) and they are pushed in using the feet, thus avoiding bending down. Brussel sprouts are planted after early potatoes, cauliflowers are also planted in June and late autumn and winter cabbages are planted after maincrop potatoes in July. The Brussel sprouts are later undersown with phacelia, but the cabbages and cauliflowers are not, because green manure seeds may germinate in the crop (see 3.5.10). Harvesting occurs throughout the winter and the purple sprouting broccoli is allowed to flower in the spring to encourage beneficial insects.

Shortly afterwards the brassica stems are turned in (the phacelia having been winter killed) and the onions and leeks are planted into the fifth course of the rotation. The onions, planted as sets, are grown through plastic black mulches because this assists with improving soil temperature, moisture retention, weed control and the later drying of the crop once it has been pulled manually (as there are no drying stores). Strips of red clover are grown in between the plastic sheets (see 3.5.7) for added nitrogen fixation. The clover strips are where the tractor wheelings were when the plastic was laid. The leeks are grown on a ridge system. The leeks are of three different varieties that are set to mature at different times in the winter and early spring. They are generally undersown with a winter cereal in October, usually rye. The late sowing of the green manure is because alliums do not like competition in their root zones and so the leeks are allowed to mature to some extent before undersowing.

The winter cereal is turned in during the following spring. The rye among the leeks is allowed to grow up to a point of flowering before being cut down. It provides a bulk of organic matter. In the sixth course of the rotation the parsnips are planted where the onions were the previous year and carrots where the leeks were. These umbellifers do well in the lower fertility situations. They are not undersown. They are left in the ground and harvested when needed. As the harvesting is mechanical, often in wet conditions,

Figure 6.1 Diagrammatic representation of the Tolhurst field-scale rotation

⇩ Direction of rotation

1. Green manure ley	2. Green manure ley	3. Potatoes	4. Brassicas	5. Alliums	6. Umbellifers	7. squashes and sweetcorn
		¼ First earlies followed by red clover when lifted	¼ brussel sprouts 3 types 1. Mature Nov 2. Mature Christmas 3. Mature Jan / Feb	½ onion sets / black plastic with clover strips White onions Red onions Dried and stored	½ parsnip after onion	½ squashes Uchiki kuri Butternut Sweet mama Little gem Pyjama Dried and stored
		¼ Second earlies followed by red clover when lifted	⅛ cauli 2 types 1. Mature autumn 2. Mature early spring ⅛ purple broccoli	½ leek 3 types 1. Mature Nov 2. Mature Jan/Feb 3. Mature April Lift when needed	½ carrot after leek sown June because of carrot root fly	½ sweetcorn 3 types Mature at different dates Pick when ready

1. Green manure ley	2. Green manure ley	3. Potatoes	4. Brassicas	5. Alliums	6. Umbellifers	7. squashes and sweetcorn
		½ Maincrop followed by a cereal when lifted because it is too late for clover to germinate	½ overwinter cabbage • Red • White • Savoy Brassicas not generally undersown – cut when ready / will field store to some extent	Onions clover strips grow on. Leave plastic in situ good for earthworm breeding Leeks undersown with a cereal late October	Not undersown Stored in the ground and lifted when needed	Both undersown at the beginning of July with red clover or Lucerne. This forms the first year of the green manure ley

subsoiling may need to be carried out because of compaction, smears and tractor wheeling damage.

The final field crops in the stockfree-organic rotation are sweetcorn and squashes. Three different varieties of sweetcorn are sown successively to mature at different times over a three-month period and are undersown with the red clover or lucerne when they are about 30cm high.

Numerous varieties of squashes are grown spaced in one-metre rows, with a metre and half between the beds and are later undersown with the red clover or lucerne. The undersowing date is critical for squash. It has to be done as soon as the plants are established but before they go rampant with growth, usually in the second half of June. The squashes are an attractive addition to the vegetable boxes and can be stored until the following April. The undersowing of the sweetcorn and squashes is the start of the thirty-month ley and therefore begins the seven-year rotation. In sequencing (see table 6.3) year one and year eight are the same.

Table 6.2 Sequencing of the field-scale rotation over eight years

Year	Plot 1	Plot 2	Plot 3	Plot 4	Plot 5	Plot 6	Plot 7
1	Clover	Clover	Potatoes	Brassicas	Alliums	Umbell	Sq /s.c
2	Clover	Potatoes	Brassicas	Alliums	Umbell	Sq /s.c	Clover
3	Potatoes	Brassicas	Alliums	Umbell	Sq /s.c	Clover	Clover
4	Brassicas	Alliums	Umbell	Sq /s.c	Clover	Clover	Potatoes
5	Alliums	Umbell	Sq /s.c	Clover	Clover	Potatoes	Brassicas
6	Umbell	Sq /s.c	Clover	Clover	Potatoes	Brassicas	Alliums
7	Sq /s.c	Clover	Clover	Potatoes	Brassicas	Alliums	Umbell
8	Clover	Clover	Potatoes	Brassicas	Alliums	Umbell	Sq /s.c

6.3 Garden crop rotation in the walled garden at Tolhurst Organic Produce

The following vegetables are all tended by hand and so can be grown at close spacings. They are mostly grown at a standard spacing to allow for a regular pass of the wheel hoe.

Plot 1 - Red Clover or lucerne (pure stand).

Plot 2 - Brassicas (raising the bare root transplants for the field) and then overwinter kales (Russian, curly green, calvenero) and other oriental leaf crops.

Plot 3 - Alliums (mainly leek bare root transplants for the field-scale growing) followed by overwinter clover or cereal green manure.

Plot 4 - Beet family: leaf beet (perpetual spinach), chard and bunched beetroot.

Plot 5 - Umbellifers (early bunched carrot, celeriac, celery) followed by overwinter phacelia, buckwheat or cereal green manure.

Plot 6 – Legumes: broad beans, French beans and peas undersown to clover.

Plot 7 – Brassicas: calabrese broccoli, kales and kohl rabi followed by an overwinter cereal.

Plot 8 – Legumes: runner beans undersown with red clover or lucerne.

Plot 9 – Courgettes: grown in the red clover or lucerne ley.

The main fertility-building phase begins in eighth course of the rotation when runner beans are undersown with clover or lucerne. The green manure forms the paths between the bamboo structures supporting the runner beans. The next year a strip is taken out of the clover by a pedestrian-pushed rotovator but the green manure paths still remain for the courgettes, which are later undersown. The final year of the ley is the first course of the rotation. The strips / leys are regularly mown during their three year lifetime. Lucerne is the preferred green manure in this three-year fertility building, but it requires very dry conditions and therefore is more suited to the higher plots in the walled garden rather than the bottom plots, which can flood.

The overwinter green manures are primarily for growing in between successive crops. The cereal green manures such as rye or oats are particularly good for 'mopping up' residual fertility late in autumn and are excellent for weed control in spring. Phacelia is good for weed control in autumn. Vetch is a nitrogen fixer and can be sown as late as mid September and still give a good nitrogen fix in spring.

Figure 6.2 Diagrammatic representation of the Tolhurst garden crop rotation for the walled garden

1. Red clover or lucerne ley	2. Autumn brassicas – cabbages oriental leaf N.B. lettuce wherever there is space	3. Alliums Bare root transplant raising for field scale leeks followed by overwinter clover or cereal
4. Beet family Bunched beetroot Perpetual spinach (leaf beet) White, ruby and rainbow chard	5. Umbellifers early carrot celery, celeriac followed by overwinter phacelia, buckwheat or cereal	6. Legumes broad beans - one sowing peas - two sowings undersown with clover
7. Brassicas Broccoli, kohl rabi June sow kales	8. Runner beans 3 successional sowings undersown with red clover or lucerne (year one of ley)	9. Courgettes strips removed from red clover or lucerne and then at a later date the red clover is allowed to grow back around with bare patches resown

6.4 Protected cropping rotation

As all stockfree-organic growers know, the big difficulty when designing a protected cropping rotation is the predominance of just a couple of crop families. In the summer months the tomatoes, peppers and aubergines are all from the solanaceae family and over the autumn and winter the winter salad leaves are brassica top heavy.

Getting around these problems is no easy task. The rotation may involve some level of compromise, but under Stockfree-Organic Standard 7.3 the stockfree-organic grower is restricted from the monocropping of annual crops in the greenhouse and polytunnel. With the prohibition of the steam sterilising of soils under Stockfree-Organic Standard 11.4 it is difficult to see how a stockfree-organic grower could monocrop. As protected cropping rotations tend to be complex a definitive rotation is not suggested as they are too dependent on the individual grower and the market for the produce. However, there should be a regime of green manuring, adding well-made plant-based composts and remembering to keep brassicas and alliums 48 months apart. Crop pairings could include (although this list is not intended to be exhaustive):

- Tomatoes (early and maincrop), peppers and aubergines – undersown to yellow trefoil or Kent wild white clover.
- Early crucifers, main season brassica salad leaves / braising mix and overwinter brassica salad leaves - radish, kohl rabi, turnip, mustard leaves, mizuna, rocket and komatsuna.
- Early lettuce, main season non-brassica salad leaves and overwinter non-brassica salad leaves – early little gem lettuce, lettuce leaves, endives, claytonia, spinach, amaranth, sorrel, and corn salad.
- Overwinter carrots, early alliums, early beetroot, maincrop celery - overwinter carrots, spring onions, bunched beetroot and celery followed by a cereal green manure.
- Legumes and autumn oriental brassicas - French beans, followed by Chinese cabbage and pak choi.
- Cucurbits - early courgette, early summer squash and maincrop cucumber undersown with red clover.

6.5 Traditional four course rotation

The rotation often taught in standard texts is the four course rotation. It is quite easy to understand, but the difficulty with it is that it does not seem to allow enough space for potatoes and brassicas, the two mainstays of the British diet!

Plot 1 – Potatoes
Plot 2 – Legumes / Alliums
Plot 3 – Brassicas
Plot 4 – Roots and salads
Plot 5 – Fertility building ley (the Soil Association recommendation)

The Soil Association recommends that the land is divided into five so that one of the plots is fertility building for one year. It is the recommendation of this book that a one-year building fertility ley is not sufficient and that a two-year fertility building should be placed in longer rotations, if possible.

6.6 Beyond the rotation towards polyculture

Martin Wolfe[1] has argued that not only should we try to move away from the monoculture of chemical and GM-led agriculture but also away from modern organic rotations, and head towards a modern organic polyculture. Rotations are a central plank of organic systems but they represent only a small step from continuous monoculture towards polyculture. In a rotational system there is interaction among crops but the interaction is limited to the relationship between the amount and range of living and dead organic matter left by each crop in turn. Possible management methods for polyculture include:

- *Mixed cropping* where two or more crops are wholly interspersed to maximise their interaction (see mixed cropping 8.8 and undersowing 8.9).
- *Row intercropping* where different crops are planted in different but adjacent rows.
- *Strip intercropping* where different crops are grown in adjacent strips (see the Organic Grower's of Durham system described below).

These techniques obviously do not suit the use of machinery. However, the Organic Growers of Durham have managed to adapt these ideas to commercial cropping.

6.7 Organic Growers of Durham strip rotational system

When the present system of mulching was introduced in 1999 (see 2.9 and 3.6.2) a particular form of strip rotation was introduced, not directly for fertility, disease control or any of the usual reasons, but purely to facilitate the mulching process. The field is split into 64m x 2.4m strips that are fifty metres long. The principles of strip rotations are the same as block rotations, in terms of sequencing e.g. a strip that grew potatoes in Year 1 will be growing brassicas in Year 2 etc. However, rather than having only four blocks in the entire field, there are numerous strips with each four strips acting as mini-block rotations.

Figure 6.3 Diagrammatic representation of Organic Growers of Durham strip rotation system

a	b	c	d	a	b	c	d	a	b	c	d	a	b	c	d
Potatoes	Brassicas	Alliums / salads	Direct sow	Potatoes	Brassicas	Alliums / salads	Direct sow	Potatoes	Brassicas	Alliums / salads	Direct sow	Potatoes	Brassicas	Alliums / salads	Direct sow

← Direction of rotation in subsequent years

The first course of the rotation (a) is potatoes, because they are more capable of growing through the very thick layer of mulch that is applied (see 2.9). By the second year this mulch has already rotted down to about half the thickness. The second course of the rotation (b) consists of brassicas, because they lend themselves to being planted into quite a thick layer of mulch. Alliums and salad crops, on the other hand, are not so happy in a thick mulch, so they are planted in the third course (c) through black plastic, when the mulch has rotted even further and is no more than a couple of centimetres deep. By the fourth year (d) the hay / straw mulch is practically all incorporated, so the black plastic is removed and the soil is suitable for the direct sowing of crops like parsnips, carrots, peas and beans. Other crops, like spinach, chard, courgettes and tomatoes are put into the third course for no better reason than to equalise the size of the four courses.

1 Elm Farm Bulletin (1999).

Chapter Seven

Weed control

7.1 Introduction

Weeds are an important part of the food web, directly providing seeds for mammals and birds and indirectly providing the habitat for insects, which are also a food source for mammals and birds. When soil is bare, weeds will germinate. If these are not removed, the weeds act naturally in the best interest of the soil by covering it and preventing erosion, improving its structure (in the same way that green manures can), encouraging soil life, drawing up nutrients from the subsoil (if the weeds have taproots) and at death adding to organic matter levels. If the area is left for several years, the pioneer weeds will be replaced by woody shrubs, eventually culminating after decades in the climax vegetation of the forest. The autumn leaves then continue the job of building soil fertility that was started naturally by the weeds.

The stockfree-organic grower blocks the natural route towards fertility by removing or smothering weeds. When it comes to germination, weed seeds have a head start over crop seeds because they are already moist. Weed competition can have quite dramatic effects on crop growth. After three weeks weeds will compete with crops for light, nutrients and moisture causing weak growth making pest and disease attack more likely.

Roberts[1] cites research where weeds were carefully removed from separate plots of an onion crop at different times during the growth. It was found that once competition had started, the final yield of bulbs was being reduced at a rate equivalent to almost 4% per day, so that, by delaying weeding for a fortnight, the yield was cut to less than half compared to the plot that was kept weed-free all the time. He goes on to record that, by early June, in some plots the weight of weeds per unit area was twenty times that of the crop and the weeds had already taken from the soil about half of the nitrogen and a third of the potash that had been applied.

Perennial weeds with persistent underground roots or rhizomes such as couch grass, bindweed, ground elder, nettles, Japanese knotweed and horsetail are able to store reserves of food and are thus able to grow faster and more vigorously than annual weeds and annual crops. There is also evidence that the roots of some perennials such as couch grass exude allelopathic chemicals, which inhibit the growth of other nearby plants.

Weeds are important indicators of soil conditions and type, for example fat hen will often indicate high levels of available nitrogen, sorrel likes acid conditions, redshank shows poor drainage and mayweed thrives in compacted areas. A thorough understanding of the role weeds play as indicators can be extremely helpful in building up a picture of the soil's characteristics. The

© Graham Burnett

character and life cycles of weeds is dealt with comprehensively by John Walker in his book *Weeds – an earth friendly guide to their identification, use and control*[2] and is not further discussed in this chapter.

7.2 The principles of weeding

The stockfree-organic grower can have no control over the transportation of weed seeds by wind, water, birds and animals but can prevent them from growing into a problem. Since there are many types of weed, with much variation in growth patterns, they cannot be controlled by a single method. The use of several recommended practices will ensure that the stockfree-organic grower can effectively reduce the weed competition. Total weed control may not always be achievable or desirable.

Primarily the design of a rotation is important in reducing weed problems. Rotations play an essential role in weed control (see chapter 6 for examples) by preventing repeat conditions that favour a specific weed becoming well established. A well-designed rotation costs very little for a large level of weed management[3]. Allowances have to be made in rotation design to enable weeds to be effectively controlled by cultivations. Differing levels of fertility will encourage / discourage different weeds types. The effects of poor rotation design is often clearly demonstrated within conventional cereal growing where after many years the land becomes heavily infested with perennial weeds.

Cultivations are generally considered to be the next most effective way after rotations to control weeds. As with any type of cultivation there will inevitably be some soil damage. The more pernicious the weed such as docks or couch grass then the more aggressive the cultivation will need to be to bring the problem under control. In some instances priority will need to be given to controlling a bad infestation (see 7.4.4), which will mean that at some later point in the rotation there will need to be a restorative period to repair the physical damage that has been done to the soil e.g. the establishment of a green manure for a period of time (see 7.6).

The system of crop transplanting / direct sowing also needs careful consideration with respect to weed control. Crops grown in very closely spaced rows are much more difficult to keep weed-free than crops in widely spaced rows. It may be necessary to allow more space between crops on land that is very heavily contaminated with weed seeds or where the physical nature of the soil prevents accurate mechanical weed control.

The most important time to tackle weeds is when they are small seedlings at the cotyledon stage (looking like cress in a punnet) before the first true leaves have appeared, because at that point they are not competing with the crops. When small weeds are damaged, they die and their debris is returned to the soil enhancing fertility and improving the soil structure at the surface. When larger perennial weeds are removed there becomes an issue as to what do you do with this waste material. Removing larger weeds reduces fertility.

Weeding stages:

1. Wait two weeks – it is simply a case of surface cultivation with a hoe / tine where the slightest knock will kill the white stringy seedling.
2. Wait two months – the weeds have to be pulled out, twisted or shallowly dug out, which is more time-consuming and a strain (if weeding by hand) or more expensive (if using machinery).
3. Wait six months – the weeds will need to be dug out or ploughed in, which is the most time-consuming and expensive of all the three options.

Optimum weeding is governed by making the best use of time and resources. For example, three hoeing sessions at stage (1) may take less time and fewer resources than one weeding at stage (3). Early season weed competition is critical and this is the time to direct all your energy into weed control. Weeding is best in hot dry conditions so there is a balance to strike between waiting for good weather and letting the weeds get too big[4].

A situation may develop where a crop becomes heavily infested with weeds at an early stage. This is usually due to a problem with either a high weed seed bank or a lack of opportunity to develop a stale seedbed. It can be a particular problem with carrots that are slow to emerge and offer little smothering effect over the weeds. Trying to rescue such a crop is usually not economically viable, the crop will need to be cultivated in and if time allows re-drilled. It is pointless to waste days of labour hand weeding such a weedy crop, because as fast as you are clearing the weeds they are growing ahead of you. Young plants can have their yield potential severely damaged by weed competition at an early stage in their development.

Weed freedom throughout the life of a crop is an impossible dream. Results from the weed competition experiments at the Horticultural Research Institute and HDRA[5] have shown that there are periods when a crop needs to be weed free to prevent yield losses. Most vegetable crops needed to be weeded regularly, especially if they are to be undersown (see 7.7). Potatoes, the most competitive vegetable crop, have a wide weeding window, between two and eight weeks after 50% crop emergence. Yield losses of up to 20% occurred in unweeded or late-weeded crops. Unfortunately, there are no blue prints as to the 'critical weed-free period' for all crops but you would expect at least three weedings before July with spring-sown crops. Fortunately with weed diligence, the weed burden gets less over the years.

7.3 Recommended – stale seedbed techniques

Stockfree-Organic Standard 10.2(a)	
Stale seedbed techniques allowing a weed strike.	
Wider environmental impact	Reducing weed competition without the use of herbicides.
Advantages for the grower	Saving on weeding costs later on. Gives the crop seedlings a head start.
Disadvantages for the grower	Need dry weather conditions.

The stale seedbed technique exhausts the weed 'seed bank' at the surface. The first flush of weeds is scratched out of the surface, which reduces subsequent weed germination by 20%[6]. This will give the crop, especially if it is directly sown, more than a fighting chance against the weeds.

- Prepare a seedbed (see 2.7.2 to 2.7.6) two weeks ahead of direct sowing or transplanting.
- The more level the seedbed, the more effective the weed control later.
- Once the fast emerging weeds appear (at about 10 days), carefully cultivate the area on a dry day by scratching it to a depth of 1cm, using a metal rake, chain harrow, harrow comb or other non-powered harrow, taking care to disturb only the very surface layer of the soil.
- Allow the weeds to wilt and die and then direct sow / transplant into the

seedbed. There is no need to prepare the seedbed again with a secondary cultivation with powered machinery.

- Repeat and prepare a stale seedbed for a second time if there has been a prolonged wet period.
- It is important that the soil is left bare for the minimum amount of time since every cultivation is damaging.

Balsari et al[7] have found that, when creating stale seedbeds, mechanical surface cultivation with a tine harrow has a cheaper operational cost than flame weeding with similar results in terms of weed control. Under Stockfree-Organic Standard 10.4(a) flame weeding is a restricted practice.

7.4 Recommended – Pre-emergence and post-emergence operations

Stockfree-Organic Standard 10.2(b) Pre-emergence and post-emergence operations	
Wider environmental impact	Use of machinery fuel but can use biodiesel.
Advantages for the grower	Allows for high yielding stockfree-organic crops.
Disadvantages for the grower	Timing can be critical - need dry weather conditions.
	Weeding equipment, especially inter row can be expensive although more affordable, 'low tech' alternatives are available.

7.4.1 Hand hoeing

A hand hoe is a sharp blade fixed to a handle, which slices the weed seedlings just below the surface. The action of the hoe should be to skim and not chop, making work fast and efficient.

- The Dutch or push hoe is readily available from all garden centres, however, there are superior hoes available.
- Wolfe™ has developed a double-edged stirrup hoe that we prefer and it can take different attachments. It has a particularly efficient push-pull action and is available in various sizes.

- Oscillating stirrup hoes (available though the *Organic Gardening Catalogue*) are particularly good for tackling larger weeds but require more effort and are harder work on the arms.

John Walker[8] recommends that you:

- Keep the hoe blade sharp at all times with a small file.
- Hoe when it is sunny and breezy so that larger weeds will wilt and die.
- Do not hoe after rain because the surface is too wet and foot traffic is likely to increase compaction.
- Ensure the blade skims below the surface, cutting the weed seedlings off cleanly.
- Take extra care when hoeing near crop plants to avoid damage. (This is where stirrup hoes come into their own if they brush against crops.)

Eliot Coleman[9] discusses the 'hoeing stance'. A long handled hoe will facilitate good posture in an upright position. The shaft should be held by both hands 50cm apart with both thumbs pointing up the handle. The accurate strokes should be smooth, similar to a sweeping motion. Jerky or chopping movements should be avoided. The aim is not to move piles of earth around but to skim the surface. Hoeing should be enjoyable, providing gentle exercise rather than becoming an arduous and back-breaking task.

Hand hoeing is limited by area, so when growing on an intensive scale the wheel hoe is the best tool for inter-row work. Glasser™ wheel hoes can be imported from the US through Johnny's Selected Seeds[10]. Hoeing (either by hand or wheel hoe) can be speeded up if crops are sown in straight rows and crops are equidistant apart; this can be aided by a studded roller. The hoe can then be taken in a north-south direction for each row and then an east-west direction, so that that the inter-row and intra-row spacings are the same. The loss of yield due to standardised spacing is more than compensated for by the decreased costs of weeding[11].

7.4.2 Ploughing

Ploughing buries weed seeds, weed seedlings and other surface materials, instantly putting them below a level from which they can emerge. This book recommends shallow ploughing no deeper than 15cm. Ploughing is most

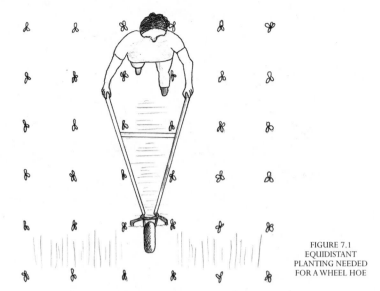

FIGURE 7.1
EQUIDISTANT
PLANTING NEEDED
FOR A WHEEL HOE

effective for small seeded weeds or annual grass weeds. However, when dealing with tap-rooted perennial weeds with side branches like dock or creeping thistle, burying alone will not work (see 7.4.4).

7.4.3 Common implements for inter-row weeding with tractors[12]

Inter-row weeding machines are most effective at killing weeds when they have between zero and three true leaves. It is important to work as closely as possible to the crop row, which should limit the amount of hand-hoeing and intra-row weeding needed and will also increase soil nitrification close to the crop. The need for very accurate drilling / transplanting is essential.

- Check for the symmetry of crop rows around the centre of the tractor / bed so that the weeder can go up and down the rows[13].

Ensuring the crop is not damaged while taking the weeder close to it requires accurate steering, which means straight lines, slow work rates and high running costs.

Weed harrows - The traditional and still most common types of weeding implements are weed harrows with their fixed, sprung or rotating tines or teeth that work both between and within rows simultaneously. They have the advantage of speed and low cost. They have a cutting, uprooting and weed-covering action and usually give good weed control.

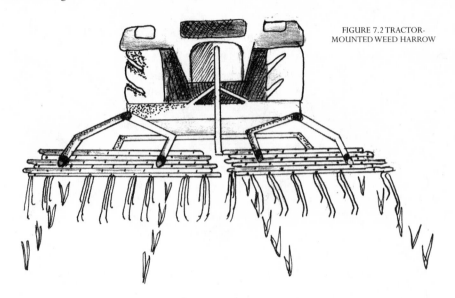

FIGURE 7.2 TRACTOR-
MOUNTED WEED HARROW

Hoes - Steerage hoes are mounted on independent units fitted with their own wheel depth, each covering a row. Hoe types fall into two groups: sweeps and ducksfoots.

- Sweep hoes have weeding blades in either an L or A shape and are designed to work just below the surface, causing little soil disturbance. The blades cut the roots of the weeds and have an action that is unaffected by the size of the weeds. Fibrous rooted weeds are more difficult to control. Sweep hoes are suitable for inter-row work on the flat.
- The ducksfoot hoe is normally fitted to a spring tine and has a more aggressive action, causing soil disturbance. It is therefore not suitable for use in narrow rows.
- At Tolhurst Organic Produce the ducksfoot has been particularly effective in conjunction with building ridges for field-scale vegetable production. As the ducksfoot and large spring tines travel down the row, they throw soil and small weeds onto the ridge, therefore achieving effective weeding and building the ridge at the same time. It is possible to use the ducksfoot in a high forward gear, although careful steering must also be observed. This equipment is inexpensive.

Brush weeders - consist of rotating nylon brushes that brush 3-5 cm deep over the topsoil and uproot and destroy small weeds. Brush weeders generally have vertical nylon brushes mounted on a horizontal axle rotating in the driving direction. The brushes can be adjusted to cater for different row widths. Shields protect the crop from the rotating brushes. The brush weeder is superior in wet conditions but in dry conditions can create too much dust, spoiling edible leaves, and is also relatively expensive to buy.

For further information about weeding machines consult Charles Merfield's *Organic Weed Management: a Practical Guide*[14], which provides a thorough analysis.

7.4.4 Harrowing and rotovating
Power harrowing and rotovating are not suitable for either inter-row work or removing the first flush of weeds from the stale seedbed. Their aggressive action will also only serve to dry out the soil and bring more weed seeds to the surface. However, harrowing and rotovating can have their uses in controlling difficult weeds.

The primary approach to managing perennial weeds with cultivation is to exhaust the plant by separating the above-ground and underground parts and then exhausting the food reserves in the underground parts. Fallows are very effective, especially on shallower and vertical perennial weeds but are very hard on the soil. As they also remove land from production they should only be used when there is a serious problem[15].

FIGURE 7.3
COUCH GRASS

For tackling ground infested with perennial weeds with shallow and deep interconnected root systems, e.g. couch grass and nettles:

* For deep roots subsoiling may be useful but must be followed by a bastard fallow or the problem will get worse[16].
* Rotovate or power harrow the weeds to

a depth of up to 8cm in May. Do not cultivate any deeper than the roots.

- Observe a bastard fallow for June and July. You want to place the roots on the surface to dry out. Cultivate with spring tines to a depth of around 12cm in opposite directions every fortnight.
- Sow an overwinter green manure in August (see 3.5.4.)

For tackling ground infested with tap-rooted weeds e.g. docks:

- Many tap-rooted weeds cannot recover if they are destroyed to a depth of 10cm although such deep rotovating will cause damage to the soil. Therefore weaken by defoliation and chopping.
- Rotovate or power harrow to a depth of 6 cm at two-week intervals in July.
- Plough and prepare for the drilling of an overwinter green manure.

These techniques for perennial weed control are, however, dependent on good weather[17]. Commercial growers with weeds like bindweed, where the roots break easily, may have to learn to live with the problem as the techniques described in this section will not work. Regular hoeing may help as bindweed has a relatively short window of growth.

7.4.5 Topping
There is much in the adage 'one year seeding, nine years weeding' and stockfree-organic growers have to be realistic in that they may not always be able to remove seedlings in their early stages. Therefore, preventing seeding becomes the priority.

- Cut the heads off perennial weeds no later than when they are at their flowering stage.
- For docks, thistles and nettles use a machete or secateurs and place heads in a bag. Ensure the seeds of older plants do not spill onto the soil.
- Mow green manures to prevent annual weeds going to seed.

7.4.6 Hand weeding
Weeding in-between rows is quite straightforward, providing that the rows are straight. However, intra-row weeds growing in-between the crops are more difficult to control and therefore it may be necessary to hand hoe in-between or pull the weeds by hand.

If all else fails it may be necessary to physically dig the weeds out, especially if they have tap roots. The best way to get docks out is to wait until after rain.

- Two people with spades stand opposite each other.
- The spades are dug into the ground, at an angle with the aim of getting underneath but avoiding slicing the roots.
- Both spades act as levers and the joint force makes the docks easier to get out.

The Lazy Dog Tool Company[18] has also invented tools for removing established weeds with tap roots and rhizomes.

Weeds with rhizomes and root systems that easily break, like bindweed and horsetail, require a different technique. These weeds are tricky customers, since leaving the smallest amount of rhizome in the soil will result in further weeds. Chopping up such weeds exacerbates the problem. If you have time and the area is not too large, cover with plastic to get the greenery to die back and then fork out the roots. Forking, which involves lifting, turning and breaking up the soil to remove the weeds, is the traditional way of clearing weed-infested ground. By loosening the soil and breaking it into crumbs, it is possible to remove the tiniest bits of roots. However, this form of meticulous weeding is limited by scale.

7.5 Recommended - Pre-germination, propagation and transplanting

Stockfree-Organic Standard 10.2(c) Pre-germination, propagation and transplanting	
Wider environmental impact	More compost and water resources required than direct sowing.
Advantages for the grower	Reliable technique for ensuring a head start on the weeds.
Disadvantages for the grower	Resources and cost.

Seedling weeds can be difficult to tell apart from germinating crops, therefore hampering weeding because the stockfree-organic grower may fear removing the crop as well as the weeds. An often overlooked tool in reducing weed competition is to establish a good crop stand through transplanting (see 5.3.5) that will shade out the weeds quickly.

For certain crops, particularly potatoes, carrots, parsnips and crucifers, direct sowing is the only option. In these circumstances it is important to mark the rows so that weeding can occur whilst the seedlings are emerging. Marking can occur by:

- tractor wheelings;
- planting into a ridge;
- leaving the line up along the seed drill;
- covering the seed drill with seed compost.

7.6 Recommended – Green manure leys maintained for several years in rotation and repeatedly mowed

Stockfree-Organic Standard 10.2(d) Green manure leys maintained for several years in rotation and repeatedly mowed.	
Wider environmental impact	Avoids transporting bulky organic wastes. Requires machinery fuel.
Advantages for the grower	Fertility building and reducing the weed seed bank part of the same strategy.
Disadvantages for the grower	Requires maintenance. Cost.

After a ley break the weed population is likely to be at its lowest. However, establishing a ley can be very vulnerable to dock infestation, because there is the potential for huge numbers of dock seeds in the soil to germinate in spring and autumn. Fortunately, dock seedlings cannot compete well with grasses at this stage and so good establishment will reduce the likelihood of early invasion[19].

- Destroy roots of old docks (see 7.4.4).
- Prepare a firm seedbed to ensure rapid development of the green manure.
- Use a generous grass seed mix where docks are a particular problem.

Well-established leys have a 'cleaning effect' (see 6.2 and 6.3 for examples of best practice when integrating a ley into a rotation) as the tough roots of green manures like lucerne will even compete with perennial weeds. Tight mowing to the soil level is a tried and tested method (see 3.5.6) for killing annual weeds in green manure leys (see 7.6). Depending on scale of growing, the equipment needed for mowing is either:

- a tractor-mounted flail mower (ideal for in situ mulching);
- a pasture topper (adequate for in situ mulching);
- a sit-on mower;
- a general garden mower;
- a strimmer;
- a scythe or
- a pair of shears.

It may still be necessary to go and dig up the odd dock (see 7.4.6) and nuisance perennial weed.

7.7 Recommended - Undersowing crops with green manures e.g. clover

Stockfree-Organic Standard 10.2(e) Undersowing crops with green manures e.g. clover.	
Wider environmental impact	Avoids transporting bulky organic wastes.
Advantages for the grower	Fertility building and reducing the weed seed bank part of the same strategy.
Disadvantages for the grower	Maintenance.

The emphasis on undersowing (see 3.5.10) in stockfree-organic systems means that hoeing and inter-row work become essential at the beginning of the season during the early stages of crop development. After undersowing (usually late June / July) further weeding should not be necessary, except for the odd hand-roguing of perennial weeds.

- The green manure seeds must be undersown into a clean seedbed.
- The last surface cultivation should be the day before undersowing.

Once the crop canopy and clover work together the weeds will have serious competition, whilst at the same time gaining all the other advantages of undersowing (see 3.5.10). The other advantage of undersowing is covering the soil over winter, and the ground cover in spring will compete with any emerging weeds.

FIGURE 7.4 CHICKWEED

© Graham Burnett

If for some reason undersowing has not taken place, e.g. in a cauliflower crop where the broadcast green manure seeds could germinate in the heart of the brassica, it is good practice to allow a ground cover of weeds to establish. For example, a covering of chickweed can be very useful in preserving soil structure and mopping up excess nutrients, performing the same role as the undersown green manure.

7.8 Recommended – Mulches of straw and hay

Stockfree-Organic Standard 10.2(f) Mulches of straw and hay

Wider environmental impact	Transport of bulky materials.
Advantages for the grower	
	No need for surface cultivation techniques.
Disadvantages for grower	Land out of production when the weeds are the being smothered.
	Getting access to enough suitable materials may limit scale.
	Need to ensure that it is light excluding.

This chapter so far has described the physical control of weeds by damaging them using cultivation. However, weeds can also be controlled by smothering. Weed seeds need light to germinate and mulching techniques prevent sunlight reaching the soil surface. These techniques are discussed in detail in the sections 2.9 and 3.6.2.

Authors disagree whether you should cultivate before setting up the mulching system or at the very least dig out the perennial weeds. It depends on how long you want to wait. Some stubborn weeds, like horsetail or couch grass, will take at least two years to rot, possibly four. Once the site is reclaimed from weeds the mulching needs continual topping-up to ensure that it is still excluding light. A single hand-roguing will probably be needed of perennial weeds that have managed to push their way through the mulch.

7.9 Recommended - Alternating weed suppressing with weed susceptible crops

Stockfree-Organic Standard 10.2(g) Alternating weed suppressing with weed susceptible crops	
Wider environmental impact	Not quantified.
Advantages for the grower	Improves soil structure.
Disadvantages for the grower	Increase complexity of the rotation.

As already stated, rotation is the greatest means of preventing weed problems. Vegetable crop rotations should include smother crops like a green manure ley, potatoes and brassicas. Carrots and onions do not compete well with the weeds and therefore inter-row weeding and plastic mulches (for alliums only) come into their own. Once lifted, short-lived crops like radish, lettuce and small-leafed spinach can be followed immediately by another crop. These catch crops then provide the additional benefit of depleting the weed seed bank as effectively as a short fallow period.

7.10 Ensuring composting reaches at least 60°C so that plant-based composts do not contain weed seeds

Stockfree-Organic Standard 10.2(h) Ensuring composting reaches at least 60°C so that plant-based composts do not contain weed seeds	
Wider environmental impact	Not quantified.
Advantages for the grower	Fewer weed seeds.
Disadvantages for the grower	Managing a heap is time-consuming.

Weed control starts with the soil fertility programme. Chapter 4 examines best composting practice to create compost that does not contain pathogens or viable weed seeds. This involves:

- using selected ingredients including crop wastes, grass clippings, legume-rich hays and straw;
- mixing plant-based ingredients ('greens' and 'browns');
- composting plant-based materials and leaf mould separately;
- building a heap of sufficient volume, at least one cubic metre;
- turning the heap to assist with aeration;
- monitoring temperature rises;
- covering the heap or windrow to prevent it from becoming waterlogged.

7.11 Permitted practices – use of plastic mulches

Wider environmental impact	Fossil fuel intensive manufacture.
	Pollution risks with manufacture.
	End of life disposal.
Advantages for the grower	Warms the soil.
	Excludes the weeds.
Disadvantages for the grower	Cost.
	End disposal.

7.11.1 Plastic mulches for alliums
Many commercial stockfree-organic growers use black plastic to grow bulb onions. At Tolhurst Organic Produce we use a roller with studs on. Once the plastic is laid, the roller can be run over it to puncture the plastic at the correct spacing for onions. We then use onion sets and simply push them through the plastic, which is a quick operation by hand. Once the onions have grown, the bulbs are lifted and left to solar dry on top of the plastic, showing that you do not need sophisticated drying facilities for onions. The plastic is sometimes left in situ until the following year, because it encourages earthworm breeding. It also helps break the cycle of perennial weeds. Recently we have been experimenting with the use of biodegradable plastic mulches.

7.11.2 Plastic mulches where they raise soil temperature for season extension of harvesting e.g. during early spring
Practices for improving season extension and alternatives to plastic are discussed in chapter 12.

7.11.3 Plastic mulches for perennial plants
Many perennial crops like strawberries, rhubarb, cane and bush fruit are grown through long-lasting woven mulches, which are water permeable, like Terram™ or Mipex™.

7.13 Routine use of plastic mulches

Stockfree-Organic Standard 10.4 reads:
Restricted
(b) routine use of plastic mulches.

Arguments of the Standards Working Group:

- For: reduces the need to weed and raises soil temperature.
- Against: manufacture and end disposal are polluting.

Reason for restriction: the use of plastic has been permitted for alliums, season extension and perennial crops. These are essential techniques for improving all-year-round supply. Using plastic has to be weighed against importing food. However, plastic, as discussed in chapter 10, has become the scourge of organic agriculture and so restrained use is to be encouraged.

7.12 Restricted practice – flame weeding

Stockfree-Organic Standard 10.4 reads:
Restricted
(a) flame weeding.

Arguments of the Standards Working Group:

- For: essential for achieving stale seedbeds.
- Against: unacceptable practice due to its indiscriminate nature, having effect on insects, small mammals, toads and reptiles.

Reason for restriction: the Standards Working Group took the wildlife implications to be paramount and, following on from the research of Balsari et al[20] (who found that physical cultivation has cheaper operation costs than flame weeding), it is not considered to be entirely necessary.

7.14 Prohibited – The use of any herbicide

Worldwide, herbicides (weedkillers) account for nearly a half of all agricultural chemicals applied[21]. When herbicide is applied to plants, most is either taken up by plants or degraded by microbial and chemical pathways. But a proportion is dispersed to the environment. Some of that is vapourised, eventually returning to the earth as rainfall, some remains in the soil, while some reaches surface and groundwater by runoff and leaching.

The concentration of banned herbicides has increased over time, with particular concerns in the Netherlands over paraquat and diquat in sandy soils attaching themselves to soil particles. Modern herbicides, however, are much more mobile and readily transfer from soil to water. Isoproturon, mecoprop, atrazine and chlorotoluron are frequently associated with breaches in drinking water quality. The herbicides atrazine and simazine have been found to be four times higher than EU standards in East Anglian chalk aquifers[22].

1 ROBERTS, H.A. (1991) in BLEASDALE et al The Complete Know and Grow Vegetables. OUP.

2 WALKER J (2003) Weeds an Earth Friendly Guide to their Identification, Use and Control. Cassell Illustrated.

3 MERFIELD C (2002) Organic Weed Management: a Practical Guide. Available at www.merfield.com/research/organic-weed-management-a-practical-guide.pdf

4 MERFIELD C (2002) Organic Weed Management: a Practical Guide. Available at www.merfield.com/research/organic-weed-management-a-practical-guide.pdf

5 BOND W et al (1988) Choosing Your Moment – Optimum Timing for Weed Control. Organic Farming 60: 22-23.

6 CLOUTIER D & LEBLANC ML (2002) Effect of the Combination of the Stale Seedbed Technique with Cultivations on Weed Control in Maize. 5th European Weed Research Society workshop on Physical Weed Control.

7 BALSARI P et al (2002) Mechanical and Physical Weed Control in Maize. 5th European Weed Research Society workshop on Physical Weed Control.

8 WALKER J (2003) Weeds an Earth Friendly Guide to their Identification, Use and Control. Cassell Illustrated.

9 COLEMAN E (1995) The New Organic Grower – a Masters Manual of Tools and Techniques for the Home and Market Gardener. Chelsea Green publishing company.

10 Johnny's Selected Seeds, 955 Benton Avenue, Winslow, Maine 04901-2601 USA. www.johnnyseeds.com

11 MERFIELD C (2002) Organic Weed Management: a Practical Guide. Available at www.merfield.com/research/organic-weed-management-a-practical-guide.pdf

12 Information from PULLEN D (1999) Field Work – a Look at the Performance of Different Field Weeders. Organic farming 61: 18-19 and BEVAN J (2000) Tackling weeds in the row. Organic farming 67: 17-19.

13 MERFIELD C (2002) Organic Weed Management: a Practical Guide. Available at www.merfield.com/research/organic-weed-management-a-practical-guide.pdf

14 Available at www.merfield.com/research/organic-weed-management-a-practical-guide.pdf

15 MERFIELD C (2002) Organic Weed Management: a Practical Guide. Available at www.merfield.com/research/organic-weed-management-a-practical-guide.pdf

16 MERFIELD C (2002) Organic Weed Management: a Practical Guide. Available at www.merfield.com/research/organic-weed-management-a-practical-guide.pdf

17 ELM FARM RESEARCH BULLETIN (2001) Managing Docks through Cultivation. 54:8-9.

18 The Lazy Dog Tool Company, Hill Top Farm, Spaunton, Appleton Le Moors, North Yorkshire YO62 6TR. Tel/fax: 01751 417 351 www.sg.clara.net/lazydogtoolcompany.

19 HOPKINS A & BOWLING P (1988) Pernicious Weeds. Organic Farming 60: 26-27.

20 BALSARI P et al (2002) Mechanical and Physical Weed Control in Maize. 5th European Weed Research Society workshop on Physical Weed Control.

21 DINHAM B (1996) Growing Food Security. Pesticides Trust and PAN, London.

22 PRETTY J (1988) The Living Land. Earthscan publications.

Chapter Eight

Diseases, competing molluscs, insects, mammals & birds

8.1 Introduction

This chapter looks at functional biodiversity and at techniques to reduce the incidence of disease, competing molluscs, insects, mammals and birds. Chapter 9 looks at environmental conservation for its own sake.

In natural ecosystems pest and diseases have the specific role of attacking weak points making space for better-adapted species. Stability is achieved through balance, with pests and disease pathogens themselves being controlled by other organisms. A soil with an active microbial population is likely to have individual micro-organisms kept in balance by the action of their antagonists. Usually their role is beneficial, so the existence of a pest or disease could be an indicator of previous or current mismanagement, e.g. monoculture, and will need to be addressed.

> **Stockfree-Organic Standard 11.1 reads**
> Disease and insect pest control is largely a matter of prevention rather than cure.

In established stockfree-organic systems, pests and diseases are generally not a problem. This stems from the fact that a healthy plant, given optimal soil conditions and balanced nutrition, will be better able to resist slugs, competing insects and pathogens. Stockfree-organic growing involves recognising the basic premise that diversity creates stability and spreads risk. Creating a complex system of checks and balances within a living and vibrant eco-system requires a systems-based approach[1], rather than tackling one problem in isolation.

Contrary to conventional approaches, where synthetic chemicals kill both beneficial and competing organisms indiscriminately, the systems-based approach seeks to develop an understanding of the webs of interaction. For example, the eradication of competing insects is undesirable, for without them the beneficial predatory and parasitic insects that depend upon them as food or hosts would not be able to survive. The grower therefore works to create a system where competing insects are kept at manageable levels.

This chapter is a general reference guide, rather than a detailed encyclopaedia of strategies for coping with pests and diseases.

8.1.1 Encouraging beneficial insects

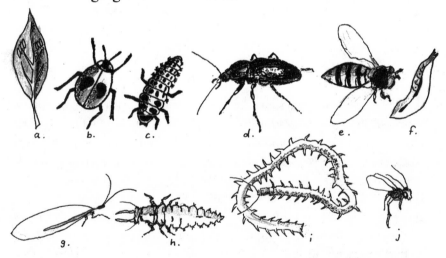

FIGURE 8.1 – BENEFICIAL INSECTS (NOT TO SCALE): LADYBIRD EGGS, LADYBIRD, LADYBIRD LARVAE, GROUND BEETLE, HOVERFLY, HOVERFLY LARVAE, LACEWING, LACEWING LARVAE, CENTIPEDE, PARASITIC WASP

Most beneficial insects will appear naturally on the registered holding, providing that you provide their required diversity of plants and habitats. Get to know which creatures are most helpful and then provide them with food, water and a comfortable home.

8.1.1.1 Ladybirds
- Ladybirds, and in particular their larvae (which are active between May and July), are voracious predators of aphids and will also consume mites, scale insects and small caterpillars. This beetle, recognisable to most people by its red and black markings, can also be yellow or orange.
- The larvae are initially small and spidery, growing up to 17mm long. They have a tapering segmented grey / black body with orange / yellow markings.
- Ladybirds can be encouraged by cultivating a patch of nettles.
- They like to hibernate en masse in houses, hedgerows, hollow stems, between sheets of loose bark, slate or corrugated card.

8.1.1.2 Ground beetles
- Ground and carabid beetles are shiny purple-black backed beetles up to 2.5cm long. They are mostly nocturnal, preying on slugs and caterpillars as well as smaller competing insects.
- Slimmer rove beetles are brown and black, looking like earwigs with pincers. They eat slugs' eggs and grubs in the soil.
- Beetles tend to live in soil or under debris and can be encouraged with compost heaps, mulches or places where it is moist or shady, e.g. beetle banks (see 8.5.1).

8.1.1.3 Hoverflies
- Hoverflies resemble small slim wasps but are slightly darker with only one set of wings. They have characteristic hovering rather than darting flight patterns.
- The hoverfly is the most important predator of the aphid. There are over 100 species of hoverfly whose larvae principally feed upon aphids, one larva devouring up to 800 during its 10 – 12 day larval period[2].
- The larvae also eat fruit tree spider mites and small caterpillars.
- Eggs are minute (1mm), pale yellow white and laid singly near aphid colonies.
- Larvae are 8 -17mm long, disguised to resemble bird droppings, are legless with no distinct head and are semi-transparent in brown or green.
- Adults feed on nectar and pollen, which they require for egg production.
- Hoverflies can be encouraged by growing open attractant flowers (see 8.5.4 and 8.7).

8.1.1.4 Lacewings
- It is the larva and not the adult lacewing that is the voracious eater of aphids.

- Lacewings are sheer shimmering insects with large flimsy wings and yellow eyes. They are nectar feeders and pollinators, which can be encouraged in the same way as hoverflies (see 8.5.4 and 8.7).
- They will overwinter in lacewing hotels, which can be bought from organic product stockists. However, it is very cheap to make them from plastic soft drink bottles with the bottoms cut off and stuffed with straw or corrugated card. They are then hung from trees or in polytunnels.

8.1.1.4 Centipedes
- Centipedes are long and segmented, with one set of legs per segment (millipedes have two) and are fast moving.
- Most are yellow or brown.
- They often prey on slugs and snails.
- Encourage them in the same way as beetles.

8.1.1.5 Parasitic wasps
- Parasitic wasps are a diverse range of wasps, which lay their eggs on or in the body of an insect host, which is then used as a food by developing larvae that look similar to maggots.
- Parasitic wasps take much longer than predators to consume their victims, for, if the larvae were to eat too fast, they would run out of food before they became adults.
- Such parasites are very useful, as they are very efficient hunters. As they fly from place to place, the adults require high amounts of energy in the form of nectar, pollen and sap. They are encouraged by flowering plants (see 8.5.4 and 8.7).

8.1.2 Encouraging beneficial creatures
8.1.2.1 Frogs and toads[3]
- Frogs and toads are particularly successful at controlling aphids and scale insect infestations.
- Toads are commonly recommended for pest control on small organic horticultural units.
- They are opportunist eaters, i.e. they attempt to catch and eat anything that is small enough for them to swallow, and they regularly eat flies and their larvae (of which there are many competing species), spiders and aphids.
- They will also eat beetles, which is a mixed blessing, for, as well as eating

weevils and mealworms, they will eat ladybirds. On balance they do more good than harm.

- They rely on ponds for breeding, but the rest of the year can be found in damp, warm and shady places.
- Ensure there are suitable terrestrial habitat features, including secure damp places where adults can shelter and hibernate. For example, leave fallen wood and rocks to provide daytime hiding.
- Allow travel between terrestrial and aquatic habitats by linking them with hedgerows, ditches or dry stone walls.
- Most male frogs hibernate at the bottom of a pond, while toads and female frogs overwinter in damp hidden places such as under stones or old logs.
- Ensure that you have several suitable ponds, which will also become an important watering hole for beneficial insects and creatures (see 8.10 and 9.21).
- Allow undisturbed areas around ponds.

8.1.2.2 Newts
- Newts look like lizards but have no scales and move very slowly.
- These amphibians' favourite foods include slugs, snails, worms and a variety of insects.
- The adults spend the summer and autumn on land, hiding under stones or in thick grass and emerging at night to feed, however, not much about their feeding habits is known.
- Most hibernate on land, returning to pools to breed in the spring.
- Ensure that you have a suitable pond, which will also become an important water hole for all the beneficial insects (see 8.10 and 9.20).
- Ensure that there are secure damp places where adults can shelter and hibernate.

8.1.2.3 Slow worms

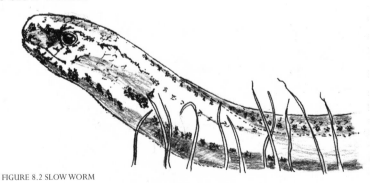

FIGURE 8.2 SLOW WORM

- Slow worms look like snakes but are technically legless lizards. They vary in colour from metallic grey to coppery dark brown.
- Slugs form a major part of a slow worm's diet.
- They are shy creatures but they will bask in the partial sunlight of long grass but spend much of their time underground, where they also hibernate.
- Ensure that you provide long grass and stones in a warm sunny spot.
- Their young need somewhere warm and insulated like a compost heap.

8.1.2.4 Hedgehogs

- Hedgehogs are a favourite British mammal. They hide during the day under shrubs in hedge bottoms or in long grass.
- They hunt at night, travelling up to several miles for food.
- The hedgehog's diet includes slugs, millipedes, caterpillars, insects, bird eggs and small mammals including mice.
- Ensure that you provide daytime shelter and hibernation sites such as low thick shrubs, leaves behind a shed and log piles. They can be encouraged to overwinter in polytunnels providing suitable sites are maintained and are not disturbed. They will often come out at night during warm spells to forage around the tunnel floor.

8.1.2.5 Bats

- Bats are the most effective controllers of summer biting insects such as mosquitoes and midges.
- In the first two hours after dusk a pipistrelle bat (the most common species) will consume eight to ten insects per minute. This is also the time when codling moths are at their most active.
- Bats roost mainly in warm dry hollows in trees and in crevices in buildings.
- Put up a bat box if there are no natural roosts.
- Erect three boxes for every one inhabited, as bats like to choose different sites. In all cases it is important to ensure that bat boxes are firmly anchored to their support to prevent any movement occurring.

8.1.2.6 Birds

Whilst birds are often thought of as troublesome, birds on the whole should be encouraged onto the registered holding. Particularly:

- song thrushes and blackbirds, which will eat small slugs and caterpillars;

- small birds, e.g. bluetits, robins and sparrows, which will pick off aphids and codling moth cocoons. They will also pick over freshly dug earth for pests;
- starlings, which will feed on leatherjackets;
- even seed-eaters like finches will feed their young on insects.

To encourage them provide different levels of vegetation, e.g. a tall tree, shrubbery and undergrowth, bird boxes, birdbaths, winter feeding stations and provide seed and fruit-bearing flowers and shrubs (see 9.5). An experiment[4] in the Netherlands showed that the presence of great tits in an apple orchard reduced the amount of caterpillar damage to fruit and increased the yield from 4.7kg to 7.8kg a tree.

8.2 Recommended - Balanced rotational cropping to break pest and disease cycles

Stockfree-Organic Standard 11.2(a) Balanced rotational cropping to break pest and disease cycles.

Wider environmental impact	Reducing pest and disease cycles without the use of pesticides.
Advantages for the grower	Very effective method.
Disadvantages for the grower	Rotational difficulties in protected cropping where pest and disease problems may be even more prominent.

Any cropping activity inevitably involves a simplification of the ecosystem and the antagonistic relationships (see 8.1) are adversely affected. Rotations are one way of attempting to restore biological diversity to a cropping system. The basic principle of crop rotation is to keep closely related annual crops together and grow them on a different piece of land each year in a regular sequence. The most commonly recognised benefit is that it helps to avoid the build-up of soil borne pests such as eelworms and pathogens such as onion white rot, which attack only closely related crops. Rotations are not, however, the only way of introducing biodiversity.

8.3 Recommended - Dividing up large fields with hedgerows

Stockfree-Organic Standard 11.2(b) Dividing up large fields with hedgerows.

Wider environmental impact	Reducing pest and disease cycles without the use of pesticides. Increasing farm biodiversity.
Advantages for the grower	Very effective method for achieving predator-pest balance. Windbreaks.
Disadvantages for the grower	Reduced cropping area. Initial planting costs. Regular maintenance.

Good hedgerow management will support an abundance of insects, provide habitat for a range of birds and mammals, and provide a rich supply of food for some species throughout the year. Many species of predatory insects, e.g. rove beetles and common earwigs overwinter almost exclusively in field boundaries and hedge banks. The main aim of hedgerow management should be to maintain a range of different types and sizes of hedgerow, to support a wide variety of wildlife. Consult BTCV's Hedging Handbook available at http://handbooks.btcv.org.uk for best practice.

8.4 Recommended - Dividing up large fields with trees

Stockfree-Organic Standard 11.2(c) Dividing up large fields with trees.

Wider environmental impact	Reducing pest and disease cycles without the use of pesticides. Increasing farm biodiversity.
Advantages for the grower	Very effective method for achieving predator-pest balance and windbreaks. Sustainable source of fuel wood.
Disadvantages for the grower	Reduced cropping area. Initial planting costs. Regular maintenance.

Alder windbreaks provide a habitat for beneficial insects and creatures. Alan and Debra Schofield of Growing with Nature, Lancashire were awarded the Lorraine Award 1997 for their conservation work. Their stockfree-organic holding excels because of its predator-encouraging ecosystem. Due to a lack of hedgerows or trees as boundaries when they started over 20 years ago, 500 trees were planted on the 1.5 ha nursery in alleys alongside the growing areas. This practice is known in agroforestry as alley cropping (see 9.14).

The windbreaks are predominantly nitrogen-fixing grey alder, which helps with the on-farm fertility and water regulation. Other trees within the windbreaks include damson, cherry, plum, oak, holly and sycamore. Windbreaks have been planted running north to south with twenty metres between the breaks and one metre between the trees in the row. Trees are coppiced and pollarded, with every third being taken down to ground level and every fourth to chest height. Small prunings are left on the floor to provide shelter for small mammals and overwintering predators.

Underneath the trees natural succession has been encouraged with the revival of native wild flowers and also deliberate introductions. The trees are interspersed with a wide variety of shrubby plants and grasses. These strips are very species-diverse and provide a habitat for birds, small mammals and invertebrates. Nettles have also colonised the area and the aphids tend to live on these and not on the crops.

8.5 Recommended – Providing permanent predator belts, including incorporating undisturbed perennial plants, shrubs and trees.

Beneficial insects will move within and between crops providing that a field edge, bank or strip is close by.

Stockfree-Organic Standard 11.2(d) Providing permanent predator belts, including incorporating undisturbed perennial plants, shrubs and trees.

Wider environmental impact	Reducing pest and disease cycles without the use of pesticides. Increasing farm biodiversity.
Advantages for the grower	Very effective method for achieving predator-pest balance.
Disadvantages for the grower	Reduced cropping area. Initial planting costs.

8.5.1 Beetle banks

Beetle banks are the popular name for grass strips which incorporate tussocky grasses. Beetle banks enhance the populations of ground beetles (over 1,000 beetles per metre squared) and other predatory insects and also provide a good habitat for small mammals like field mice or voles, which in turn may promote raptor populations. The provisions of perching posts can make the strips attractive to owls and kestrels[5].

Beetle banks tend to be on raised banks, as the grass species cannot tolerate wet ground.

- Allow two plough passes to face each other to create an earth ridge approximately 40cm high and 1.5 m to 2 m wide.

Banks can either be drilled or hand sown at a rate of $3g/m^2$:

- September is the best month to sow.
- The grass mix should include up to 30% of tussock-forming species such as cocksfoot or timothy grass.
- Creeping red fescue can provide ground cover between tussocks.
- A pre-mixed beetle bank mix is often available from seed merchants.
- Plugs / pots of herbaceous plants (see 8.5.4) may also be inserted to provide extra floral resources.

Maintenance of the beetle bank is simple.

- Three cuts may be necessary in the first summer (when the sward reaches 10 cm in height) to encourage the grasses to tiller and to help control invasive annual weeds.
- Once established, you should only cut the grass strips when there is a need to get the dead tussocks to regenerate. (This is likely to be no more than once every three years).
- Regular mowing will cause a reduction in the natural habitat.
- Therefore the beetle bank should be left with bare patches being reseeded and suckering or woody plant invasion being controlled by localised cutting[6].

8.5.2 Nettle strips

Stinging nettle strips near vegetable beds have proved invaluable at Tolhurst Organic Produce. Nettles are truly multipurpose weeds and have an important role in attracting beneficial insects to the growing area. Their hollow stems are the ideal habitat for overwintering beetles, and peacock, small tortoiseshell and red admiral caterpillars will feed on the leaves.

Their thick growth provides shade and seclusion for frogs, toads and other wildlife. Aphids feeding on the young shoots in spring are an important food source for ladybirds coming out of hibernation. The ladybirds will then migrate to the crops to reduce all aphid populations.

[FIGURE 8.3 NETTLE]

- It is better to cut them in succession and definitely before they go to seed.
- Strimming can damage the entrance to the hollow stem and so scything is preferred.

8.5.3 Wildflower meadow strips

Wild flower strips[7] should be used to attract nectar-feeding beneficial insects and provide a habitat for mammals and ground nesting birds. The key to creating a successful wildflower strip or meadow is low fertility and management. In a highly fertile environment the dominant species, e.g. nettles, thistles and coarse grasses, will take a hold.

It is important to:

- create wild flower strips or meadows in a sunny area;
- find a suitable site, e.g. strips in the field, a well-used farm track or footpath[8];
- use a mix of fine grasses, such as fescues and bents with 10 - 15 wildflowers. The proportions are typically 85% grasses with 15% wildflowers by weight;
- know that most sown mixtures take five or six years to settle down and therefore ox-eye daisy is likely to dominate in the early years;
- use a local seed source with native stock where possible because British insects prefer them and there is a risk that non-native stocks might cross with existing populations of wild flora.

Late summer / early autumn sowings are preferable to a spring sowing. If sowing in spring, break the dormancy of the wildflower seeds by putting them in the refrigerator for six to eight weeks.

To sow into a bare soil ensure:

- reduced fertility – this can be done by removing turfs;
- a fine firm seedbed;
- freedom from perennial weeds;
- a selection of appropriate species;
- that the grass seed is drilled and the wild flower seed is broadcast before rolling. It is advisable to mix the wildflower seed with sand to help distribution.

Management:

- mow three times in the first year and remove the cut material to control the weeds;
- in subsequent years remove the material in late October;
- promote the scattering of seeds when collecting material;
- do not apply plant-based compost for at least five years.

8.5.4 Perennial and biennial flowering plants and shrubs suitable for attracting beneficial insects and pollinators [9]

Table 8.1 Perennial and biennial flowering plants for beneficial insects

Plant	Origin	Description	Soil type
Californian poppy, *Eschscholzia*	Non-native	It is in flower from July to September, and the seeds ripen from August to September. The flowers are hermaphrodite (have both male and female organs) and are pollinated by bees.	Prefers sandy soils.
Coltsfoot, *Tussilago farfara*	Native	Bright yellow, early spring flowering, dandelion-like flowers. Seeds are favoured by birds. Deep rooting rhizomes can become troublesome.	Suit most soils.
Cowslip, *Primula veris*	Native	Delicate yellow flowers appear in the spring, popular with bees. Foliage provides food for butterflies. Prefers partial shade.	Neutral to alkaline.
Cranesbill, *Geranium pratense*	Native	Blue / purple flowers in the summer. Foliage is food for butterfly larvae.	Prefers rich, moisture retentive soil.
Hemp agrimony, *Eupatorium cannabinum*	Native	Pale mauve flowers are attractive to many insects, and therefore birds. Prefers damp ground.	Near ponds or streams.
Evening *Oenothera biennis primrose* Biennial	Native	Tall-growing plant with pale yellow flowers, highly perfumed at night. Seeds are attractive to birds, flowers to night moths.	Suit most soils.

Plant	Origin	Description	Soil type
Fennel, *Foeniculum vulgare*	Native	The scented yellow flowers are especially attractive to hoverflies, parasitic wasps and bees throughout the summer. Seeds are popular with birds, hollow stems are important for hibernation of beetles such as the ladybird.	Suit most soils.
Foxglove, *Digitalis purpurea*	Native	Tall spike of purple flowers late spring/late summer are popular with bees. Suitable for shady area.	Prefers nutrient-rich, moist soil.
Grasses, e.g. cocksfoot, Yorkshire fog,	Native	Caterpillars of butterflies such as speckled wood and scotch argus feed on the leaves of such grasses. Tussocks also provide habitat for beetles, spiders, frogs and toads.	Well-drained soil. Prefers full sun.
Honesty, *Lunaria annua binennial*	Non-native	Purple flowers followed by easily recognised silver coin-like seed-pods that last all winter. Birds such as the bullfinch feed on seeds. Can grow in semi shade.	Suit most soils.
Michaelmas daisy, *Aster spp*	Non-native	Purple to pink flowers attract butterflies and hoverflies in the autumn. Aster x frikartii is a very useful bee and butterfly attractant. Britain's only native aster, Aster tripolium has pale mauve flowers and is only suitable for salt marsh sites.	Suit most soils.
Stinging Nettle, *Urtica dioica*	Native	Provides food for the early nettle aphid and therefore ladybirds. Caterpillar of the small tortoiseshell butterfly eat the foliage before pupating. Can grow in semi shade.	Suit most soils.

Plant	Origin	Description	Soil type
Primrose, *Primula vulgaris*	Native	Pale yellow flowers appear in the spring and are attractive to bees. Leaves are food for butterflies. Can grow in full sun or semi shade.	Nutrient-rich, moist soil, neutral to acid.
Goldenrod, *Solidago virgaurea*	Native	Flowers are attractive to many insects. Common on heaths and dry banks.	Suit most soils.
Teasel, *Dipascus fullonum* Biennial	Native	Pale mauve flowers July to August followed by tall candelabra of dried flower heads providing seeds throughout the winter for birds such as goldfinches. Bumblebees and other insects feed on the pollen.	Neutral to alkaline.
Thrift, *Armeria maritime*	Native	Pale pink flowers popular with bees, flowering March to September. Useful for rock gardens and dry stone walls. Prefers full sun.	Requires well-drained, poor soil.
Violet, *Viola odorata*	Native	Food for butterflies including the High Brown Fritillary. Prefers woodland semi-shaded sites. Soil must have plenty of organic matter.	Neutral to alkaline.
Wallflower, *Erysimum cheiri*	Naturalised	Seeds are popular with birds. The scented flowers provide nectar to many insects early spring. Full sun.	Poor soil, neutral to alkaline.
Stinking hellebore, *Helleborus foetidus*	Native	Pale green flowers (January to March) are important for early bees. Prefers semi shade.	Well-drained alkaline soils.

8.5.5 Overwinter hibernation

Piles of logs and strategically-sited compost heaps will offer year-long protection and a place for beetles, hedgehogs, toads, frogs, slow worms and toads to hibernate.

8.6 Recommended – Providing annual predator belts by leaving uncultivated field margins and strips between beds

---

Stockfree-Organic Standard 11.2(e) Providing annual predator belts by leaving uncultivated field margins and strips between beds

Wider environmental impact	Reducing pest and disease cycles without the use of pesticides. Increasing farm biodiversity.
Advantages for the grower	Very effective method for achieving predator-pest balance. Low cost.
Disadvantages for the grower	Reduced cropping area.

Just a one-metre uncultivated strip next to a hedge and strips in between beds, can benefit wildlife-boosting beneficial insects and spider populations. The area should be allowed to regenerate naturally. John Walker[10] has argued that naturally occurring weeds growing wild and free really make a difference over deliberately planted species. This is because they have always been there, evolving and adapting over time to make the best of the specific growing conditions around them. This technique can also encourage local wildflowers. A deliberately planted beetle bank or wildflower strip in such circumstances would dominate and would suppress the germination of potentially rare plants.

8.7 Recommended – Planting attractant species of flowers in strips, e.g. phacelia[11]

Stockfree-Organic Standard 11.2(f) Planting attractant species of flowers in strips, e.g. phacelia

Wider environmental impact	Reducing pest and disease cycles without the use of pesticides.
	Increasing farm biodiversity.
Advantages for the grower	Very effective method for attracting beneficial insects.
	Increasing the aesthetic beauty of the registered holding.
Disadvantages for the grower	Reduced cropping area.
	Initial seed costs.
	Annual maintenance.

It is important not to underestimate the importance of sowing attractant species of flowers. In experiments it was found that using cornflower, marigold and chamomile attracted a great number of hoverflies and parasitic wasps. Combining these three species around orchard trees reduced the numbers of pear sucker by half compared to plots with bare earth[13].

8.8 Recommended – Companion planting and mixed cropping

Companion planting is the growing of specific combinations of plants to the benefit of one or both. The companion may be an attractant flower, or another crop. Companion planting with flowers is to be encouraged as a technique to enhance functional biodiversity. However, companion planting with crops (more appropriately called 'mixed cropping') is impractical in a commercial situation because of difficulties with rotations. Also general information, on which all experts agree, about which crops favour other crops is untested and contradictory.

8.9 Recommended - Undersowing crops with clover e.g. white clover under brassicas

> **Stockfree-Organic Standard 11.2(h) Undersowing crops with clover e.g. white clover under brassicas**
>
> | | |
> |---|---|
> | Wider environmental impact | Reduces soil erosion. |
> | Advantages for the grower | Multi benefits to soil structure, fertility building and helping predator–pest balance. |
> | Disadvantages for the grower | Timing is critical (see 3.5.10): sow too early and the green manure can overwhelm the crop; sow too late and there might not be enough time to get establishment before winter. |

Stan Finch[14] has pioneered research into the benefits of undersowing for reducing competing insect problems. Many researchers have shown that the numbers of competing insects found on brassica crop plants are reduced considerably when the crop is:

- allowed to become weedy;
- intercropped with another plant species or
- undersown with a living mulch such as clover.

However, there is still considerable debate about how this works and could include a combination of:

- the undersown crop physically impeding the competing insect species;
- visual camouflage;
- the odours of the host plant being masked by those of the undersown crop;
- root exudates from the clover altering the chemical physiology of the host plant or;
- volatile chemicals released by the undersown crop directly deterring the competing insect species.

In all tests (except one in which the brassica plants were about three times as high as the clover background) 39-100% fewer pests were found on the host plants presented in clover than those presented on bare soil. The differences were not accounted for by an increase in natural predators and therefore, lower colonisation accounted for fewer pest species.

However, undersowing with clover only reduced the small white butterfly oviposition (laying of eggs) by 40-60%, which may be insufficient to reduce the damage to acceptable levels for crop sales. In these circumstances netting needs to be considered but ensure that the netting has a narrow mesh or the cabbage white butterflies will push their way through. The long-term solution includes encouraging natural predators like parasitic wasps (see 8.1.1.5).

8.10 Recommended - Installing some body of non-running water to attract beneficial insects and creatures

Agriculture intensification has led to a general reduction in the number of ponds and water quality of habitats for amphibians and drinking holes for beneficial insects and creatures. Amongst the problems reported are contamination of ponds and other water bodies by agrochemicals and reduction of suitable habitats for both breeding and feeding by drainage. Nutrient enrichment can affect breeding success when excessive weed growth shades spawning areas.

Table 8.2 Annual flowers suitable for attracting beneficial insects[12]

Annual flower	Origin	Description	Soil type
Annual convolvulus, Convolvulus tricolour	Non-native	Relative of bindweed. Requires a sheltered and sunny position. Particular favourite of hoverflies.	Low-to-medium fertility.
Cornflower, Centaurea cyanus	Native	Beautiful blue flowers in summer attractive to hoverflies. Seeds attractive to birds. Prefers full sun.	Neutral to acid.

Annual flower	Origin	Description	Soil type
Cosmos, *Cosmos bipinnatus*	Non-native	Open attractant flowers (many colours) liked by all pollinating insects. Prefers full sun.	Prefers sandy soils.
Fiddleneck, *Phacelia tanacetifolium*	Non-native	Pale mauve flowers are available throughout the summer and attractive to hoverflies and bees. Also used as a green manure.	Suit most soils.
Forget-me-not, *Myosotis arversis*	Native	Pale blue flowers favoured by bees. Birds such as the bullfinch enjoy the seeds.	Prefers damp soils.
Pot marigold, *Calendula officinalis*	Non-native	Orangey-yellow flowers. Very prolific as long as you deadhead. Liked by all pollinating insects. Can grow in semi shade.	Suit most soils.
Poached egg flower, *Limnanthes douglasii*	Non-native	Bright yellow, white-edged flowers, very attractive to insects, and can flower for nearly twelve months of the year. Also useful as winter ground cover.	Prefers well-drained soils.
Sunflower, *Helianthus annuus*	Non-native	Bright yellow flowers in the summer attract butterflies and bees. Seeds are popular with birds. Large seed heads can be stored for use in winter. Requires full sun.	Fertile well-draining soil.
Tobacco, *Nicotiana sp*	Non-native	Several species available, many are night scented. Popular with butterflies and night flying moths, including the convolvulus hawkmoth. Can grow in light shade to full sun.	Suit most soils.

Stockfree-Organic Standard 11.2(i) Installing some body of non-running water to attract beneficial insects and creatures

Wider environmental impact	Reducing pest and disease cycles without the use of pesticides. Increasing farm biodiversity.
Advantages for the grower	Very effective method for achieving predator-pest balance.
Disadvantages for the grower	Reduced cropping area. Initial start up costs.

To redress this decline it is important to[15]:

- establish ponds in groups of five or more, rather than scattering them around the registered holding;
- have a variety in the depth of ponds because frogs will spawn in the shallows whilst toads use mainly deep water;
- use a variety of water plants;
- have open stretches of water;
- do not deliberately introduce fish as they will eat the tadpoles.

Consult BTCV's Urban Handbook available at http://handbooks.btcv.org.uk for best practice.

8.11 Recommended - compost
The value of mature compost for fungal disease control has been well known for several years. Spreading well-made compost will also do much for improving resistance to competing insects and diseases. However, to attain these benefits proper composting must take place or disease problems can get worse (see 4.2 to 4.7).

Stockfree-Organic Standard 11.2(j) Compost has been shown to encourage beneficial antagonistic micro-organisms and have an inoculating effect against disease

Wider environmental impact	Composting – converting waste into useful products.
Advantages for the grower	Increasing the biodiversity of the soil. Applied through irrigation water.
Disadvantages for the grower	Need quality compost. Benefits not yet widely known, very little quality information on the subject.

8.12 Recommended - Appropriate choice of crop varieties, e.g. using resistant varieties

Stockfree-Organic Standard 11.2(k) Appropriate choice of crop varieties, e.g. using resistant varieties

Wider environmental impact	Reducing pest and disease cycles without the use of pesticides.
Advantages for the grower	Very effective technique used by all organic growers.
Disadvantages for the grower	Trade-off where variety may be lacking flavour, yield or quality. Development of new pathogen strains.

No matter how diverse and healthy the ecosystem may be, there will always be a background presence of pest and diseases. Some level of pathogen population is not only acceptable but desirable to encourage immunity against detrimental effects. Indeed, most of the plants for food crops will tend to have been selected because they are trouble-free and those that are more susceptible to attack will have fallen by the wayside over time.

For food crops there has been considerable research and selective breeding carried out in order to find cultivars that are resistant or immune to competing insect and disease damage. However, there can be a 'trade-off', because those varieties that have increased immunity or resistance may be lacking in other qualities such as flavour, yield or quality. Another drawback is that resistance can be short-lived, as new pathogen strains quickly develop and further research and breeding is constantly needed. In general it is probably fair to say that resistance will not fully guarantee total crop protection, but rather choosing resistant varieties should be considered as a part of the systems-based approach, especially against virus diseases.

8.13 Recommended - the use of strategic planting dates

Stockfree-Organic Standard 11.2(l) The use of strategic planting dates

Wider environmental impact	Reducing pest and disease cycles without the use of pesticides.
Advantages for the grower	Very effective technique used by all organic growers.
Disadvantages for the grower	May disrupt continuity of supply.

Sowing times can be adjusted in order to avoid the periods when certain competing insects, molluscs and diseases are most active. For example:

- The carrot root fly can be devastating, wiping out a whole crop of carrot seedlings. Strategic sowing is essential. The first generation usually flies during late May, whilst the second flight peaks in September. Therefore, sowing as early as possible before the first flight, or the safer option of sowing after the first flight in June, will help prevent infection.
- The pea moth lays its eggs on pea flowers in early to mid summer. Peas sown as first earlies or as an autumn crop (see 11.13.2) should avoid the worst of the damage.
- Flea beetles can attack radish, turnips, kohl rabi and swede. Sow as early as possible and then cease sowing between May and July. After this period the flea beetle becomes dormant. Therefore late swedes raised as transplants can avoid the worst of the problems.
- Powdery mildews are worst when the soil is very dry. Sow peas early and swedes and turnips late.

8.14 Recommended - Good husbandry and hygienic practices

Stockfree-Organic Standard 11.2(m) Good husbandry and hygienic practices	
Wider environmental impact	Reducing pest and disease cycles without the use of pesticides.
Advantages for the grower	Very effective technique used by all organic growers.
Disadvantages for the grower	Time consuming. Need to pay attention to detail.

Good husbandry is a generic term that could include a whole host of techniques. The premise for this book begins with the need to look at soil care. A healthy soil produces healthy plants which are less susceptible to soil-borne organisms. An organically-enriched soil with good structure is likely to prevent nematode infestation[16]. Attention to soil structure, drainage and cultivation techniques that minimise compaction will also help with the growth of the plants. Plant and row spacings need to be adequate for crop growth, photosynthesis and air movement (see Chapter 11).

When plants become stressed, they are more likely to be attacked by competing insects and diseases. The stress is thought to be a stoppage in the synthesis of protein, which results in a build-up in the plant tissues of free nitrogen. Competing insect infestations are more likely when there are easily available nitrogenous compounds[17]. If plants are under stress, it is a good idea to spray them with seaweed extract (see 3.9.3) to encourage the continuation of protein synthesis[18] and to avoid such future stresses.

The basic rule in gardening that diseased and damaged crops need to be physically removed and destroyed is not true in commercial situations as this would be impossible to achieve. Therefore, it becomes more important to observe well-designed and long rotations. Monitoring crops can assist with future control strategies. Records of actions taken are the key to successful prevention. Revisiting records, even if they are several years old, will ensure that you are more proactive and vigilant, e.g. daily inspecting crops that you know in the past have been susceptible to a problem.

8.15 Recommended – Physical barriers, e.g. netting and fleeces

Stockfree-Organic Standard 11.2(n) Physical barriers, e.g. netting and fleeces

Wider environmental impact	Reducing pest and disease damage without the use of pesticides.
Advantages for grower	Very effective techniques used by all organic the growers.
Disadvantages for the grower	Cost. Requires maintenance. Should be used in conjunction with other techniques.

Very fine mesh covers like Enviromesh™, Wondermesh™ and horticultural fleece are available to protect crops against competing insects including flea beetle, carrot root fly and cabbage caterpillars. They have the advantage over traditional cloches in that, as they allow the rain to penetrate.

The following should be observed:

- lay covers after transplanting or direct sowing;
- when using covers in protected cropping (polytunnel or greenhouse), attach to wire hoops with clothes pegs;
- when using covers outdoors, weigh down (with stones or bags of soil) or bury the edges. Burying can shorten the life of the fleece and pegging can lead to the material ripping;
- ensure that there is enough slack in the fleece to allow for the crop to grow;
- in the height of summer netting may be more appropriate (see section 8.25), as it can protect crops from larger competing animals.

8.16 Common competing molluscs and insects[19]

 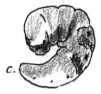

 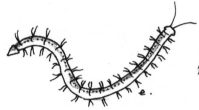 

FIGURE 8.4 COMMON COMPETING MOLLUSCS AND INSECTS – SLUG, SPIDER MITE, CUTWORM, WIREWORM, MILLIPEDE AND VINE WEEVIL

8.16.1 Slugs

For many gardeners slugs are a most difficult problem. However, in a commercial stockfree-organic situation they should not pose such a problem providing that the pH is maintained between 6.5 and 6.8. It is useful to have some understanding of a slug's lifestyle and the patterns that they follow.

Slugs are soft-bodied molluscs with a permanently moist / slimy skin and tend to dry out easily, so during the day they will shelter in damp places, under stones or vegetation or in cracks in the soil. At night they will come out to feed, searching by smell for suitable food plants. Young seedlings and lettuces seem to be particular favourites. They will graze on that plant until dawn, and then return to the same shelter. On subsequent nights they will pick up their own trail of slime and return to the same plant. Other slugs will also pick up this trail, resulting in a concentration of slugs.

There are probably as many slug control techniques as there are organic gardeners and therefore only the techniques suitable for commercial growers are looked at. None are guaranteed 100% effective, but by using a combination of some of methods described it will be possible to at least minimise the damage that slugs cause:

- tillage in early spring is particularly effective at killing slugs eggs;

- fine tilth and a firmly-rolled bed (see 2.7.4 and 2.7.6) eliminates cracks for small slugs to burrow;
- planting out established transplants gives the crops a greater ability to withstand attack;
- water transplants in the morning so there is no film of water left on the soil or leaves by the evening;
- frequent hoeing, especially before undersowing, will expose eggs and adults to predators.

A nocturnal trip around beds with a torch and bucket can yield huge numbers of slugs. This is labour-intensive and messy, but effective in breaking the back-and-forth habit of slugs who have established both a shelter and a good food source. Carried out every few days in spring, it also gradually reduces the population. For those who do not wish to venture out after dark, pieces of slab wood, black plastic, slate or even grapefruit halves can be left adjacent to growing areas, where the slugs will congregate during the day time. They can then be picked off every few days. However, the downside is that this is providing them with shelter right next to their food source and so needs to be fairly closely monitored.

Beer / yeast or milk traps have long been recommended as a technique by traditional organic growers but can only be used under restriction by commercial stockfree-organic growers if the economic viability (see 8.18) of the enterprise is threatened. Care must be taken as they can indiscriminately kill beneficial beetles as well and so there must be a lip in place so that the beetles do not fall in.

Slugs move on a trail of slime, therefore dry, drying, acidic or irritant materials such as quartz sand (see 8.15), pine needles, wood ash, human hair, bran or lime placed around vulnerable plants will impede and discourage them. Unfortunately, however this method will only be effective until the next rainfall or the material becomes wet, when the slugs will be able to glide straight across. Surrounding susceptible plants with copper wire is also said to provide a barrier, possibly due to emitting a slight electrical charge, which repels the slug invaders.

The long-term solution is to encourage the natural predators of molluscs by making them feel at home. Installing a pond (see 8.10) will attract newts, growing long grasses will attract slow worms whilst piles of brushwood or leaves situated in secluded corners or under hedges are very welcoming to hedgehogs. Centipedes and beetles will also consume vast quantities of slug eggs and other pests, so their presence should be encouraged by providing them with plenty of sheltering places and beetle banks. Birds too can be encouraged onto the registered holding by providing hedges, nesting boxes and winter feeding stations.

8.16.2 Aphids

Aphids are the most frequently occurring pest in temperate countries. Aphids damage many crops by piercing and sucking the cell contents from the plant so that growth is reduced. They have an impressive capacity for population growth, commonly increasing up to 12 times a week under ideal conditions. This can lead to the leaf distortion, with accumulations of cast skins and the aphids' deposits of honeydew that attract sooty moulds. Although plants can look rough with sooty moulds, these do not damage the plant tissues. Once the aphids disappear, the sooty mould often dries up and falls off the plant. Of more significance is the fact that aphids transmit plant viruses.

Unfortunately aphid levels can rocket out of control before the predators establish themselves. Warm, dry weather conditions favour aphid infestations, although certain aphid species are active all year, especially on protected crops during mild winters. Traditional organic growers reach for the biological control agents immediately (see 8.18), but these are restricted under Stockfree-Organic Standard 11.3 (a).

The stockfree-organic grower needs to be proactive by:

- providing nettle strips, which are the single most important technique (see 8.5.2);
- ensuring that there is not too much nitrogen in the system (see 12.2) or the crop will grow sappy;
- ensuring that the crop is not under stress (see 8.14);
- using the methods described in 8.1.1 and 8.1.2 to encourage bluetits, ladybirds, hoverflies, lace wings, predatory wasps, toads and frogs;
- avoiding the use of fleece as it creates the ideal micro-climate for aphid

breeding and prevents the natural predators from getting in. In these circumstances netting is better;

- ventilating protected structures;
- growing resistant varieties;
- using strategic planting dates, e.g. autumn sown broad beans are less attractive to black fly;
- monitoring crops for the first signs of attack i.e. looking for smallish bleached and crumbled areas on the leaves;
- scraping off aphid colonies.

8.16.3 Whitefly

Whiteflies are often categorised as aphids as they too have sucking mouthparts that feed on plant sap. Fortunately, whiteflies do not seem to cause the same level of damage and usually fly off when disturbed. They can be controlled in the same way as aphids.

8.16.4 Red spider mite

Red spider mite is generally a problem for protected cropping. The leaves become light and mottled, with tiny greenish mites appearing on the underside of leaves. You may need a lens to spot them, but you are more likely to see their silken webbing when their infestation is in an advanced stage. In a commercial setting cleaning the greenhouse or polytunnel in the autumn is a waste of time, unless you fumigated and killed all the beneficial insects as well, which is prohibited under the Stockfree-Organic Standards. The worst effects can be prevented by misting plants with water twice a day during warm weather and the mites can be scraped off or removed by a water jet. The long-term strategy is long rotations and creating habitats for beneficial insects within the protected cropping environment.

8.16.5 Carrot root fly[20]

Carrot root flies complete two generations each year (see 8.13). Peak numbers of eggs are laid usually during May and August. As the temperature levels are higher and there is low soil moisture for the second generation, many carrot fly maggots die. Therefore it is the first generation that the stockfree-organic grower needs to concentrate on by:

- selecting a sowing date that avoids the peak period of egg laying, i.e. early June;

- using barriers like fleece, Enviromesh™ or Wondermesh™;
- growing away from field boundaries (if possible) as these tend to be the overwintering habitat for the flies.

Resistance to carrot fly in carrots has been studied at HRI Wellesbourne for more than 25 years and partial resistance has been identified in about 20 carrot varieties, most of which are Nantes types.

8.16.6 Cutworm
Cutworms are the caterpillars of certain moths that feed on plants at ground level, cutting or severing them from their roots. The caterpillar of the turnip moth is the most harmful cutworm. They are a grassland pest and will generally only be a problem after long-term leys. However, every ten to thirteen years there will be a population explosion and they may damage other crops, with lettuce being particularly vulnerable.

Eggs are laid on the leaves and stems of plants or on soil and plant debris. The larvae then hatch and first feed above ground level. After their second moult the larvae burrow into the soil and acquire the cutworm habit. They are up to 3cm long, although are often found in a C shape, and because of their dull colouring they are difficult to see in the soil[21]. There can be up to four generations a year. Cutworms can be hand-picked by gently raking near the seedlings. Harrowing or rotavating to form seedbeds will also reduce populations. The long-term strategy is to encourage ground beetles, birds and predatory wasps.

8.16.7 Wireworm
Wireworms are the slim orange-brown larvae of the click beetle (up to 2.5cm long) and are a particular menace when growing after old pasture. Click beetles lay their eggs in summer and the larvae will feed in March to May and in September to October for up five years before turning into beetles and flying elsewhere. When you clear grass, they will feed on whatever comes next and particularly like potatoes and other root crops.

- When you clear old pasture it is a good idea to grow a green manure crop of mustard before planting vegetables. This encourages the wireworms to complete their life cycle in record time and fly away.

- Harvest crops by September to limit damage from autumn feeding.

8.16.8 Eelworms
Eelworms are species of tiny transparent nematodes that attack tomatoes, potatoes and cucumbers. Composting is the key, because they cannot survive in an organically-enriched soil which has plenty of mycelium-forming fungi. Eelworms are less likely in long rotations. Root exudations of African marigolds (tagetes erecta) will also kill pest nematodes and so can be grown in a block to reduce populations in the worst affected areas. If you are unfortunate enough to get eelworm damage then it will be necessary to destroy the crop.

8.16.9 Millipede
These slow moving insects (with two sets of legs per segment) feed mainly on dead plants or extend the wounds caused by other creatures in roots and tubers. They can be a particular nuisance with the seeds of peas and beans, where they eat pieces of them away so that they germinate poorly. The cultivation of land will expose them to their predators, which include birds, hedgehogs and ground beetles.

8.16.10 Vine weevil
Vine weevils are matt black, about 10mm long, with a noticeable snout. They climb to make holes and irregular notches in plant foliage, which the crop can often survive. It is their larvae which cause the real problems. They are 10mm long legless maggots with a creamy white body and brown head. The larvae tunnel into the soil, feeding on plant roots. As the weather cools, they burrow further down to overwinter and the following spring complete their life cycle. The first sign of attack can be when plants keel over and, when pulled up there is an absence of roots. Cultivation with machinery will help control populations of larvae. It is possible to hand-pick vine weevils as they do not move too quickly. When using propagation compost check for vine weevil larvae.

8.17 Common disease problems
Diseases symptoms are caused by bacteria, viruses and fungi.

Bacteria are tiny simple organisms. Some of the most common problems caused by them include soft rots, leaf spots, cankers and galls. They are unable to break through a plant's skin and so their main entry is though a wound caused by other organisms, e.g. aphids or by pruning.

Viruses are smaller than bacteria and are often named after the plant they were initially, or are most commonly, found in. They can only multiply within other plant cells. Once a plant is infected, the virus spreads throughout the plant and nothing can cure it, so prevention is the only course of action.

The majority of viruses are spread by aphids and eelworm. Only a few viruses are distributed in pollen and seed, while some rely on humans to spread. This is why it is important to buy vegetative reproductive material that is certified as virus-free. Some symptoms can be confused with mineral deficiencies, although a virus is likely to appear on one or two plants, whereas a deficiency will appear on a whole row.

Preventing viruses:

- control aphids (see 8.16.2) and eelworms (8.16.8);
- break the cycle by removing susceptible plants;
- observe long rotations;
- grow virus-resistant cultivars;
- buy certified virus-free vegetative reproductive material;
- grow new plants from seed.

The majority of plant diseases are fungal where microscopic threads grow through plant tissue. Fungi spread from plant to plant mainly in the form of spores though the air, water or soil. The majority can live on dead or alive plant material, so crop debris can be a reservoir for fungal infection. Typical fungal infections include:

- spots - death of plant tissue;
- canker and scabs – abnormal increase in tissue;
- silvering or yellowing;
- wilting;
- wet rots – damping off;
- powdery and fluffy moulds – mildews and grey moulds[22].

8.17.1 Blight (phytophera infestans) prevention in potatoes

A systems-based approach to blight control starts with the correct choice of variety. Some cultivars have a high resistance and these should not be placed adjacent to susceptible ones. Chitting is essential (see 11.1.5), even with maincrop, to advance the crop and establish a decent yield prior to blight. Optimum fertility, based on rotation and fertility-building, is important, as potatoes are very demanding of nutrients if a good yield is to be attained (see 6.2 and 11.1.1).

Monitoring for blight should be done daily as soon as a Mills period is evident, which means the incidence of warm damp weather conditions and the presence of blight spores. Depending on the resistance degree of varieties, a decision has to be made as to whether it is prudent to mow the foliage or to leave it to die back naturally. At Tolhurst Organic Produce we stopped mowing potato haulm years ago. We always get blighted foliage to a lesser or greater degree, in 2005 it was 100% blighted by early August but we still harvested 16 tons /acre with maincrop and that is in the stoniest part of the field. In our experience leaving haulm does not make for more blight and removing it just spreads the spores even more. We've never had much of a problem except for the odd tuber rotting in the ground but maybe this is down to the health of our soils.

The crop must not be lifted for at least three weeks after the foliage has died down naturally. The haulm must have died completely prior to harvesting. The disease survives over winter in infected potato tubers which remain in the soil or in discarded heaps, so it is important to remove all tubers when harvesting and not to compost potatoes or tomatoes in the general compost. The Standards Working Group considered the issue and suggests that diseased or damaged potatoes are sent to landfill, composted under cover or laid on the soil surface to allow the frost to kill them. Donating waste potatoes to an animal farmer or burning them is not allowed under the Stockfree-Organic Standards.

8.17.2 Downy mildew (Perenospora spp. Bremia spp.) prevention[23]

Downy mildew appears as a fluffy mealy white mould on the under surface of the infected leaves. On first inspection they seem similar in appearance to powdery mildews. However, under a lens they can be seen to have many individual spore-bearing heads, whereas powdery mildew moulds have a thick velvety appearance with few distinguishable heads.

The downy mildew that affects brassicas (Perenospora parasitica) can attack at the seedling stage. Therefore:

- it is preferable to raise bare root transplants outdoors in a nursery bed (see 5.4);
- or follow best transplant raising practice (see 5.3.5);
- ventilate transplants well;
- do not overcrowd transplants;
- use larger blocks or modules;
- avoid water dripping onto the seedlings;
- use capillary or drip irrigation, as opposed to overhead sprinkling or watering with a watering can;
- if infection occurs, remove the plants immediately.

Seedlings are infected through the roots and, once inside the plant, downy mildew spreads to the leaves. The spores are then spread to neighbouring brassicas by wind or water splash. Warm damp conditions particularly favour the spread of this disease. The symptoms are less well-defined in mature crops and can be confused with potash or magnesium deficiency. There is very little a grower can do as heavy fogs, light rains and prolonged dew (the favoured conditions for infection) are outside your control. The fungus only survives on living tissue and soft rots are often visible at the death of the plants.

8.17.3 Powdery mildew (Erysiphe spp. Sphaerotheca spp, Podosphaera spp) prevention
Powdery mildews are very common with some species being specific to the crops that they attack. They prefer warm dry weather and dry soils. The typical symptoms include a white coating, blossoms withering and leaves dropping as the whole plant weakens. Growing resistant cultivars is a good idea, as well as irrigating in dry weather. Once the disease has occurred, it is best to pick off or prune out infected leaves as appropriate.

8.17.4 Grey mould (Botrytis cinerea) prevention
Grey mould is a ubiquitous disease thriving in cool, damp and crowded conditions and spoiling soft fruits, protected solanaceae and lettuce. All symptoms are associated with a fluffy grey mould. Grey mould is a weak pathogen and usually infects through a wound already made by something else. Cut out patches, e.g. in the stems of tomato plants, and rub in soil for inoculation. Good hygiene is

essential for preventing this disease by removing dying and dead plant material, particularly in protected cropping. Improving airflow will also help though venting, using fans, reducing overcrowding and pruning.

8.18 Restricted - Natural pesticides, insecticides and biological controls

> **Stockfree-Organic Standard 11.3 (a) reads:**
> Restricted
> All natural pesticides, insecticides and biological controls - the use of which are only permitted in cases where the viability of the enterprise is threatened.

8.18.1 Natural pesticides and insecticides

So-called natural pesticides have given organic agriculture a bad name, allowing conventional thinking to dominate where individual pest species can be eradicated by the natural sprays as opposed to the synthetic sprays. Natural sprays may be less harmful or persistent than other pesticides, but they also kill indiscriminately. They treat the symptom and not the cause. Using natural pesticides ignores the systems-based approach, where the stockfree-organic grower strives for predator-pest balance. If an organic grower feels the need to regularly use such products, this suggests that there are ecosystem deficiencies on the registered holding. For these reasons the use of derris, pyrethrum, sulphur, soft soap and insecticidal soap are restricted solely to spot-spraying when the viability of the enterprise is threatened. The onus will be on the stockfree-organic grower to prove this and you will need to apply to the approved certification body for a restricted practice form.

All copper mixtures, which have been allowed under restriction in traditional organic systems, have been prohibited in stockfree-organic systems because of their persistent nature and toxicity to fish.

8.18.2 Biological control agents

Naturally occurring biological control agents, 'bugs that eat bugs' can be bought commercially by mail order. Their application is detailed in the *Organic Farm Managers Handbook*[24]. All biological control agents are restricted to use only when the viability of the enterprise is threatened. The onus will be on the stockfree-organic grower to prove this and you will need to apply to the approved certification body for a restricted practice form.

8.19 Restricted – Ducks which are kept to eat slugs and snails

Ducks have been a popular answer to slugs by commercial organic growers and leading permaculturists. Under Stockfree-Organic Standard 11.3(b) they can be kept under restriction. If you are a registered grower and are keeping ducks or poultry to control competing molluscs, it is important to obtain written permission from the approved certification body. The decision will be made on a case-by-case basis taking into consideration whether there could be an infringement of Stockfree-Organic Standard requirement 1.1 - You must not keep animals for food production or commercial gain on the registered holding.

8.20 Prohibited practices for diseases, insects and mollusc control

Under Stockfree-Organic Standard 11.4 the following are prohibited:

(a) All synthetic biocides.
(b) All biocides based on animal derivatives.
(c) Steam sterilisation of soils.
(d) Hypochlorite-based disinfectants for sterilising buildings and equipment.
(e) Copper sulphate, copper oxychloride, copper ammonia carbonate.
(f) Nicotine.
(g) Formaldehyde and phenols for soil sterilisation.
(h) Methyl bromide and other chemical soil sterilisers.
(i) Slug and snail-killers based on metaldehyde or aluminium compounds.
(j) Beeswax pruning agent.
(k) Hydrolysed proteins.

Slug pellets, in particular, are worth singling out for special consideration. Iron phosphate is a slug pellet that is allowed in traditional organic systems although its use in commercial growing may prove cost prohibitive. In conventional systems, the two main chemical slug controls are metaldehyde and methiocarb. They are highly poisonous to slugs and worms, which can then be eaten by predators like song thrushes and hedgehogs. The poisons then bioaccumulate in the creatures higher up the food web.

8.21 Introduction to competing animal and bird control

Stockfree-Organic Standard 12.1 reads:
As a Stockfree-Organic grower you should not deliberately kill or maim any animal. Where crops may be destroyed and/or consumer health is at risk, then all competing animals should be prevented from causing damage by the installation of physical barriers.

The Stockfree-Organic Standards are based on a principle of compassion. Many commercial stockfree-organic growers do not cull competing animals and birds because they have struck a balance, providing areas in which to tolerate their presence and areas from which they are excluded. Where health factors feature, e.g. in food storage areas, the stockfree-organic grower should ensure that these are small rodent-proof. Where economic viability is the issue, excluding deer, rabbits and badgers from growing areas with fencing and excluding birds with netting will ensure protection for the crops.

8.22 Recommended – Attracting natural predators

Stockfree-Organic Standard 12.2(a) Attracting natural predators

Wider environmental impact	Reducing animal and bird competition and promoting balance without the need for culling.
Advantages for the grower	Relatively low cost. Fits in with environmental conservation objectives.
Disadvantages for the grower	Takes years to achieve balance.

Many of the techniques for attracting natural predators of competing rabbits, rodents and birds have been discussed in the context of pest and disease control. For example, raptors can be encouraged by:

• perch posts erected along beetle banks and grass margins;
• a single owl / raptor willow basket can be placed five metre high in a tree[25].

Predators of rabbits and rodents, particularly foxes and stoats, can be

FIGURE 8.5 STOAT

encouraged by having a variety of habitats on the registered holdings. The size of the holding obviously makes a difference, since very large holdings with several hundred hectares are able to accommodate woodlands, grasslands, wildflower meadows, ponds, scrub, young broadleaf woodlands, beetle banks, agroforestry and wildlife margins. However, on smaller holdings the key is having a variety of undisturbed habitats, particularly wildlife margins, hedges, ponds and woodland areas, e.g. a small copse.

8.23 Recommended - Fencing

Stockfree-Organic Standard 12.2(b) Fencing	
Wider environmental impact	Reducing animal competition without the need for culling.
Advantages for the grower	Most effective technique for protecting cropping areas.
Disadvantages for the grower	High initial cost. Maintenance.

Consult BTCV's Fencing Handbook available at http://handbooks.btcv.org.uk for best practice. Also BTCV's Tree Planting and Aftercare Handbook outlines how to use tree guards.

8.24 Recommended – Electric fencing

Stockfree-Organic Standard 12.2(c) Electric fencing

Wider environmental impact	Reducing animal competition without the need for culling.
Advantages for the grower	Most cost effective technique for high value crops.
Disadvantages for the grower	Regular maintenance.

If your field requires year-round protection, fencing and netting are your only options. If protection is only needed for part of the year (e.g. protecting the sweetcorn from badgers), then an electric fence may be more cost effective. Consult BTCV's Fencing Handbook available at http://handbooks.btcv.org.uk for the different types of electric fencing available

8.25 Recommended – Netting and wire mesh

Stockfree-Organic Standard 12.2(d) Netting and wire mesh.

Wider environmental impact	Reducing bird competition without the need for culling.
Advantages for the grower	Most cost effective technique for high value crops.
Disadvantages for the grower	Regular maintenance.

Generally speaking, birds are a great asset on the registered holding but they can become a nuisance. Wood pigeons, for example, can devastate brassica crops, fruit bushes (stripping the bushes of buds, leaves and fruit) and directly sown peas and beans. Blackbirds and starlings can attack tree and bush fruit, stripping cherries and leaving peck marks on apples and pears, making them susceptible to rots. Jays are a particular problem in relation to peas and beans, since they will peck developing seed pods and devour the seed inside.

Unlike most competing insects, birds generally cause the most damage during the winter, when there is little else around for them to eat. Developing fruit buds and brassicas are particularly vulnerable, especially after snowfall, as they are often the only edible plants visible. Rows of seedlings that are particularly at risk from bird damage can be covered with netting although it can soon become a wildlife hazard. Flying birds will generally bounce off nets and wire that is held taut but can become ensnared if it is loose and this can lead to their deaths.

8.26 Recommended - Sonic repellents

Stockfree-Organic Standard 12.2(e) Sonic repellents	
Wider environmental impact	Reducing bird and rabbit competition without the need for culling.
Advantages for the grower	Useful technique for vulnerable crops.
Disadvantages for the grower	Birds and rabbits can get used to them. Cost. Noise nuisance to human neighbours.

Gas cannons are mechanical devices that produce loud banging noises by igniting either acetylene or propane gas. They are effective to a distance of between 60 and 120 metres. Gas cannons may keep birds and rabbits away, but they need to be moved around every couple of days and the timing of the bangs should be varied. It is preferable to use them in conjunction with other techniques[26]. They can also pose a noise nuisance to human neighbours and it is important to erect straw baffles around them, with the open direction pointing away from the houses.

Bio-acoustic sonic devices transmit sounds of biological relevance, e.g. recorded bird alarm and distress calls, which exploit the competing bird's instinct to avoid danger. Such biologically meaningful sounds are more repellent than other sounds and have a wider working distance - up to 300m. However, they are not effective on pigeons or Canada geese. There is no evidence that ultrasonic repellents repel birds[27].

8.27 Recommended – Raptor models and balloons

Stockfree-Organic standard 12.2(f) Raptor models and balloons

Wider environmental impact	Reducing bird competition without the need for culling.
Advantages for the grower	Most cost effective techniques for reducing pigeon damage.
Disadvantages for the grower	Cost.

The mimicry of raptors will evoke fear in competing birds, particularly pigeons and crows. A still plastic model is not likely to effective. However, a plastic owl with a crow in its talons and moving wings (that move with the wind or are battery driven when there is no breeze) is likely to reduce damage in a vegetable crop by up to 81%. The effectiveness of raptor models increases if they are animated and if they are moved regularly. They are a relatively cheap option[28].

Balloons tethered in a crop are also an effective deterrent. Eyespots, arranged horizontally and containing concentric rings of bright colour, appear to be very effective at mimicking the eyes of large raptors. They have a working distance up to 40 metres. Although easy to set up and move around, balloons can be damaged in high winds and can deteriorate in sunlight leading to loss of helium and therefore height.

8.28 Recommended – Scarecrows

Stockfree-Organic Standard 12.2(g) Scarecrows

Wider environmental impact	Reducing bird competition without the need for culling.
Advantages for the grower	Useful technique for vulnerable crops.
Disadvantages for the grower	Birds get used to them.

Predator models, such as scarecrows, are the traditional technique for scaring birds. They are usually based on human effigies and can cost nothing to make. However, motionless devices are likely to be effective for only a short period of time. The effectiveness of scarecrows will be enhanced if fitted with loose clothing and bright streamers. Commercially available inflatable effigies that emit sounds and lights have become available[29].

Cheaper options for small areas include plastic bags on bamboo canes and CDs on string. Mirrors and reflectors work on the principle that the bright flashes of light will invoke fear in the competing bird and are thought to be particularly effective against pigeons, starlings and crows[30].

Cats can be scared by draping cycle inner tubers near their favourite plants, as they apparently think that they are snakes. Moles can be scared away by placing children's seaside windmills or upturned glass bottles in the most recent molehills, because the sounds and vibrations may deter the moles.

8.29 Recommended - Sealed containers for the produce

Stockfree-Organic Standard 12.2(h) Sealed containers.	
Wider environmental impact	Reducing rodent competition without the need for culling.
Advantages for the grower	Effective technique.
Disadvantages for the grower	Cost.

The stockfree-organic grower should aim for rodent-free food stores. If this is not feasible because of the type of building then using sealed containers is the next best solution. As all animals hunt by scent, properly sealed containers can reduce the likelihood of rodent attack in food stores.

8.30 Restricted - Trapping

Stockfree-Organic Standard 12.3(a) reads:
Restricted
The trapping of competing animals should only occur as a last resort if a crop may be destroyed or human health is at risk (e.g. when the Environmental Health Authority may question practices).

As was stated in the introduction to 8.21, the basic tenet of competing animal and bird control is compassion. Therefore, trapping is to be used as a last resort, where all else has failed, and in most cases it should not come to this. If, however, food stores are being overrun by rodents or where the Local Health Authority may also intervene to shut down enterprises then trapping is allowed under restriction. If you are a registered grower, before considering trapping it is important to obtain written permission from the approved certification body. In all cases, humane live trapping with relocation will be the preferred method of control.

8.31 Restricted - Dogs or cats

Stockfree-Organic standard 12.3(b) reads:
Restricted
Dogs or cats which are kept to control competing birds and mammals.

Most farms keep dogs and / or cats particularly for controlling rodents around the farm buildings. However, cats in particular bring their own problems, since they will also kill songbirds, amphibians and other beneficial animals, e.g. butterflies. Since dogs and cats have extremely unpleasant fouling habits, some members of the Standards Working Group called for these animals to be banned altogether from registered holdings.

After consultation with commercial growers it was found that many keep companion animals as pets, and therefore distinguishing between companion dogs and cats and working dogs and cats on registered holdings may be difficult. If you are a registered grower and are keeping dogs or cats to control competing birds and mammals, it is important to obtain written permission from the approved certification body. The decision will be made on a case-by-case basis, taking into consideration whether there is the opportunity for the dog or cat to be used for cruel sports like fox hunting, badger baiting and shooting, e.g. gun dogs. If a grower has a domestic animal used for cruel sports, they will not be able to hold the Stockfree-Organic Symbol.

8.32 Prohibited practices for competing animal and bird control
Under Stockfree-Organic standard 12.4 the following are prohibited:

(a) The intentional maiming of any species of animal except after veterinary advice for compassionate reasons.
(b) The intentional killing of any species of animal other than those referred to in 11.3, 12.3 or after veterinary advice for compassionate reasons.
(c) Killing of animals in the name of sport on the registered holding.
(d) Poisoning animals.
(e) Shooting animals.

1 Sometimes described as a holistic approach.

2 Quoted in HAWARD R (2000) Habitat Management for Crop Production. Organic Farming 66: 15 -17

3 Advice taken from WILKINSON J et al (1996) Amphibians on Pest Patrol. New Farmer and Grower. Winter 20-21.

4 Quoted in MILLER I (2003) Birds, Bats and Beasts. Organic Farming Summer: 22 – 23.

5 MARSHALL J (2001) We Can Work It Out – Beetle Banks. Organic Farming. Summer: 26 – 28.

6 Advice is taken from THOMAS S & HOLLAND J (2001) How to Establish and Maintain a Beetle Bank. Organic Farming Summer 28-29 and the RSPB website.

7 Advice taken from the RSPB website and UGLOW J (2003) Wildflower Meadows. EFRC Bulletin 68: 20-21

8 These areas are disturbed too often to make them suitable for the tussocky margin of the beetle bank.

9 Advice taken from HDRA- the Organic Association website. www.hdra.org.uk

10 WALKER J (2003) Weeds – an Earth Friendly Guide to their Identification, Use and Control. Cassel illustrated.

11 Advice taken from HDRA- the Organic Association website www.hdra.org.uk with flowers added by the authors.

12 Advice taken from HDRA- the Organic Association website www.hdra.org and the Plants for a Future database www.scs.leeds.ac.uk/pfaf/index.html.

13 Quoted in HAWARD R (2000) Habitat Management for Crop Production. Organic Farming 66: 15 -17.

14 FINCH S & EDMONDS GH (1994) Undersowing Cabbage Crops with Clover – Effects on Pest Insects, Ground Beetles and Crop Yields. IOBC / WPRS Bulletin 17(8) 159 – 167.

15 WILKINSON J et al (1996) Amphibians on Pest Patrol. New Farmer and Grower. Winter 20-21.

16 Van DER LAAN PA The Influence of Organic Manuring in the Development of the Potato Root Eelworm, Heterodera rostochiensis. Nematology 1 (1956) 113-115 quoted by Eliot Coleman.

17 WHITE TCR (1984) The Abundance of Invertebrate Herbivores in Relation to the Availability of Nitrogen in Stressed Food Plants. Oecologia 63: 90-105 quoted by Eliot Coleman.

18 COLEMAN, E (1995) New Organic Grower. A Master's Manual of Tools and Techniques for the Home and Market Gardener. Chelsea Green publishing.

19 Advice is adapted from RYRIE C (2001) Pests. Gaia books and PEARS P and STICKLAND S (1995) Organic Gardening. Mitchell Beasley.

20 Advice taken from COLLIER R et al (1999) Stop Your Carrot getting Stick. Organic farming 63: 18-19.

21 CASPELL N (1999) Protect your Brassicas Organic Farming 62:22-24

22 Information about fungal, bacterial and virus disorders adapted from PEARS P and STICKLAND S (1995) Organic Gardening. Mitchell Beasley.

23 Advice taken from Anon (1996) Downy Mildew New Farmer and Grower: Summer -26.

24 OFMH is regularly updated by LAMPKIN N, MEASURES M and PADEL S and is produced by the University of Wales, Aberystwyth and the Organic Advisory Service at Elm Farm.

25 Information taken from MILLER I (2003) Birds, Bats and Beasts. Organic Farming Summer: 22 – 23.

26 BISHOP J et al (2003) Review of International Research Literature Regarding the Effectiveness of Auditory Bird Scaring Techniques and Potential Alternatives. Available from DEFRA.

27 For further information see BISHOP J et al (2003) Review of International Research Literature Regarding the Effectiveness of Auditory Bird Scaring Techniques and Potential Alternatives. Available from DEFRA.

28 Available from Network Pest Control Systems Limited, 1030 Centre Park, Slutchers Lane, Warrington, Cheshire, WA1 1QR, Tel: 01925 411 823.

29 Available from CLARRATTS LTD, Hollow Farm, Toseland, St Neots, Huntingdon, Cambridgeshire, PE19 6RU. Telephone: 01480 476376.

30 quoted in BISHOP J et al (2003) Review of International Research Literature Regarding the Effectiveness of Auditory Bird Scaring Techniques and Potential Alternatives. Available from DEFRA.

Chapter Nine

Environmental conservation

9.1 Introduction

Biodiversity describes the variety of living organisms within a given ecosystem, including the numbers of species, the population of each species and the genetic variation within species. As already highlighted in Chapter 8, the links between biodiversity and the efficiency of the organic system should not be underestimated. Environmental conservation of biodiversity is an important part of a sustainable organic system.

> **Stockfree-Organic Standard 9.1 reads:**
> Growers should actively encourage wildlife and biodiversity on their registered holding.

The benefits for biodiversity of stockfree-organic systems could include[1]:

- increased numbers of invertebrates through an absence of pesticides;
- increased weed abundance and plant foods for invertebrates through an absence of herbicides;
- increased invertebrate foods for birds, mammals, amphibians and reptiles generally;
- increased variation in vegetation structure for wildlife;
- improved predator-pest balance;
- benefits for earthworm populations and other soil life;

- increased soil fauna food for invertebrates, birds and mammals;
- increased invertebrates, beetles, small mammals, ground-nesting birds with the provision for grass-margin habitats;
- greater species diversity within hedgerows and ditches;
- taller, thicker hedgerow structures which are beneficial to many bird species;
- greater species diversity by practising agroforestry and planting trees;
- prohibition of GM technology removes a threat to biodiversity.

9.2 Statutory and stockfree-organic standard obligations

> **Stockfree-Organic Standard requirement 9.2 reads:**
> Growers are expected to abide by all legal and statutory environmental requirements.

The Environment Agency provides the website Netregs at www.environment-agency.gov.uk/netregs, which outlines the environmental regulations that affect agriculture. The site also looks at best practice and provides links to the 'Codes of good agricultural practice'.

> **Stockfree-Organic Standard principle 9.3 reads:**
> Concern for the environment should manifest itself in a willingness to consult appropriate conservation bodies.

The nature conservation and archaeological value of all habitats should be assessed before undertaking any management changes on the registered holding. This standard goes beyond what is legally required of the stockfree-organic grower.

Information can be gained from the following agencies:

- ADAS: Woodthorne, Wergs Road, Wolverhampton, WV6 8TQ, Tel: 0845 7660085.
- Barn Owl Conservation Network: Sheepdrove Organic Farm, Lambourn, Berkshire, RG17 7UU, Tel: 01488 73335.
- The Bat Conservation Trust: 15 Cloisters House, 8 Battersea Park Road,

London, SW8 4BG, Tel: 0845 130 0228.

- BTCV: Conservation Centre, 163 Balby Road, Doncaster, South Yorkshire, DN4 0RH, Tel: 01302 572 244.
- English Nature: Northminster House, Northminster Road, Peterborough, PE1 1AU, Tel: 01733 455000.
- Environment Agency (England and Wales): Advice on recycling and correct disposal of fuel and oil Tel: 0845 933 3111.
- Farming and Wildlife Advisory Group (FWAG): NAC Stoneleigh, Kenilworth, Warwickshire, CV8 2RX, Tel: 024 7669 6699.
- Farm Management Improvement Divisions (DEFRA): practical advise on how to avoid water, air and soil pollution from farm waste, Tel: 020 7238 5395.
- National Farm Waste Management Register: Professional advice available from members of the register, Tel: 01844 234852.
- The National Trust: The Estates Department, 33 Sheep Street, Cirencester, Gloucestershire GL7 1RQ, Tel: 01285 651 818.
- Organic Advisory Service: Elm Farm Research Centre (EFRC): Hamstead Marshall, Newbury RG20 OHR, Tel: 01488 658279.
- Organic Centre Wales: Institute of Rural Studies, University of Wales, Aberystwyth, Ceredigion SY23 3AL, Tel: 01970 622100, Email: organic-helpline@aber.ac.uk
- Organic Conversion Information Service (OCIS): England - Tel 0117 922 7707, Scotland – Tel: 01224 711 072, Wales – Tel: 01970 622100, Northern Ireland – Tel: 028 9070 1115.
- RSPB Agricultural adviser: UK Headquarters, The Lodge, Sandy, Bedfordshire, SG19 2DL, Tel: 01767 680551.
- Soil Association: 40-56 Victoria Street, Bristol, BS1 6BY, Tel: 0117 914 2407.
- The Wildlife Trusts: The Kiln, Waterside, Mather Road, Newark NG24 1WT, Tel: 0870 036 7711.

9.3 Recommended - Leaving an undisturbed field margin around all fields for wildlife conservation

Stockfree-Organic Standard 9.4 (a) Leaving an undisturbed field margin around all fields for wildlife conservation (b) Leaving strips of undisturbed vegetation across the field

Wider environmental impact	Increasing on-farm biodiversity.
	Important habitat for declining bird species.
Advantages for the grower	Refuge for mammals and unfledged birds.
	Low cost.
Disadvantages for the grower	Reduced cropping area.

A two-metre strip of undisturbed field margin will increase the effectiveness of a hedge. As discussed in 8.6 even a one-metre strip can be an important refuge for invertebrates (which will feed chicks), spiders, mammals and birds such as partridges. Grass seeds in summer are also important for seed eating birds. It is important not to plough up to the hedge base, as this will damage the roots of the hedgerow.

9.4 Recommended - Leaving strips of undisturbed vegetation across the field

Beetle banks (8.5.1), nettle strips (8.5.2), wildflower strips (8.5.3) and attractant flower strips (8.7) are discussed in the previous chapter. These, coupled with strips of undisturbed vegetation, can provide important wildlife corridors in the field, linking hedges (see 9.12 and 9.13) and rows of trees (see 9.14). Having adjacent linear field margin habitats, such as hedges, ditches, and grass strips, greatly enhances the potential of both habitats.

Mid-field strips are particularly useful for skylarks, as they tend to avoid field margins. They also provide a good habitat for predators, allowing them to move out and into the crop quickly. Partridges may also prefer such areas to field margins.

9.5 Recommended - Planting attractant species for beneficial insects, e.g. phacelia, and for birds, e.g. teasel

<table>
<tr><td colspan="2">Stockfree-Organic Standard 9.4(c) Planting attractant species for beneficial insects, e.g. phacelia, and for birds, e.g. teasel</td></tr>
<tr><td>Wider environmental impact</td><td>Reducing pest and disease cycles without the use of pesticides.
Increasing farm biodiversity.</td></tr>
<tr><td>Advantages for the grower</td><td>Very effective method for attracting beneficial insects and birds.
Increasing the aesthetic beauty of the registered holding.</td></tr>
<tr><td>Disadvantages for the grower</td><td>Reduced cropping area.
Initial seed costs.
Annual maintenance.</td></tr>
</table>

Pauline Pears and Sue Stickland[2] recommend choosing flowers, shrubs and trees that attract insects and birds. For example the following provide nectar and pollen throughout the season for beneficial insects like bees, hoverflies and parasitic wasps:

- Alpine strawberry *(Fragaria vesca)*
- Angelica *(Angelica archangelica)*
- Annual convolvulus *(Convolvulus tricolour)*
- Baby blue eyes *(Nemophila menziesii)*
- Buckwheat *(Polygonum fagopyrum)*
- Californian poppy *(Eschscholzia)*
- Chevril *(Anthriscus cerefolium)*
- Dill *(Anethum graveolens)*
- Fennel *(Foeniculum vulgare)*
- Fleabane *(Erigon)*
- Golden rod *(Solidago)*
- Hazel *(Corylus avellana)*
- Lovage *(Levisticum officinale)*

- Michaelmas daisies and other asters *(Aster)*
- Pearl everlasting *(Anaphalis)*
- Phacelia *(Phacelia tanacetifolia)*
- Poached egg plant *(Limnanthes douglasii)*
- Pot marigold *(Calendula officinalis)*
- Shasta daisy *(Chrysanthemum maximium)*
- Sunflower *(Helianthus annuus)*
- Sweet cicely *(Myrrhis odorata)*
- Thyme *(Thymus vulgaris)*
- Viper's bugloss *(Echium vulgare)*
- Willow *(Salix)*
- Yarrow *(Achillea millefolium)*

The old cottage garden flower mixes are good for attracting beneficial insects and look particularly beautiful as borders to vegetable beds. They also tend to produce good seed heads, providing not only a good food source for goldfinches and greenfinches, but also allowing the stockfree-organic grower to save the seed from year to year.

Butterfly plants include:

- buddleias
- sedums
- alliums
- hebes
- heliotropes

Flowers that provide seeds for birds include:

- Cornflower *(Centurea cyanus)*
- Cosmos *(Cosmos atrosanguineus)*
- Cranesbill *(Geranium spp)*
- Evening primrose *(Oenothera)*
- Fennel *(Foeniculum vulgare)*
- Forget-me-not *(Myosotis)*
- Globe artichoke *(Cynara cardunculus scolymus)*
- Globe thistle *(Echinops ritro, E. bannaticus)*
- Golden rod *(Solidago)*
- Honesty *(Lunaria biennis)*
- Lavender *(Lavandula)*
- Michaelmas daisies and other asters *(Aster)*
- Rose campion *(Lychnis conoria)*
- Scabious *(Scabiosa caucasia)*
- Snap dragon *(Antirrhinum)*
- Sunflower *(Helianthus annuus)*
- Teasel *(Dipsacus fullonum)*
- Yarrow *(Achillea millefolium)*

Trees and shrubs that provide fruit and berries for birds include:

- Berberis – all berrying varieties *(Berberis)*
- Cotoneaster *(Cotoneaster)*
- Crab apple varieties 'John Downie' *(Malus)*
- Elder *(Sambucus nigra)*
- Guelder rose *(Viburnum opulus)*
- Hawthorn *(Cratagus monogyna)*
- Holly – native species *(Ilex aquifolium)*
- Japanese quince *(Chaenomeles)*
- Pyracantha *(Pyracantha)*
- Rowan / mountain ash *(Sorbus)*
- Skimmia *(Skimmia japonica)*
- Snowberry *(Symphoricarpos)*
- Species rose *(Rosa rugosa)*
- Virburnum *(Virburnus davidii)*

9.6 Recommended – Planting or encouraging indigenous flora of the area

Stockfree-Organic Standard 9.4(d) Planting or encouraging indigenous flora of the area

Wider environmental impact	Increasing local biodiversity. Reversing a decline in species.
Advantages for the grower	Very effective method for attracting beneficial insects. Increasing the aesthetic beauty of the registered holding.
Disadvantages for the grower	Reduced cropping area. Initial seed / plant costs. Annual maintenance.

The Natural History Museum provides an excellent website, where you can search for all the native flora and fauna of your area by postcode. It is available at: www.nhm.ac.uk/science/projects/fff/SearchPC.htm

It will search for local native annual, biennial and perennial plants, shrubs and trees, as well as local amphibians, birds, butterflies, mammals and reptiles.

9.7 Recommended – Installation of bird and bat boxes and winter-feeding stations for birds

Stockfree-Organic Standard 9.4(e) Installation of bird and bat boxes and winter-feeding stations for birds

Wider environmental impact	Increasing bird and bat populations.
Advantages for the grower	Most effective techniques for encouraging birds and bats.
Disadvantages for the grower	Initial cost of materials. Bird feeding requires a regular commitment throughout the winter.

Consult BTCV's *Woodland Manual* available at http://handbooks.btcv.org.uk for best practice.

9.8 Recommended – Avoiding the disturbance of ground-nesting birds when cultivating and mowing

Stockfree-Organic Standard 9.4(f) Avoiding the disturbance of ground-nesting birds when cultivating and mowing

Wider environmental impact	Increasing ground nesting populations.
Advantages for the grower	Most effective technique.
Disadvantages for the grower	Loss of cropping area. Regular observations and time required to mark nests.

Ground-nesting birds like lapwings may have their nests destroyed when preparing land for spring-sown crops or when mowing green manure leys and hay fields between March and July. On a field scale their nests can be marked by bamboo canes and a five-metre machinery exclusion zone can be put around them. When mowing green manure leys it is important to try to leave seven weeks between cuts. This allows skylarks, in particular, to complete a breeding cycle between the two cuts.

9.9 Recommended – Mowing from the centre of the field outwards

Stockfree-Organic Standard 9.4(g) Mowing from the centre of the field outwards so that unfledged birds and mammals can escape to the uncut refuges

Wider environmental impact	Increasing bird and mammal populations.
Advantages for the grower	Improves biodiversity.
Disadvantages for the grower	None.

There may be unfledged birds and young hares on green manure leys at the time of mowing or haymaking. You can assist their escape by mowing from the centre of the field outwards, as this allows the animals to move to the uncut refuges like the margins and strips in the field (see 9.3 and 9.4). You can also leave strips in the green manures (see 3.5.6).

9.10 Recommended – Timing mowing operations to allow wildflower meadow grasses and flowers to set seed

See 8.5.3 for practices for establishing and maintaining wildflower meadows and strips.

Stockfree-Organic Standard 9.4(h) Timing mowing operations to allow wildflower meadow grasses and flowers to set seed

Wider environmental impact	Wildflower meadows can last a long time.
Advantages for the grower	Improves biodiversity. Seeds for birds.
Disadvantages for the grower	Initial establishment costs. Maintenance costs.

9.11 Recommended – Allowing undisturbed areas for natural regeneration of wild plants

Stockfree-Organic Standard 9.5(a) Allowing undisturbed areas for natural regeneration of wild plants

Wider environmental impact	Giving local plants an opportunity to thrive.
Advantages for the grower	Improves biodiversity. Low cost.
Disadvantages for the grower	Reduced cropping area.

See 8.6 for explanations.

9.12 Recommended – Maintaining traditional boundaries such as hedges, ditches and stone walls, which act as important wildlife corridors.

Stockfree-Organic Standard 9.5(b) Maintaining traditional boundaries such as hedges, ditches and stone walls, which act as important wildlife corridors. These will provide the refuge and hibernation facilities for beneficial vertebrate and invertebrate life.

Wider environmental impact	Improves biodiversity.
Advantages for the grower	Very important for improving the conservation value of the registered holding.
Disadvantages for the grower	Reduced cropping area.

Field boundaries provide important links between other semi-natural habitats and are commonly called 'wildlife corridors'. If there are isolated habitats on the registered holding, it is important to consider whether new wildlife corridors can be instated or whether potential wildlife corridors are being lost through poor management or even over-management, e.g. trimming for aesthetic reasons.

Hedgerows are particularly important[3] as they:

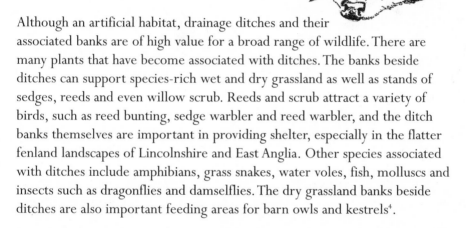

- provide an important wildlife habitat;
- create a specific micro-climate by reducing wind speeds in the field;
- support natural pest control;
- protect against soil erosion.

Consult BTCV's Hedging Handbook available at http://handbooks.btcv.org.uk for best practice.

Although an artificial habitat, drainage ditches and their associated banks are of high value for a broad range of wildlife. There are many plants that have become associated with ditches. The banks beside ditches can support species-rich wet and dry grassland as well as stands of sedges, reeds and even willow scrub. Reeds and scrub attract a variety of birds, such as reed bunting, sedge warbler and reed warbler, and the ditch banks themselves are important in providing shelter, especially in the flatter fenland landscapes of Lincolnshire and East Anglia. Other species associated with ditches include amphibians, grass snakes, water voles, fish, molluscs and insects such as dragonflies and damselflies. The dry grassland banks beside ditches are also important feeding areas for barn owls and kestrels[4].

9.13 Recommended – Reinstating hedges where appropriate

Stockfree-Organic Standard 9.5(c) Reinstating hedges where appropriate.	
Wider environmental impact	Improves biodiversity.
Advantages for the grower	Very important for improving the conservation value of the registered holding.
Disadvantages for grower	Initial start up costs, although these can be the offset by grants.

Consult BTCV's Hedging Handbook available at http://handbooks.btcv.org.uk which offers full descriptions of hedge species. The handbook also gives technical explanations about planting and ground preparation for a hedge.

9.14 Recommended – Practising agroforestry techniques, e.g. alley cropping with row of trees

Stockfree-Organic Standard 9.5(d) Practising agroforestry techniques, e.g. alley cropping with rows of trees

Wider environmental impact	Improves biodiversity.
Advantages for the grower	Very effective method for improving biodiversity. Windbreaks. Sustainable source of fuel wood.
Disadvantages for the grower	Reduced cropping area. Initial planting costs. Regular maintenance.

Agroforestry is the growing of trees and agricultural / horticultural crops on the same piece of land to gain mutual interactions which will benefit the whole growing system. Agrisilvicultural systems involve crops (arable or horticultural) that are grown simultaneously with a tree / woody perennial crop.

With small-scale systems, the pattern of trees and crops can be very complicated, as shown in Robert Hart's *Forest Gardening*[5]. On a commercial growing scale less-complex systems, with ordered tree arrangements, allow for the use of machinery. A common arrangement is alley-cropping – rows of trees with wide alleys in-between providing beds for the annual crops.

Tree rows should be:

- spaced at a minimum of 14 metres apart to allow enough room for cultivation operations in the alleys;
- aligned north to south.

Single, double or triple rows can be used[6]. The trees may be used for the production of timber, fuelwood, nitrogen fixing, fruit or nuts. The trees can be established using mulching and then the natural flora can generate underneath, allowing a predator belt to develop. The example of Growing with Nature with their single tree rows of nitrogen-fixing grey alder, twenty metres apart with one metre between the trees, is discussed in section 8.4. Alan and Debra Schofield pollard and coppice their tree rows and use the products for fuel wood and creating log piles for habitat.

The benefits of alley cropping with rows of trees include[7]:

- nutrient resources can be shared through leafmould (see 4.2) and chipped branch wood (see 3.8);
- trees provide windbreaks;
- trees provide predator belts;
- tree roots contribute to the long-term process of soil development;
- more carbon is fixed in the soil;
- to a considerable extent trees and crops use light and water resources at different times of the year;
- employment opportunities are provided in winter and
- wildlife habitat and aesthetic quality are improved.

The disadvantages include:

- high management input;
- difficulties in drought periods;
- delayed return on the investment and;
- high planting costs.

The Agroforestry Research Trust[8] recommends that tillage be used on the alleys between the trees because zero tillage beds are likely to fill with fine tree roots. It is also important to avoid cultivations directly under the tree canopy, as this will damage the trees. Therefore, there must be separation between the trees and the alleys as the crop roots and tree roots do not want to be competing in the same zone for moisture.

Pollarding and coppicing of the trees are essential practices to stop the interference with annual crops and to create long-lasting systems. Yields of alley crops are not reduced by shading until the tree height reaches the alley width. The practice of allowing the trees to continue to grow and then converting the system to silvopastoral using livestock is prohibited under the Stockfree-Organic Standards.

9.15 Recommended – Replanting indigenous shrubs and trees

Stockfree-Organic Standard 9.5(e) Replanting indigenous shrubs and trees

Wider environmental impact	Increasing local biodiversity. Reversing a decline in species.
Advantages for the grower	Very effective method for attracting beneficial insects.
Disadvantages for the grower	Reduced cropping area. Initial plant costs.

See 9.6. Of all field boundaries woodland edges are considered to offer the greatest contribution to biodiversity. Plants for a Future[9] (PFAF) have produced a briefing sheet '*The Woodland Edge Garden*', which details suitable species, including edible ones, which could also be included within agroforestry techniques (see 9.15.).

9.16 Recommended – Coppicing and other traditional management practices of existing woodland

Stockfree-Organic Standard 9.5(f) Coppicing and other traditional management practices of existing woodland

Wider environmental impact	Maintaining biodiverse woodlands.
Advantages for the grower	Improvement in woodland skills.
Disadvantages for the grower	Possibly need to pay for professional services.

Best practice for woodland management includes[10]:

- the management of trees in accordance with local custom;
- replanting programmes using indigenous species (see 9.6);
- protection of newly planted or regenerated woodland against competing animals;
- use of planting material from recognised local suppliers;
- retention of deadwood and log piles;
- cultivating the beds at the point where the outermost canopy of the trees is no longer above them.

Consult the BTCV's *Woodlands Handbook* and *Tree Planting and Aftercare Handbook* available at http://handbooks.btcv.org.uk for best practice.

9.17 Recommended - Tree planting and fencing newly planted trees against competing animals

Stockfree-Organic Standard 9.5(g) Fencing newly planted trees against competing animals	
Wider environmental impact	Maintaining biodiverse woodlands.
Advantages for the grower	Trees more likely to survive.
Disadvantages for the grower	Cost and time.

Consult the BTCV's *Tree Planting and Aftercare Handbook* available at http://handbooks.btcv.org.uk for best practice.

9.18 Recommended - Hedge trimming and ditch and dyke clearance between January and February

Stockfree-Organic Standard 9.5(h) Hedge trimming and ditch and dyke clearance between January and February

Wider environmental impact	Maintaining biodiverse hedgerows and ditches.
Advantages for the grower	More effective habitats.
Disadvantages for the grower	Possibly need to pay for professional services.

Consult the BTCV Hedging Handbook available at http://handbooks.btcv.org.uk for best practice.

9.19 Recommended - Clearing ditches in phased operations, leaving a portion uncleared each year, e.g. clearing opposite sides of ditches in successive years

Stockfree-Organic Standard 9.5(i) Clearing ditches in phased operations, leaving a portion uncleared each year, e.g. clearing opposite sides of ditches in successive years

Wider environmental impact	Maintaining biodiverse ditches.
Advantages for the grower	More effective habitats.
Disadvantages for the grower	Time.

It is important to leave drainage ditches uncleared for periods of time, especially if the ditch side has a tussocky grass sward. Allowing this to develop can increase insect and small mammal populations, leading to an improved raptor habitat. Therefore, it is important to[11]:

- clear ditches on a rotational basis between January and February;

- leave 10% of the vegetation undisturbed to allow re-colonisation by plants and amphibian species;
- re-profile sections of ditches, providing shallow ledges rather than traditional steep sides, which will reduce erosion and provide a better wildlife habitat.

These management reductions will also bring about a time and resource saving for the stockfree-organic grower.

9.20 Recommended – Maintaining and creating water bodies for beneficial amphibians, reptiles and insects

<table>
<tr><td colspan="2">Stockfree-Organic Standard 9.5(j) Maintaining and creating water bodies for beneficial amphibians, reptiles and insects.</td></tr>
<tr><td>Wider environmental impact</td><td>Increasing on-farm biodiversity.
All insects and creatures need water.</td></tr>
<tr><td>Advantages for the grower</td><td>Very effective method for improving biodiversity.</td></tr>
<tr><td>Disadvantages for the grower</td><td>Reduced cropping area.
Initial start up costs.</td></tr>
</table>

Created watercourses can offer habitats to uncommon plants, mammals such as water voles, breeding wildfowl, amphibians and invertebrates such as dragonflies. Maintaining or excavating a new water feature is one of the most important practices you can undertake to increase biodiversity. However, it is important that you[12]:

- avoid excavating wetland areas;
- establish ponds in groups of five or more rather than scattering them around the registered holding (they do not need to be large);
- have a variety in the depth of ponds; frogs will spawn in the

shallows, whilst toads use mainly deep water;
- have open stretches of water;
- construct irrigation lagoons with consideration for wildlife, adding profiled banks and ensuring that some water is always retained;
- link water features with hedges, grassland and woodland features;
- allow natural colonisation with plants;
- avoid contaminating ponds with deliberately introduced plants and fish;
- avoid run-off entering into the watercourse (see 4.8 and 4.9).

Consult the BTCV's Urban Handbook available at http://handbooks.btcv.org.uk for best practice.

9.21 Recommended practices relating to farm buildings

Stockfree-Organic Standard 9.6 (a) The siting and construction of new farm buildings should be done sensitively, taking account of their environmental and aesthetic impact. (b) Maintaining existing old buildings in their original form. (c) The provision of roosts and nest sites for bats and barn owls in new buildings and conversions.	
Wider environmental impact	Increasing on-farm biodiversity.
Advantages for the grower	Very effective method for improving encouraging barn owls, swallows and bats.
Disadvantages for the grower	Extra caution is needed.

Buildings are an important feature in environmental conservation. They can provide nest sites for birds such as swallows and barn owls and also roost sites for bats. It is important to encourage such sites in farm buildings. For example, removing a windowpane or leaving a window slightly ajar can help swallows find a suitable nest site.

9.22 Restricted - Removal of hedgerows, banks or ditches

Stockfree-Organic Standard 9.6 (a) reads:

Restricted

Removal of hedgerows, banks or ditches. Proposed measures must be discussed with a conservation advisor. Consideration should be given to the need for compensatory environmental work.

As discussed in 9.2 stockfree-organic growers should talk to a conservation advisor before undertaking any management changes on the registered holding. This is particularly relevant to hedgerows that are protected in law.

9.23 Restricted - Removal of trees

Stockfree-Organic Standard 9.6 reads:

Restricted

(b) Clear felling of woodland

(c) Felling of mature trees that are not endangering safety.

As discussed in 9.2 stockfree-organic growers should talk to a conservation advisor before undertaking any management changes on the registered holding.

9.24 Prohibited practices that are harmful to environmental conservation

Under Stockfree-Organic Standard 9.8 the following are prohibited:

a. Hedge trimming, tree felling, ditch and dyke clearance between 1st March and 31st August.
b. Annual trimming of all hedges unless required by Local Authorities for road safety.
c. Ploughing species-rich meadows agreed with a statutory conservation body to be of conservation interest.
d. New or improved drainage affecting areas of significant conservation value.
e. Exploitation of peat bogs that are of conservation interest.
f. Damage to or disturbance of the nesting and roosting sites of owls, bats

and other protected species.

g The use of wood preservatives that are harmful to bats and other wildlife on new or existing building or fence posts, etc.

h Levelling of ridge-and-furrow fields and cultivation of sites of ancient monuments, archaeological sites and earthworks.

Among the Standards Working Group it was the unanimous view that these practices should be prohibited. For example, annual flailing decreases the longevity of hedges. Again the standards can be seen to go beyond what is legally required of the stockfree-organic grower. Even conventional farmers may need to take note, since 9.8(c), (d) and (e) are covered by EU regulation 97/11/EC (effective since 1st February 2002). Agricultural projects for improving the productivity of extensively managed, unimproved or semi-improved land will often require an environmental impact assessment. Details are available from DEFRA.

1 Adapted from the SOIL ASSOCIATION (2002) Improving Biodiversity on Organic Farms. Soil Association Technical Guides.

2 PEARS P & STICKLAND S (1995) Organic Gardening: The Royal Horticultural Society Encyclopaedia of Practical Gardening. Mitchell Beazley.

3 Adapted from SOIL ASSOCIATION (2002) Improving Biodiversity on Organic Farms. Soil Association Technical Guides.

4 Adapted from the Cambridge County Council's website.

5 HART, R (1997) Forest Gardening. Green Books.

6 It depends on the tree crop that is sought by the stockfree-organic grower, e.g. a high-value timber crop can be sandwiched between rows of coniferous trees to help straighten the timber tree.

7 WOLFE, M (1998) Agroforestry: a Way Forward on Organic Farms? New farmer & Grower 58: 30 – 31.

8 Agroforestry Research Trust, 46 Hunters Moon, Dartington, Totnes, Devon, TQ9 6JT, 01803 840776.

9 Plants for a Future is a resource and information centre for useful plants, promoting ecologically sustainable vegan-organic horticulture and agriculture with an emphasis on tree, shrub and other perennial species. Their research is recorded on a database comprising 7500 species edible and useful plants. For more information contact Plants for a Future, Blagdon Lodge Cross, Ashwater, Beaworthy, Devon. EX21 5DF. Tel: 0845 458 4719. Website: - www.pfaf.org

10 Adapted from SOIL ASSOCIATION (2002) Improving Biodiversity on Organic Farms. Soil Association Technical Guides.

11 Adapted from SOIL ASSOCIATION (2002) Improving Biodiversity on Organic Farms. Soil Association Technical Guides.

12 Adapted from SOIL ASSOCIATION (2002) Improving Biodiversity on Organic Farms. Soil association technical guides and WILKINSON J et al (1996) Amphibians on Pest Patrol. New Farmer and Grower. Winter 20-21.

Chapter Ten

Environmental accounting

10.1 Introduction to environmental benefits of organic farming

By practising organic growing you are already making a less negative environmental impact in comparison to conventional growing relying on synthetic inputs. Organic production techniques do not rely to the same extent on fossil fuel intensive and polluting inputs. For example, in Germany, some water companies have realised that it is cheaper to pay farmers to convert to organic systems than to clean up the water pollution of conventional farms. Pesticides in particular are responsible for:

* the wide-spectrum killing of beneficial insects and flora;
* failing to reach target organisms and consequently being lost to the environment;
* contamination of lakes, ponds, rivers and ground waters;
* residues in fish and predatory animals;
* human illness connected to organophosphate sheep dips;
* poisoning and deaths of agricultural workers in developing countries;
* increased pesticide resistance of target species;
* food contamination.

The 'polluter pays' principle is not part of conventional agricultural policy and therefore it is the water consumer and tax payer who pay for nitrate / pesticide removal and the health scares. These problems can be avoided in stockfree-organic systems with careful management to avoid pollution risks.

10.2 Recommended practices

Under Stockfree-organic Standard 8.1 it is recommended that:

(a) Wherever possible, using renewable energy sources such as human, wind, solar and water power in the place of fossil fuels.
(b) Reusing and recycling waste materials rather than burning them or sending them to landfill.
(c) Obtaining supplies as locally as possible and in any case in the UK.
(d) Selling the products of the holding as locally as possible and in any case and in any case in the UK.

The following can be used as a checklist to avoid pollution:

1. Conserving materials
   - fewer inputs;
   - durable and / or reusable inputs;
   - inputs that contain fewer materials e.g. less packaging;
   - inputs that contain fewer environmentally damaging constituents.

2. Increasing the generation of on-farm fertility
   - green manuring, composting, mulching, chipped branch wood.

3. Reducing water pollution from plant-based composts
   - adequate storage;
   - prevent leachate from windrows / heaps entering water courses and ground water;
   - avoid spreading compost within 10 metres of ditches, watercourses and boreholes;
   - avoid spreading compost on frozen or saturated ground.

4. Reducing nitrate pollution
   - avoid over winter leaching by keeping the ground covered with overwinter green manures;
   - avoid turning in leys in Autumn;
   - avoid anaerobic conditions in the soil due to compaction and water logging;

- improve soil structure to enhance nitrogen-holding capacity in the soil;
- improve the organic matter levels of the soil to enhance the mineralisation / immobilisation nitrogen cycle.

5. Reducing eutrophication – phosphorus enrichment of water courses
    - prevent water erosion - soil particles being washed into watercourses;
    - soil protection strategies;
    - ground cover in the form of green manures or mulches, especially over winter;
    - attach filters to field drainage pipes.

6. Reducing waste flows from
    - growing operations;
    - storage and packing operations;
    - ensure all produce has a market (see chapter 13).

7. Reducing direct fossil fuel use on the holding
    - human labour over machinery where possible;
    - use intermediate technology e.g. a wheel hoe;
    - correct cultivation equipment;
    - fewer passes with machinery;
    - machinery and tractors at the most efficient speed and load;
    - keep internal combustion engines optimally tuned and well maintained;
    - avoid unnecessary idling of engines;
    - water conservation strategies, especially with irrigation equipment;
    - shut off electrical appliances when not needed.

8. Renewable energy
    - human labour over machinery where possible;
    - use intermediate technology e.g. a wheel hoe;
    - solar uses of power e.g. solar drying of onions, solar panels;
    - wind turbines;
    - water turbines;
    - change electricity company[1] to one that uses more renewable sources of energy.

9. Transportation
- reduce distance inputs travel;
- reduce food miles;
- aim for multi purpose trips with vehicles;
- move towards foot and cycle power.

10.3 Prohibited practices
10.3.1 Topsoil heavy metal contamination
The growing of produce in topsoil that is contaminated with heavy metals above these maximum levels is prohibited:

Topsoil contamination of agricultural land (that has only ever been used for agriculture) is not generally considered to be a problem by certification bodies and tests are not required. However, contamination is more likely where the site for growing has had a former industrial use (heavy industry or manufacturing industry) or has been

	Soil mg/kg	kg/ha
Zinc	150	336
Chromium	150	336
Copper	50	110
Lead	100	220
Nickel	50	116
Cadmium	2	4.4
Mercury	1	2

used as a landfill site. The incidence of contamination is a particular problem in urban areas. In these circumstances it will be necessary to research the former use of the site, via an environmental search and have a soil analysis done.

10.3.2 Plant-based composts with heavy metal contamination
The use of plant based composts that are contaminated with heavy metals above these maximum levels is prohibited.

The cost of having contamination criteria for plant-based compost may fill small-scale growers with dread, especially if you use bought-in compost from different sources. Fortunately, green waste compost, free from animal-inputs, attaining the Soil Association certified product symbol will have acceptable heavy metal levels.

	mg/kg of dry matter
Zinc	200
Chromium (VI)	0
Copper	70
Lead	45
Nickel	25
Cadmium	0.7
Mercury	0.4

For unapproved bought-in composts stockfree-organic growers will need to assess the risk of contamination and seek approval from the certification body. The contamination criteria are important to prevent the use of compost that is from non-segregated waste streams.

- If you are collecting the materials yourself from outside sources e.g. garden green waste, seaweed, spent hops or chipped branch wood then tests will not be insisted upon as long as you know the circumstances under which the material has been collected.
- Segregated vegetable waste (e.g. from a greengrocers), community composting and sites dedicated solely to segregated garden green wastes are excluded from testing provided that the supplier signs an undertaking that the compost is not contaminated with animal products.
- Householder's kitchen waste, even if this is raw vegetable wastes from a vegan household, is classed as catering waste and is covered by the Animal By-products Order (see 3.7.1).
- If you are buying from a compost manufacturer e.g. a local authority where no testing has occurred, and where you cannot know the circumstances under which the plant-based material has been collected, then you will need to carry out heavy metal contamination tests at your expense.

10.3.3 Spray drift contamination

Spray drift contamination can occur from pesticides and herbicides on the registered holding. Effort must be made to provide an effective windbreak until the time when a hedge is established. A ten-metre buffer zone is normally sufficient. However, there should be a twenty-metre buffer zone if the registered holding is near to a conventional orchard or other heavily-sprayed area. These prohibitions are to prevent spray drift contamination of the stockfree-organic produce.

10.3.4 Contamination of water and use of contaminated water for irrigation purposes

If the stockfree-organic grower follows recommended practices throughout the Stockfree-Organic Standards, pollution risks to water supplies are low. However, there may be issues where irrigation water is being polluted by a neighbouring farm. If you have concerns, in the first instance you should contact the Environment Agency.

10.3.5 Seeds etc containing GMOs or their derivatives

Seeds, seedlings, plant propagation materials, inoculants or other crop production inputs containing GMOs or their derivatives are prohibited in organic farming because of their:

- incompatibility with the principles of organic agriculture;
- unrecallable nature;
- potential risks they pose to the environment and human health.

10.3.6 Genetic engineering contamination

Genetic engineering may cause unacceptable contamination of the land or crops via pollen or other plant residues. Contamination can occur through the:

- cross pollination of soil flora and plants, including weeds;
- physical contamination by pollen or other plant residues.

If genetically engineered crops are being grown within a six-mile radius of a registered holding, the certification body should be notified. If agreed by the grower, this information can be passed to the Vegan-Organic Network to assist the publicising of the risk to livelihood. With widespread adoption of organic farming, the six-mile radius will prove increasingly difficult to observe, especially if genetic engineering becomes standard practice in conventional farming. The position of GMOs in agriculture will need careful consideration by policy makers in the future.

10.3.7 The burning of straw, cereal waste, stubble and other compostable materials

In Britain about fourteen million tonnes of straw are produced annually. Some is used as bedding or for feeding livestock, but about half of the straw produced is unwanted surplus. Until 1992 surplus straw was usually burnt along with the stubble in the fields at the time of harvest, leaving the field clear for planting the next crop. The burning of stubble has been banned since 1993 under the Crops Residues (Burning) Regulations 1993 and is enforced by Environmental Health Officers.

Farmers have been looking for uses for straw surpluses. Burners that can take straw bales have been developed in Denmark and the USA and even power stations powered by straw have been proposed. However, as straw is an excellent material for compost, and returns potash and phosphates back to the soil, the widespread adoption of stockfree-organic systems could provide that needed outlet for straw surpluses.

10.3.8 Environmental impact of plastic

The use of plastic in organic agriculture has been commonplace, especially in the case of growing on marginal land. However, plastic can be considered to be the scourge of organic agriculture. Life cycle analysis of plastic film products like polyethylene and PVC has shown them to be fossil fuel intensive in their manufacture with 66.80MJ of energy used for every kilogram of plastic. Plastic can also cause pollution in its manufacture and end-of-life disposal. The manufacture of plastics can give rise to emissions of, amongst other things, hydrochloric acid and chlorinated by-products including dioxin, which is feared to be carcinogenic. As well as possible hazards to human health, constituents, such as plasticisers, have found their way into sewage systems and are known to be toxic to aquatic life.

The difficulty for the stockfree-organic grower is final disposal, especially of black plastic. As it is contaminated with soil and plant residues, it is not always suitable for recycling, which often requires a clean product. New opportunities may arise, but finding a recycling company and transporting the plastic waste may prove difficult and this is why biodegradable plastic mulches are becoming more favoured. Biodegradable plastic mulches manufactured from maize starch, break down after a season. They still contain small amounts of plasticisers but are made using less fossil fuel. They are also about three times more expensive than traditional plastic mulches but having no disposal cost tends to bring the cost down to similar levels.

It is illegal to burn plastic under the Clean Air Act 1993. This Act is enforced by the local authority and it is an offence to burn waste materials in the open on trade premises if the burning produces dark smoke. Land being used for commercial agricultural or horticultural purposes constitutes trade premises under this Act.

10.4 Energy accounting to measure environmental impact

The most useful tool available to stockfree-organic growers is the measuring of energy flows, particularly fossil fuel use, into the food system of which they are a part.

10.4.1 Background

Primitive agricultural systems rely on human and animal labour. To meet their energy requirements the people and animals eat food and the energy in the food is derived from solar energy. Thus a steady-state system is maintained, in which the food system operates entirely on the incident flux of solar energy. Not only the food system, but the whole energy budget of primitive societies is limited to the incident flux of solar energy.

Industrialised societies have learned to tap the solar energy, trapped over millions of years and now lying in coal beds and oil and gas pools in the earth. Critics of modern agriculture have argued that the human removal from agriculture has come at the cost of dependency of fossil fuel stocks. One gallon of petrol contains about 155MJ (31,000 kcal) of potential energy which is the equivalent of one man working eight hours a day, five days a week for about 2.5 weeks[2].

Energy density may prove itself to be a useful indicator for where farming begins to cause pollution and more research in this area is needed. According to Slesser[3] once farming has exceeded an input of 15 gigajoules per hectare, the 'farmer is no longer keeping his messes to himself'. 'Food miles' has become the other popular yardstick for measuring environmental impact. For example, for every tonne / kilometre a lorry travels 0.00612MJ of fossil energy is used, leading to the emission of 48g of carbon dioxide and 0.95g of nitrous oxide, both of which are greenhouse gases.

When conducting energy input and CO_2 analysis of two comparable mixed farms, Köpke and Haas[4] found the organic farming system to have an energy input of 6.8GJ per hectare, 65% less than that used in the conventional system, which was 19.4GJ per hectare. The conventional system is seen to exceed Slesser's pollution threshold. The difference can be accounted for by the amount of fossil energy it takes to manufacture artificial fertilisers and pesticides and the bought-in animal feeds.

Similar research into stockfree-organic systems has not yet been conducted. However, in theory, greater energy efficiency in stockfree-organic systems is likely, especially if we consider the features of Tolhurst Organic Produce and Organic Growers of Durham:

- most of the fertility is generated on the holding through the use of green manures;
- they have limited bought-in inputs e.g. only buy in straw bales;
- the growing systems do not use animal inputs;
- the produce is marketed locally – in the case of OGD on a bicycle.

10.4.2 Input / output analysis of energy use

Following on from the pioneering work of Organic Growers of Durham (without which this chapter would not have been possible), growers can now conduct input / output analysis of the fossil fuel inputs compared to the energy outputs.

There are two pathways through which fossil energy is used on holding:

- direct e.g. diesel for tractors;
- indirect, through the use of materials like fertilisers, pesticides and plastic mulches that require fossil energy for their manufacture.

It is necessary to know the actual amount of fossil fuel resource that has to be extracted from the ground in order to make the input available. However, the extensive literature includes a very wide range of different values. For example, when calculating the energy requirement for a synthetic fertiliser, an analyst could count the energy required to manufacture it, but, to be exhaustive, the energy used for packaging and transport must also be included, as well as the energy embodied in the industrial plant where it is manufactured.

The dilemma is where to stop the regression of tracing material flows. The problem has been described as the 'partitioning problem' and the 'truncating problem'. The grower wants useful information about energy input flows and so it is necessary to make assumptions and rely on imperfect information. The same assumptions, however, have to be made every year, so that direct comparisons can be made.

Input / output analysis relates not only to the inputs / outputs on the holding but also to the inputs / outputs of:

- other industries with which the holding interacts;
- transport necessary to get inputs to the holding;
- transport to get the harvest to the consumer.

The process analysis presented in this book concentrates on the most relevant interactions through which organically produced vegetables are grown and later distributed.

It is necessary to calculate

- Inputs are assigned an energy value in megajoules (MJ) so that a Total Support Energy can be summed.
- The Total Support Energy Inputs are subtracted from the Total Energy Outputs of the vegetable harvest to find the Fossil Fuel Energy Deficit.
- The Total Support Energy Inputs are divided by the Total Energy Outputs to find The Energy Input / Output ratio.

Table 10.1 Inputs and outputs	
INPUTS (MJ)	OUTPUTS (MJ)
Mining of mineral inputs Manufacture of inputs Transport of inputs to the holding On-farm direct fossil energy use Transport of harvest	The total weight of each vegetable unit x corresponding energy coefficient
Sum to find Total Support Energy Input	Sum to find Total Energy Output

10.4.3 Calculating inputs

The grower needs to quantify how many units of inputs are used in the horticultural system from records kept for the purpose of organic certification:

- multiply the units used by the corresponding MJ energy coefficient provided in Table 10.3;
- the inputs are summed to find the Total Support Energy Input.

Table 10.2 Converting horticultural inputs into mega joules

Input	Energy	When you know this	Multiple by this figure (Energy coefficient)
Petrol (iv)	10,109 kcal/l	Litre	42.3MJ
Diesel (iv)	11,414 kcal/l	Litre	47.8MJ
Electricity (iv)	2,863 kcal/ kWh	KWh	12MJ
Paraffin (xv)		Litre	44MJ
Gas (propane) (xv)		Kg	59MJ
Gas (butane) (xv)		Kg	58MJ
Engine oil (xv)		Kg	78MJ
Car journeys (viii)	6.6 litre/ 100km	Km	2.79MJ
Train journeys (i)	0.047 kWh/ tonne/km	Km & Kg	0.00017MJ
Lorry (40 tonnes) (i)	0.17 kWh/ tonne/km	Km & Kg	0.000612MJ
Cargo Ship (i)	0.067 kWh/ tonne/km	Km & Kg	0.000241MJ
Aircraft (i)	3.15 kWh/ tonne/km	Km & Kg	0.01134MJ
Overwinter heating of glasshouse (ix)	Average of 401 and 536 MJ/m²/year	m²	470MJ

Input	Energy	When you know this	Multiple by this figure (Energy coefficient)
All round heating of glasshouse (xii)		m²	1590MJ
Ploughing (xiii)	18 litre / ha	ha	860.4MJ
Rotary cultivating (xiii)	15 litre / ha	ha	717MJ
Subsoiling (xiii)	10 litre / ha	ha	478MJ
Chisel ploughing (xiii)	9 litre / ha	ha	430.2MJ
Disc harrowing (xiii)	7 litre / ha	ha	334.6MJ
Springtime harrowing (xiii)	6 litre / ha	ha	286.6MJ
Drilling (xiii)	3 litre / ha	ha	47.8MJ
Rolling (xiii)	2 litre / ha	ha	95.8MJ
Spraying (v)		ha	34MJ
Rock phosphate (x)	1300 kcal per kg	kg	544MJ
Rock potash (iii)	2200 kcal per kg	kg	920.9MJ
Lime (xiv)	15.45 kcal kg	kg	0.065MJ
Dolomite (est) (xiv)	15.45 kcal kg	kg	0.065MJ
Seaweed meal (v)		kg	12.9MJ
Plastic mulch (vi)		kg	158MJ
Horticultural Fleece (xv)		kg	147MJ
Plastic protective netting (xv)		kg	147MJ
All seeds by weight		gram	0.0151MJ
Aluminium (vii)		kg	262MJ
Steel (vii)		kg	46.4MJ
Plastic e.g. packaging for veg (vii)		kg	9.52MJ
Timber		kg	2.5MJ
Sand and gravel (vii)		kg	0.071MJ
Cement (vii)		kg	8.4MJ
Roadstone (xv)		tonne	120MJ
Office stationery (vii)		kg	28.5MJ

References:

i ASG, Sweden, Corporate Environment Report 1996 and Energy Use and Air Pollution in UK Road Freight David Taylor and Malcolm Fergusson, WWF, 1993.

ii BERTILLISON G (1992) Environmental Consequences of Different Farming Systems using Good Agricultural Practice. Proceedings of the Fertiliser Society no. 332.

iii BERANDI – no reference found.

iv CERVINKA – no reference found.

v EDWARD-JONES G & HOWELLS O (1997) Resource Use in Organic Farming 71-88. Proceedings of the European Network of Organic Farmers (ENOF) Workshop. Ancona. 5-6 June 1997.

vi FLUCK RC et al (1978) Proceedings of Florida State Horticultural Society 90 382-385.

vii FLUCK R.C.and BAIRD (1980) Agricultural Energetics. The Avi Publishing Company Inc.

viiiLAPILLONNE B (1998) La demande d'energie dans les pays de l'OCED Energie International 1988/1999 291-300.

ix LEACH G (1976) Energy and Food Production. IPC Science and Technology Press, Guildford, Surrey.

x LOCKERETZ W (1980) in Pimental's D Handbook of Energy Utilisation ob. Cit.

xi PIMENTEL D (1980) Handbook of Energy Utilisation in Agriculture. CRC Press.

xii SHEARD GF (1975) Energy Requirements of Glasshouse Heating in Britain. SPAN 18 (1) 27-28.

xiiiSTANFIELD JR (1975) Fuel and Power in Agriculture. Span 18 (1) 23-24.

xivTERHUME – no reference found.

xv ORGANIC GROWERS OF DURHAM – personal communication.

Example: calculating energy input of spreading one tonne of lime on one hectare of land:

1000kg (weight of lime) x 0.065 (energy coefficient for its mining and crushing)	65MJ
Transporting the lime to the holding over a distance of e.g. 50km = 1000kg (weight) x 50km (distance) x 0.000612 (energy coefficient for lorry transport)	30.6MJ
Spreading (using energy coefficient for spraying) for an estimated half an hour	34MJ
TOTAL	129.6MJ

No figures are available for the following unassigned inputs into organic systems because of their proprietary nature, as their manufacture is often an industry secret. Future research into them would be useful.

- Propagation compost with peat.
- Propagation compost with green waste.
- Green waste composts.
- Compound fertilisers.
- Calcified seaweed.
- Restricted organic pesticides.

- Biological controls.

The following inputs that are allowed in traditional organic systems (generally under restriction) are prohibited in stockfree-organic systems. They also have no energy value assigned.

- Slaughterhouse by products.
- Fish emulsion.
- Conventional manures.
- Organic manures.

The transport (MJ/kg/km) involved in getting unassigned inputs (even without the energy that went into their manufacture) can still be added to the calculation. It is better to have at least some recognition of their energy input and goes somewhere towards gaining a fuller impression of the organic food system.

10.4.4 Should an energy value be assigned to labour inputs?

Organic Growers of Durham have researched the issue of attaching an energy value to human labour to give a true reflection. The different positions taken by researchers are highlighted:

1. Omit the energy cost of human labour as negligible compared to other fossil fuel inputs.
2. Assign a figure of 13 megajoules per day to the food energy used by a person doing a day's work[5].
3. Assign a figure of 594 megajoules per day to the food energy that is consumed plus part of the energy consumed by an agricultural worker in the form of clothing, transport and housing[6].
4. Assign a figure of 1500 megajoules per day calculated by Organic Growers of Durham, described below.

Organic Growers of Durham have argued[7] that even the 594 megajoules is too low because it fails to take into account that labour has to be reproduced not only from day to day, but from year to year and generation to generation. So the cost of labour has to include the cost of raising a family, of education, of health, of the welfare state and of retirement. It needs to include the energy cost of everything a person needs to live, such as a house, domestic appliances, a car or public transport. There is even a case for including the energy cost of leisure activities and holidays if these are considered necessary to keep on working.

This approach considers the agricultural worker not as an isolated individual but as a member of a society and emphasises the differences between the energy costs in different societies. In the UK for example, about ten exajoules (billion billion joules) of primary energy are consumed annually to keep our society functioning at the material standard of living we enjoy. If we divide this energy equally between the number of workers, we get a figure of approximately 1500 megajoules per day for the energy cost for human labour.

10.4.5. Calculating the harvest output

Table 10.3 Energy outputs of vegetables (information provided by Organic Growers of Durham)

Vegetable type (est = estimate)	Kgs multiplied by	Vegetable type (est = estimate)	Kgs multiplied by
Asparagus	1.08	Carrot	1.42
Aubergine	1.01	Cauliflower	1.08
Basil	0.29	Celeriac	1.01
Bean (broad)	0.95	Celery	0.53
Bean (French)	1.18	Chard, green	0.84
Bean (runner)	1.02	Chard, red (est)	0.90
Beetroot	1.75	Chicory green	0.72
Broccoli	1.26	Chicory, red	0.73
Brussel sprout	1.70	Chives	1.07
Cabbage (Chinese leaf)	0.54	Coriander	0.82
Cabbage (red)	1.17	Courgette	0.78
Cabbage (savoy)	0.95	Cucumber	0.62
Cabbage (spring)	1.09	Dill	0.70
Cabbage (summer)	0.92	Endive	0.64
Cabbage (white)	0.89	Fennel	0.50
Cabbage (winter) (est)	0.90	Garlic	4.83
Calabrese (est)	1.25	Jerusalem Artichoke	2.01

Kale	1.29	Potato (main)	3.15
Kohl Rabi	0.99	Potato (new)	3.14
Leek	1.37	Radish	0.60
Lettuce, cos	0.69	Radish – mooli	0.72
Lettuce, crisp	0.54	Rocket (herb) (est)	1.00
Lettuce, Little Gem	0.65	Rocket (veg)	0.96
Lettuce, plain	0.55	Salsify	0.79
Lettuce, red	0.64	Scorzonera (est)	0.80
Marrow	0.45	Shallot	1.94
Mint (est)	2.00	Spinach	0.99
Onion, bulb	1.36	Spinach -	
Onion, Spring	1.30	perpetual (est)	0.95
Oregano	2.76	Swede turnip	1.22
Parsley	1.49	Sweet corn	3.55
Parsnip	2.86	Tomato (red)	1.20
Pea.	2.16	Tomato (green)	1.01
Pea (sugar snap)	1.24	Turnip (white)	0.94
Pepper (green)	0.80		

The grower needs to quantify the harvest of vegetables in weight (kg) from sales invoices or other records.

- Multiply each vegetable category by weight in kilograms with the corresponding Energy Content Coefficient.

The outputs are summed to find the Total Energy Output.

10.4.6 Food miles analysis
10.4.6.1 Calculating the energy requirement of transportation through centralised distribution systems
The Food Miles Report[8] gives the following example:

'In Evesham, two supermarkets sell organic produce, some of which is grown on farms 1.5km away. But to get the vegetables from the farm to the shelf they must first travel to a co-operative in Herefordshire, then to a pack house in Dyfed, Wales, then to a distribution depot south of Manchester and finally back to Evesham'.

This example has been used as the basis of a hypothetical scenario. Joe Bloggs Organic Growers is based in Evesham and he sells 1000kg of carrots to the supermarkets. In the hypothetical scenario, 1000kg quantity will remain in tact until the distribution depot in Manchester. 50kg will then return to Evesham.

- Evesham to Herefordshire - 1000kg of carrots by lorry
  = 66km x 1000kg x 0.000612MJ/kg/km = 40.392 MJ
- Herefordshire to Dyfed - 1000kg of carrots by lorry
  = 130km x 1000kg x 0.000612MJ/kg/km = 79.56 MJ
- Dyfed to South Manchester - 1000kg of carrots by lorry
  = 238km x 1000kg x 0.000612MJ/kg/km = 145.656 MJ
- South Manchester to Evesham - 50 kg of carrots by lorry
  = 175km x 50kg x 0.000612MJ/kg/km = 5.355 MJ
- (Estimate) South Manchester centralised distribution to supermarkets -
  1000kg of carrots by lorry
  = 50km x 1000kg x 0.000612MJ/kg/km = 30.6 MJ

The total fossil fuel input to transport the carrots to South Manchester is 265.61 MJ, the equivalent of 6 litres of diesel. However, a problem arises at South Manchester as the carrots are split to go to different supermarkets. The analyst could (1) calculate the average distance travelled to any one supermarket (more research needed) or (2) make a plausible guess of 50km. Once the estimate is added the total energy for transport after harvest is calculated to be 296.21 MJ (nearly 7 litres of diesel).

10.4.6.2 Calculating the energy requirement of transport through a decentralised distribution system e.g. a box scheme

A team of student auditors from Lancaster University in 1998 conducted analysis of food miles per vegetable bag on the Growing with Nature (GWN) Nursery in Pilling near Preston, Lancashire run by Alan and Debra Schofield. The group of students looked at all the miles the food had travelled:

- distance the GWN delivery vans travelled to deliver bags to customers;
- distance the produce from other organic growers who supply GWN had travelled;
- distance the wholesaler had travelled delivering vegetables to GWN.

This was then divided by the number of vegetable bags produced in 1998. The average distance travelled to the final consumer by each vegetable bag was 3km.

If we compare this with the centralised distribution example above, we can estimate how much energy it would take to transport one tonne of carrots through Growing with Nature's distribution system. Certain assumptions had to be made:

- if the average weight of the carrots to be included in an individual vegetable bag is 500g then the 1000kg of carrots will fill 2000 bags;
- the carrots are roughly one-fifth (0.2) of the weight of the bag;
- the lorry energy coefficient 0.000612 MJ/kg/km is used because no corresponding energy coefficient for tonne/ kilometres for vans has been found.

$$\frac{2000 \times 2.5\text{kg (total weight of bags with carrots)} \times 3\text{km} \times 0.000612}{0.2 \text{ (Proportional weight of carrots)}} = 45.9\text{MJ}$$

The difference between the transport fossil fuel use for 1000kg of carrots in Example 1 (centralised distribution) and Example 2 (direct marketing to the final consumer is sizeable: 296.21 MJ (nearly 7 litres of diesel) as against 45.9MJ (nearly 1 litre of diesel).

It may be argued that Example 1 is extreme and includes a crude estimate of 50km from depot to supermarket. However, as the supermarkets rely largely on imported vegetable produce, the figure for centralised distribution may actually be generous compared to the vast majority of organically grown vegetables that are bought in UK supermarkets. More systematic research is needed in this area.

1 Ecotricity, Axiom House, Station Road, Stroud, Gloucestershire, GL5 3AP. T 01453 75611. www.ecotricity.co.uk
2 PIMENTEL D & M (1979) Food Energy and Society. Resources & Environmental Science Series.
3 SLESSER M (1975) Energy Requirements of Agriculture in Leniham J and Fletcher W.W, Food Agriculture and the Environment.
4 KÖPKE U and HAAS G (1996) Fossil Fuels and CO2 New Farmer and Grower spring 1996.
5 BORIN M et al (1997) Effects of Tillage on Energy and Carbon Balance in North-eastern Italy. Soil and Tillage Research vol 40.
6 FLUCK RC & BAIRD CD (1982) Agricultural Energetics.
7 ORGANIC GROWERS OF DURHAM (2000) The Energy Cost of Farm Labour. – A Preliminary Assessment. Growing Green International. No 6 page 5.
8 The Dangers of Long Distance Food Transport. SAFE Alliance

Chapter Eleven

UK Vegetable crops

11.1 Solanaceae
POTATOES

11.1.1 Rotation and fertility requirements

- Potatoes are the heaviest feeders in terms of taking nutrients out of the soil. It is better if they are positioned in long rotations e.g. every seven years[1].
- Green manuring:
    - Before the crop - Potatoes must be grown after a nitrogen-fixing ley preferably for two years.
    - Undersowing - Potatoes are not suitable for undersowing because they develop a wide, dense canopy.
    - After the crop - after the potatoes are lifted, an overwinter green manure can be sown to mop up excess nutrients (see 6.2).
- Compost should only be applied to green manures during the fertility building phase of a rotation and is not necessary after a two-year ley. Apply:
    - Hectare - 25 tonnes;
    - Acre - 10 tonnes.
- Potatoes prefer a pH near neutral.

11.1.2 Soil conditions
- Potatoes need a deep, loose and friable soil. For earlies, it may be necessary to plough / dig in early winter to have sufficient tilth in time. The difficulty

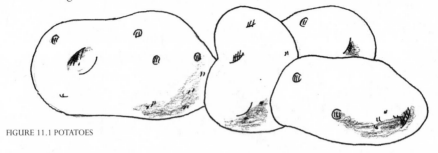

FIGURE 11.1 POTATOES

is the loss of nutrients and so is only recommended where soils freeze for long periods. Heavy clay soils are unsuitable for potato crops.

- Seedbed preparation - organic matter will be worked into the soil with initial ploughing of the ley. The aim is to produce a good, deep tilth with secondary cultivations e.g. power harrowing. Soon after bed preparation, the seed potatoes are planted from a hopper with the ridges being formed as a dual operation.

11.1.3 Zero tillage potatoes (developed by Organic Growers of Durham)

- Mulch with hay as described in 2.9.1.
- Plant the seed potatoes by pushing them through the hay until they are nearly in contact with the soil. This can be done quickly by a team of people working along the bed, planting two rows each.
- Apply the straw mulch on top of the hay and the potatoes (see section 2.9.1).
- After that the bed needs no further attention except perhaps a single hand-roguing of perennial weeds.
- To harvest the potatoes simply rake back the mulch and pick the potatoes by hand.

11.1.4 Qualities to look for when choosing potato varieties

- blight resistance;
- early bulking;
- good weed suppression.

There is an unmet demand for salad potatoes in the UK.

11.1.5 Chitting

- Chitting is important for bringing potatoes on earlier to avoid the worst of late blight.

- To encourage healthy green sprouts, keep seed potatoes in cool (about 10°C), light conditions. If they are kept in a warm, dark place, they will produce pale and weak sprouts.
- Begin chitting four weeks before planting (early January for earlies and end of January for others).

11.1.6 Planting and spacings
- Earlies can be planted from January in the favoured areas of the south through to early April in the north. The test is to place your hand in the soil. If you can hold it there comfortably for 10 seconds, the potatoes will not rot in the ground. Otherwise, it may be too cold.
- Plant the main crop from the end of March, weather permitting.
- Plant seed potatoes at an approximate density of three tonne per hectare / 1.2 tonne per acre.

11.1.7 Weed control
- Weed ten days after planting.
- Weeding with tractor mounted machinery - use chain harrows, ridgers or purpose-built weeders. After emergence inter-row work can continue with a final ridging up before the canopy of the potatoes becomes too dense for the tractor to get through.

11.1.8 Watering
- Earlies benefit from watering throughout.
- Frances Blake[2] recommends watering the main crop using irrigation equipment two weeks before harvesting to gain maximum yield benefit.

11.1.9 Common potato problems
- Slugs - tubers contain wide tunnels. For prevention see 8.16.1.
- Cutworm - tubers contain wide tunnels. For prevention see 8.16.6.
- Wireworm - tubers contain narrow tunnels. Likely pest after breaking a grass ley. Examine several mother tubers after 28 days and if there is evidence of wireworm harvest early. For prevention see 8.16.7.
- Potato cyst eelworm - Pale leaves, tiny cysts on roots, tubers abnormally small. For prevention see 8.16.8.
- Millipede - tubers contain wide tunnels. For prevention see 8.16.9.
- Blight - brown patches on leaves, brown areas under the skin of the tubers.

For prevention see 8.17.1.
- Blackleg - blackened base of stems. Physical examination of tubers before planting. Practice long rotations. No treatment, remove.
- Common scab and powdery scab of tubers - essentially cosmetic diseases use resistant varieties.
- Soft rot - Store only sound, healthy tubers and ensure the store is airy and frost-free.

11.1.10 Harvesting
- Earlies are lower yielding than maincrop potatoes.
- Earlies are ready to harvest when they start to flower. Second earlies and maincrop can be harvested after flowering.
- For potato storage see 12.12.1 and 12.15.

11.2 Protected Solanaceae
TOMATOES, AUBERGINES, PEPPERS[3]

Tomatoes, aubergines and peppers are tropical plants and therefore benefit from being grown under protection, although there are outdoor varieties available.

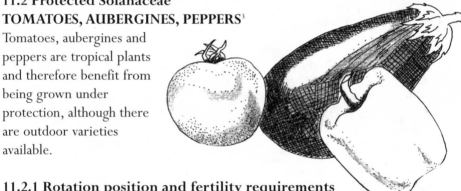

11.2.1 Rotation position and fertility requirements
- The protected solanaceae are heavy feeders.

FIGURE 11.2 TOMATO, PEPPER AND AUBERGINE

- Green manuring:
  - Before the crop - Protected solanaceae will benefit from growing after a one-year ley.
  - Undersowing - tomatoes and peppers are suitable for undersowing with low growing green manures, e.g. yellow trefoil or Kent wild white clover.
- pH range of 6.0 to 6.5
- Unfortunately the one-year ley is impractical in protected cropping as commercial growers cannot afford it. With normal cropping dig five litres / one bucket full of year-old compost for each square metre. This is
  - tomatoes up to eight trusses;
  - aubergines allowing five fruits per plant;

- peppers allowing six to ten fruits per plant;
- Tomato plants with more than ten trusses require added nutrition. This may prove difficult in stockfree-organic systems, as the base fertiliser blood, fish and bone meal has been the usual source of nutrition for extended season tomatoes. New animal-free sources of base fertiliser are still being researched (see 5.3.2). These are likely to include lucerne, soya and pea meal.

11.2.2 Potash requirements
- Potash is particularly important to the production of fruit, with a potash to nitrogen ratio of 2:1 needed. Comfrey is the stockfree-organic grower's richest source of home-grown potash, although there is a conflict between organic principles of feeding the soil, as comfrey is a soluble fertiliser. Under Stockfree-Organic Standard 5.1(a) it can be used for supplementary nutrients only.
- Making specific solanaceae compost with a high proportion of comfrey leaves is more in line with stockfree-organic principles.

11.2.3 Germination periods
- Difficult - December to January - most expensive propagating period, but may provide fruit in May.
- Medium - February to March with naturally improving light intensity and temperature.
- Good - March to April with twelve to fourteen hours of daylight.

11.2.4 Transplanting
- Prick out strong seedlings into 9cm pots once they have two leaves.
- Transplant at about ten weeks.
- Terry Marshall recommends planting tomatoes when 50% of the flowers are open.
- Eliot Coleman[5] recommends pruning off early pepper blossoms to produce more rigorous plants with better rooting systems.
- The day before planting, thoroughly water the pots and feed with seaweed.

11.2.5 Soil Conditions
- Create a warm moist soil at planting time of at least 14.5°C.
- Make it firm enough to anchor roots but to give good porous structure to permit air to reach the roots.

Table 11.1 Significant temperatures for protected solanaceae[4]

	Low	Optimum	High
Germination	15°C	20°C	25°C
Keep propagation media temperature above	14.5°C		
Chilling injury	10°C		
Death with extended exposure	5°C		
Plant into soils with a temperature above	14.5°C		
Day time air temperature	16°C	20°C	21°C
Night time air temperature		15°C	
Set automatic vents to open at		23°C	
Roots will not grow below	14.5°C		
Pollination		20°C	
Pollen death four hours at			40°C
Blossom drop if temperatures exceed			D 34°C N 20°C
Ripening for tomatoes and peppers		D 20°C N 16°C	

- Because of deep roots it will be necessary to have non-compacted subsoil (see 2.8).
- 60 to 90% of roots will be in the top 30cm of soil.
- 20 to 25% will be between 30cm to 50cm.
- The tap root will penetrate deeper.

11.2.6 Spacings
- Tomatoes
  - Most cultivars can be planted at 60cm apart with 75cm between the rows.
  - They can be either planted in staggered double rows with a path in between or two leaders can be taken from each stem to form the rows[6].
- Aubergines
  - 45cm apart with 75cm between the rows.
- Peppers
  - 45cm apart with 75cm between the rows.

11.2.7 Supporting the plants

- If using canes, ensure that cane caps or small plant pots are put on the end of canes to prevent eye injury.
- The simplest and easiest way to grow cordon varieties of tomato plants is to twist them up strings (e.g. baling twine) trapped underneath the base of the plant and tie the other end of the string to wires suspended over the row of plants. The overhead wires should be in place before planting.
- Aubergines and peppers with one or two leaders can also be strung.

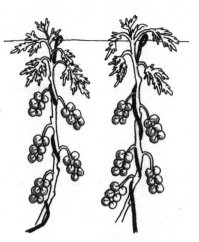

FIGURE 11.3 SUPPORTING TOMATO PLANTS

- The advantage of jute fillis is that it can be put on the compost heap with the haulms when finished. It needs to have a strong breaking resistance.
- As individual tomato plant's developing fruits can weigh up to 12kg, the greenhouse / polytunnel support structures will need to be strong. In lightweight greenhouses, canes are a better idea.

11.2.8 Watering the plants[7]

- Drip irrigation is the preferred method of watering.
- After transplanting give each plant 600ml of water carefully around the root ball.
  - For February, March and April transplants resist the temptation to water again for a week. Instead on bright days, top spray daily.
  - For May and June transplants resist watering for 3 - 5 days and just top spray daily.
- The object of restrained initial watering is to encourage the plant to root out.
- During wet humid spells in the summer, do not water.

11.2.9 Assisted pollination early in the season[8]

- Once a flower is fully open it is at its most fecund over the next 3 days. Very early in the season this may mean only a 1 in 3 chance of successful fertilisation.
- A relative humidity near 70% is needed for successful fertilisation.
- Early in the season it may be necessary to provide the conditions for fertilisation.
- You can increase humidity by watering concrete paths in the early morning OR

- in the mid morning close the ventilation for one hour. At noon top spray all the plants with a fine mist until the water runs off the leaves. Return an hour later and open the vents.
- Once the humidity is up tap the wire or canes, or the flower heads gently with a paint brush. On a good day the pollen can be seen to fly.
- If a greenhouse or polytunnel is unventilated the temperature might rise too much and four hours at 40°C will kill the pollen.

11.2.10 Training cordon varieties

- Twist the string regularly.
- Take one or two leaders for tomatoes. Take the second leader as a side shoot, choosing the most dominant side shoot, which is usually 25cm above the ground[9].
- Take two leaders for aubergines and peppers as a side shoot 25cm above the ground.
- Remove side shoots in tomatoes as soon as they are pinchable. We have stopped side shooting peppers at Tolhurst Organic Produce.
- When tomato plants reach the overhead support, ideally 2.4 metres, they can be stopped for short production or the plants can be lowered onto supports. In order to layer the plants you will need to have an extra length of twine at the top. It is possible to get special hanging bobbins for this purpose.

FIGURE 11.4 SIDE SHOOTING TOMATO PLANTS

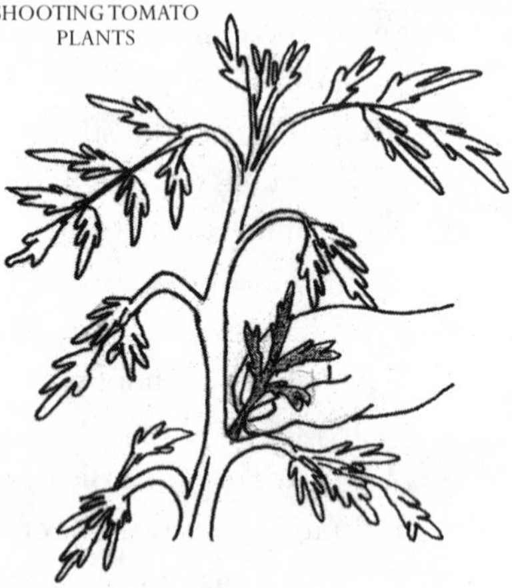

- By this stage of growth, the bottom cluster of fruit will have been harvested, and the lower stem will be bare. Untie the twine and lower the plants in the same direction along the row, taking end plants around the bend.
- For aubergines and peppers, stop them once you have reached the desired number of fruit.

11.2.11 Deleafing

- Remove tomato leaves little and often so that the plant puts its energy into producing fruit and not leaves.
- Use a sharp knife and cut cleanly through the 'collar'.
- Leaf early in the day to allow for fast healing.
- Only leaf up to a ripening truss and not above it.

11.2.12 Venting and shading

- Shading reduces midsummer temperatures and prevents wilts.
- Vent at 23°C - fitting automatic vents is a good idea.
- Venting is not just about dissipating heat when it is too hot but also supplying the crops with carbon dioxide.
- Leave vents partially open at night.
- Open vents fully early in the day.

11.2.13 Stopping protected tomato plants

- Early stopping in mid July will allow the plant to be picked until mid September.
- Late stopping in mid August will allow the plant to be picked until the end of October / early November.
- Stop the plant two leaves above the last truss.

11.2.14 Common tomato, aubergine and pepper problems

- Aphids and whitefly - infestation and curled leaves. For prevention see 8.16.2 and 8.16.3
- Red spider mite - mottled leaves and silken webbing. For prevention see 8.16.4.
- Potato blight - brown patches on leaves, soft rot on fruits. For prevention see 8.17.1.
- Botrytis - grey mouldy patches on stems, grey mould, fruits drop before maturity. For prevention see 8.17.4.
- Foot rot / stem rot - brown zone on stems, wilted leaves. Practice long rotations. Avoid over watering. Remove affected plants.
- Root rot - leaves wilted, roots brown and corky. Practice long rotations. Avoid over watering. Remove affected plants.
- Verticillium wilt - wilted leaves. Practice long rotations. Remove affected plants.
- Tomato mosaic virus - mottled or fern like leaves. Buy virus free seeds. Remove affected plants and wash hands and tools thoroughly before touching other plants.
- Blossom drop - flowers fall off before fruit sets. Too hot when pollination took place see table 11.1.
- Dry set - fruits form but remain tiny. Too hot when pollination took place see table 11.1.
- Blossom end rot - discoloured patch on the underside of the fruit. Caused

by allowing the plants to dry out and then subsequently watering too much. Keep pH between 6.5 and 6.75.

11.2.15 Harvesting

- When you pull a fruit, it is easy to snap or break the main stem. Use both hands when harvesting and with tomatoes twist the fruit and with peppers and aubergines cut with secateurs or push the fruits back against the curve of their stem.

11.3 Field scale brassicas CAULIFLOWER, CABBAGE, BROCCOLI, BRUSSEL SPROUTS, KALE

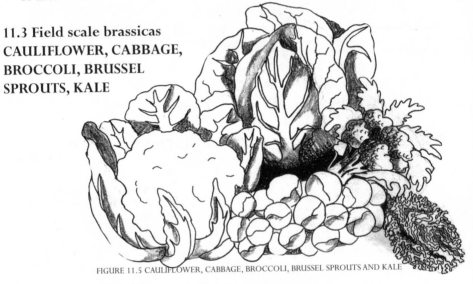

FIGURE 11.5 CAULIFLOWER, CABBAGE, BROCCOLI, BRUSSEL SPROUTS AND KALE

11.3.1 Rotation position and fertility requirements

- Summer/autumn brassicas are heavy feeders. Overwinter brassicas do not need such a rich soil.
- Green manuring:
    - Before the crop - If you are growing potatoes in rotation, the residual fertility from the potatoes plus an overwinter green manure which has been able to develop in spring should be sufficient OR
    - If you are not growing potatoes in rotation, a one-year ley before the brassicas is recommended.
    - Undersowing - All brassicas are suitable for undersowing, although broadcasting the seed can mean that clover seeds can germinate in the crop. Stan Finch[10] has found that undersowing white clover reduces the incidence of cabbage white butterfly laying their eggs.
- Compost should only be applied to green manures during the fertility

building phase of a rotation and is not necessary after a one-year ley. Apply:
- Acre - at ten tonnes per acre.
- Ten metre squared - one barrow load for summer / autumn brassicas.
- Brassicas do not like an acid soil and prefer a pH between 6.5 and 7.0.
- Cauliflowers are very sensitive to a lack of boron - light soils and wetter soils in the west may need borax additions with certified growers needing to apply to the certification body for permission to use this. This information will be available from soil analysis.

11.3.2 Sowing dates for transplants

All brassicas can be raised as bare root transplants (see 5.4).

- Cauliflower
    - Early summer - sow early October or January with heat for transplanting in March - April.
    - Late summer - sow March for transplanting in April.
    - Early autumn - sow early May for transplanting in mid June.
    - Late autumn - sow mid May for transplanting early July.
    - Winter - sow late May for transplanting July.
    - Following spring - sow late May for transplanting July but this technique will only work in frost free areas.
- Cabbage
    - Spring cabbage and spring greens (unhearted) - sow early August for transplanting late September.
    - Summer and autumn cabbages - sow April and May for transplanting in June.
    - Winter cabbages - sow mid May for transplanting in July.
- Single head calabrese broccoli
    - Sow at any time from February (with heat) until June for transplanting six weeks later.
- Overwinter purple sprouting broccoli
    - Sow in April for planting in early June choose three varieties that mature at different times.
- Brussel sprouts
    - Choose four varieties that will spread cropping from late September until March.
    - The late autumn / Christmas varieties can be sown in March for transplanting in May.
    - The winter / early spring varieties can be sown in April for

transplanting in June.
- Kale
  - Sow late May / early June for transplanting in July for an autumn crop that will overwinter.

11.3.3 Soil conditions
- Seedbed preparation using equipment - cultivate the seedbed two weeks before transplanting with the aim of removing cutworm.
- Brassicas like to be planted, deeply, into a well-consolidated seed-bed where they can anchor their roots. If there is 'rocking' in the root zone, a poor crop will result e.g. blown brussel sprouts.

11.3.4 Spacings
- Cauliflower - 60cm x 60cm for the summer crop to 70cm x 70cm for the autumn and winter crop.
- Spring greens & cabbage - 20cm x 35cm cut every second plant for spring greens and allow the remaining plants to heart up as spring cabbage.
- Cabbages - from 40cm x 40cm to 60cm x 120cm.
- Single head calabrese broccoli 40cm x 55cm.
- Purple sprouting broccoli - 60cm x 120cm.
- Brussel sprouts from 45-60cm x 120cm.
- Kale - 30cm x 30cm.

11.3.5 Choice of varieties
- Early maturing varieties of cabbage are less affected by aphids than lates.
- Smooth varieties of cabbage are less affected by aphids than blistering types, red varieties are less affected than green or white types.

11.3.6 Physical barriers
- Physical barriers can keep birds, caterpillars, aphids and molluscs away.
- It is important to cover brassicas in the early part of the season. This keeps away the flying pests but not the molluscs which prefer to shelter under wet covers. Fleeces can encourage aphid populations so narrow meshed nets may be preferred. Cabbage white butterflies may push their way through larger meshed nets.
- Netting cauliflowers later in the season can help prevent pigeon damage and will not raise air temperatures.

11.3.7 Weed control
- Weed ten days after planting.
- Weeding with machinery - aim for three passes with inter-row weeders. Ensure you lift fleeces each week to check weed and aphid infestation development.
- Weeding by hand - hoe when the weeds are just emerging, at their white stringy stage, and are easily killed.
- Before undersowing - ensure a clear seedbed before undersowing.

11.3.8 Watering
- Give newly planted transplants a good soak once in the ground.
- Sound transplanting (firm and deep) should help crops withstand drought conditions and prevent root rocking.
- Foliar dressings of seaweed can be used.
- Cauliflowers - irrigation is important in summer, especially during the critical three weeks before maturity.

11.3.9 Common brassica problems
- Slugs - seedlings and leaves eaten. For prevention see 8.16.1.
- Aphids - leaves curled and blistered. For prevention see 8.16.2.
- Cutworm - seedlings severed at ground level. For prevention see 8.16.6.
- Flea beetle - small holes in seedlings, wilted plants. Raising transplants in the greenhouse makes them soft and very vulnerable to flea beetles; therefore raising bare root transplants in nursery beds is preferable where the pest is a problem. Practice long rotations and irrigate daily during dry conditions. This pest may make it impossible to grow crucifers see 8.13.
- Cabbage root fly - roots tunnelled with maggots present. For prevention see 8.15.
- Cabbage white caterpillars - leaves holed and in severe cases eaten entirely. For barrier prevention fleece or net (see 8.15), undersow clover (see 8.9) and encourage parasitic wasps (see 8.1.1.5).
- Pigeons - seedlings eaten. For prevention see 8.25.
- Whiptail molybdenum deficiency - narrow strap-like leaves. Lime to correct on over acidic soil.
- Downy mildew - diseased leaves. Use a long rotation, raise as bare root transplants and remove badly affected leaves. For prevention see 8.17.2.
- Club root - swollen roots. Remove brassicas from the rotation as it can

take up to 30 years to reduce the spores.
- Small cauliflower heads - Cabbage root fly (see 8.15), molybdenum deficiency (lime to prevent an over acid soil), boron deficiency (see below) or not planted firmly enough.
- Cauliflowers with brown curds - with boron deficiency apply borax with permission from the certifying body.

11.3.10 Harvesting techniques
- Single cut brassicas e.g. cauliflowers, winter cabbages and brussel sprouts - a swift, single, sweeping blow with a machete at the base of the frame should be sufficient with experienced growers also using the machetes to trim outer leaves. Brussel sprout tops can also be sold as an alternative to cabbage.
- Monitoring cauliflower - Cauliflower will need cutting at least every two days in the summer and at least twice a week in the autumn.
- Main cut with later side shoots brassicas e.g. spring cabbages and single-headed calabrese broccoli - cut as above and then encourage side shooting by leaving the main stem intact. The new growth can be twisted off or cut with a small knife.
- Harvest over time brassicas e.g. kale and purple sprouting broccoli - removed by a swift downward action with the wrist.

11.3.11 Storage techniques
- Remove field heat (see 12.11) to improve storage capability.
- Eat cauliflowers, broccoli and kale fresh.
- Brussel sprouts can be cold stored for three weeks on the stem but it is better to eat them fresh.
- Overwinter cabbages can be cold stored depending on type with Dutch white varieties being able to be stored for up to five months.

11.4 Protected brassica salad leaves and braising mixtures ROCKET, LANDCRESS, CHINESE CABBAGE, PAK CHOI, ORIENTAL MUSTARDS, MIZUNA, MIBUNA, KOMATSUNA.

FIGURE 11.6 MIZUNA LEAF, KOMATSUNA LEAF, ROCKET LEAF AND LAND CRESS LEAF

11.4.1 Rotation position and fertility requirements

- All leaves can be grown as main season salads or winter salads. There are, however, two different techniques recommended depending on the time of year you are growing with main season leaves being directly sown and overwinter crops being raised as transplants, after another crop.
- The difficulties with protected cropping rotations are discussed in section 6.4.
- Fertility requirements are the same as overwinter brassicas (see 11.3.1).
- Green manuring
  - Before the crop - green manuring is not always possible because of 'back-to-back' cropping in protected cropping.
  - Undersowing - salad leaves are not suitable.
- These salad leaves are brassicas and can carry club root. If your soil is acidic, then add lime.
- For rotational purposes keep brassica salad leaves separate from other salad leaves (see 11.16).

11.4.2 Soil conditions

- A fine tilth is required for good root establishment.
- Cultivate to a depth of 10cm.
- For directly sown salad leaves observe a stale seedbed (see 7.3).
- Ensure that the beds are very level.

11.4.3 Sowing dates

- Spring and summer salad bags
  - Brassica salad leaves can be direct sown for main season salad bags where the leaves are harvested small and the crop is redrilled after each

picking. Johnny's Selected Seeds have designed two seeders specifically for this purpose[11] and recommend this technique.

- Direct sow weekly from late February to mid June.
- If the leaves get larger they can be sold as ready-to-cook braising mixes for stir fries etc.
- It is not appropriate to use spring and summer brassica salad leaves as cut and come again (CCA) crops as they will bolt, are likely to suffer tipburn and the growth may also be more fibrous due to plant stress.
- Overwinter salad bags
  - For an overwinter crop CCA brassica salad leaves should be sown as transplants after the longest day (i.e. from mid June).
  - All brassica salad leaves are particularly well suited to the UK autumn climate.

11.4.4 Spacings

- Directly sown - 5cm x 5cm.
- Transplants for overwinter
  - Rocket - 15cm x 30cm.
  - Landcress (cut over time) - 15cm x 30cm.
  - Chinese cabbage (single cut).
    - Loose headed varieties - 60cm x 60cm.
    - Headed Chinese cabbage - 40cm x 40cm.
  - Pak choi (single cut) - 40cm x 40cm.
    - Rosette varieties - 30cm x 30cm.
  - Oriental mustards (cut and come again)
    - Giant leaved varieties - 30cm x 30cm.
    - Green-in-the-snow - 30cm x 30cm.
    - Leaf - 30cm x 30cm.
  - Mizuna greens and mibuna greens (cut and come again) - 30cm x 30cm.
  - Komatsuna (cut and come again) - 30cm x 30cm.

11.4.5 Transplanting technique

- To prevent the leaves becoming contaminated with soil, the transplant plugs are planted so that the base is at the surface of the soil and no deeper than 5cm.
- Soil blocks are preferred as they can sit slightly proud of the soil surface.

11.4.6 Crop care

- Hand hoe transplants regularly.
- Avoid soil splash on the leaves by using fine spray when overhead watering OR
- Use drip irrigation to keep the humidity down.
- Avoid overwatering especially from September onwards as this tends to create favourable conditions for grey moulds.
- Fleece with the onset of the early frosts.

11.4.7 Harvesting techniques

- It is very easy to rip up the plant roots when using a knife, as they are not deeply anchored. Harvest leaves with a pair of scissors.
- Direct sown leaves
  - For the salad and braising mixes harvest the leaves at the desired size.
- For CCA leaves raised as transplants
  - It will be necessary to cut almost weekly up until the end of autumn. Growth slows down after November and stops mid-winter, starting again early February.
  - Cover the trimmed plants with a fleece between December and January. Place the fleece over a cloche frame, so that it is not resting on the crops.
  - By the end of February you will probably need to cut at least every week in favourable conditions. By mid March some of the leaves will probably start to bolt.

11.5 Crucifer (close relation to brassicas)
SWEDE, KOHL RABI, TURNIP, RADISH, MOOLI

11.5.1 Rotation position and fertility requirements

- Swede - same as summer and autumn field-scale brassicas (see 11.3.1).
- Other crucifers are short-lived crops and so do not require such a high level of fertility.

FIGURE 11.7 KOHL RABI, SWEDE, TURNIP, MOOLI AND RADISH

- Green manuring
  - Before the crop - swedes will benefit by following on from an overwinter green manure. This is not necessary with other crucifers.
  - Undersowing - crucifers are not suitable.
  - After the crop - after lifting an overwinter green manure can be planted.
- pH between 6 and 6.5 which is slightly more acidic than for other brassicas.
- Crucifers are very sensitive to a lack of boron - light soils and wetter soils in the west may need borax additions with certified growers needing to apply to the certification body for permission to use this. This information will be available from soil analysis.

11.5.2 Soil conditions
- Treat as brassicas (see 11.3.3).

11.5.3 Sowing dates
- Swede:
  - mid June for an autumn / winter crop.
- Kohl rabi:
  - succession sowings from March to June.
- Sweet turnip:
  - Protected cropping sow August for a crop the following spring.
  - Outdoors - succession sowings from March and May (to avoid the worst of the flea beetle see 8.13).
- Radish:
  - Protected cropping succession sowings from March to April.
  - Outdoors - succession sowings from April and May (to avoid the worst of the flea beetle see 8.13).
  - Can be grown as a catch crop but remember it should be treated as a brassicas crop with regards to club root.
- Mooli:
  - Sow after the longest day i.e. about July otherwise it tends to run to seed prematurely.

All are usually directly sown but swedes and kohl rabi may benefit from transplanting.

11.5.4 Spacings
- Swede - 30cm x 30cm.
- Kohl rabi - 30cm x 30cm.
- Turnip - direct sow 30cm between the rows and 10cm between seedlings.
- Radish - direct sow 30cm between the rows and 2.5cm between seedlings.
- Mooli - direct sow 30cm between the rows and 10cm between seedlings.

11.5.5 Weeding
- As with all directly sown crops it is a good idea to establish a stale seedbed (see 7.3) to reduce weed competition before sowing.
- Weed ten days after sowing / planting.
- As with other crucifers weed intensively (usually three times) because you want them to grow quickly without their growth being checked.
- Weeding swedes with machinery - aim for three passes with inter-row weeders.
- Weeding by hand - hoe when the weeds are just emerging and are at their white stringy stage when they are easily killed.

11.5.6 Watering
Swedes need lots of water and are really only suitable for growing in the wetter parts of the country and on medium to heavy soils.

11.5.7 Common crucifer problems
- Mealy aphid - infestation. For prevention see 8.16.2.
- Cutworm - severed at ground level. For prevention see 8.16.6.
- Flea beetle - seedlings and leaves peppered with holes. Use strategic planting dates (see 8.13) and cover with fleece. Raise swedes as transplants.
- Cabbage white caterpillars - leaves holed and in severe cases eaten entirely. For barrier prevention fleece or net (see 8.15), to reduce infestation undersow clover (see 8.9) and encourage parasitic wasps (see 8.1.1.5).
- Cabbage root fly - roots tunnelled with maggots present. For barrier prevention see 8.15.
- Downy mildew - greyish mould on the underside of leaves. For prevention see 8.17.2.
- Powdery mildew - white floury coating of leaves. For prevention see 8.17.3.
- Club root - swollen roots. Remove brassicas and crucifers from the

rotation as it can take up to 30 years to reduce the spores.

- Split roots - caused by heavy rain / or copious watering after a prolonged dry spell. Ensure you water regularly during dry periods.
- Woody roots - growth checked during drought periods, short of fertility or too long a delay in harvesting. Change practices accordingly.
- Brown heart - boron deficiency. Apply borax with permission from the certifying body.

11.5.8 Harvesting
- Lever with a fork.
- Swedes and mooli are usually field stored and lifted when ready.
- All other crucifers should be lifted and eaten fresh.

11.6 Field-scale alliums
LEEKS AND ONIONS

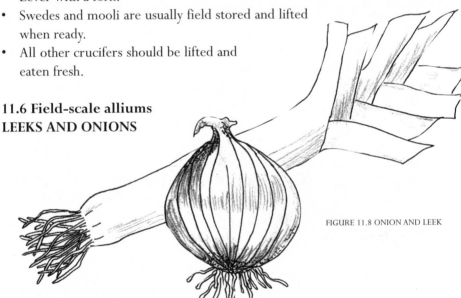

FIGURE 11.8 ONION AND LEEK

11.6.1 Rotation position and fertility requirements
- Field-scale alliums are not demanding compared to potatoes or brassicas and can make do with residual fertility.
- Alliums are very weed intolerant and so should be planted in a phase of the rotation that has a low weed burden e.g. after crops with large canopies like potatoes and brassicas.
- Green manuring
  - Before the crop - a ley is not necessary before field-scale alliums, providing that the alliums follow another heavily fertilised crops i.e. potatoes or brassicas.

- Undersowing - leeks and onions are not suitable for undersowing during the growing season because they cannot tolerate the root competition, but leeks can be undersown in October with cereals to mop up residual fertility (see 6.2).
- After the crop - after lifting onions the soil can be sown with an overwinter green manure.
- Medium pH.

11.6.2 Soil conditions

- The alliums like a free-draining soil and it is important to avoid areas of compaction.
- A fine tilth is required for good root establishment of onions.
- Ensure that the bed is level.
- It may be necessary to plant onions through black plastic to get the soil to warm up and to reduce weed competition.
- Leeks benefit from being grown on ridges.

11.6.3 Sowing dates

- Overwinter onions e.g. Japanese onions:
  - sow in August outdoors or in October under protection;
    - sow for transplants with five seeds per module OR
    - plant sets.
  - If sowing into modules the seeds should be near the surface so that when the module is transplanted, only the roots grow in the soil OR
  - Onion sets should be planted on the shallow side by pushing them gently into soft earth so that only the tips are showing.
  - Harvest July the following year and ensure that they have not started to bolt. These onions tend to fill the gap before the autumn ones are ready. The difficulty with them is that they can harbour mildew and this disease can infect other spring-planted crops. For this reason we have stopped growing them at Tolhurst Organic Produce.
- Maincrop onions:
  - For smaller onions sow five seeds per plug from February to April and the bulbs will grow together as a clump, pushing each other aside for more room[12] OR
  - Plant out sets in April. Avoid planting sets too early because they tend to bolt. Avoid planting too deeply because this will encourage thick necks.

- Autumn leeks:
  - Sow as transplants in late March / April (either in modules or as bare root) and plant when the seedlings are pencil sized.
- Winter leeks available December - March:
  - Same as autumn leeks - make sure you look at the maturity date of varieties and plant when the seedlings are pencil sized.
  - Look for varieties that resist bolting.
- Spring leeks available April and May of the following year:
  - Sow as transplants in early May for transplanting in July (either in modules or as bare roots) when the seedlings are pencil sized.
  - Look for varieties that resist bolting.

11.6.4 Spacings

- Onions
  - Bed system - 15cm x 15cm.
- Leeks
  - Bed system - 20cm x 30cm.
  - 15cm between plants in ridges.
  - Leeks are very sensitive to spacing and lower planting densities will give larger plants.
  - To blanch the stems leeks should be planted into a dibbed hole that is 20cm deep or the ridges should be made higher during weeding.

11.6.5 Weed control

- The upright growth habit of alliums makes them poor weed suppressors.
- Do not fleece because they cannot push the fleece up.
- Alliums need to be kept weed free, especially in the early stages of growth.
- Care must be taken when weeding so that the tops are not damaged.
- Weeding with machinery - aim for three passes with inter-row weeders. A slight ridging effect for leeks may be beneficial.
- Weeding by hand - hoe when the weeds are just emerging, at their white stringy stage, and are easily killed.
- Plastic mulches with onions are particularly successful. (See 10.3.8 for the discussion about the environmental impact of plastic.) When the onions are grown the bulbs can be lifted and left to solar dry on top of the plastic mulch. At Tolhurst Organic Produce we sow clover strips in between the plastic sheets and either allow the sheets to stay there over winter, which

provides favourable conditions for earthworm breeding or use biodegradable plastic mulches and sow an overwinter green manure.

11.6.6 Watering
- Onions under plastic do not need watering in.
- Watering in will help establish leeks.
- Water during dry spells in the summer to prevent checks in growth.

11.6.7 Common allium problems
- Cutworm - severed at ground level. For prevention see 8.16.6.
- Stem and bulb nematode - seedlings killed, leaves swollen or bulbs soft but not foul smelling. For prevention see 8.16.8.
- Onion fly - yellow drooping leaves or bulbs of onions tunnelled with maggots present. Onion fly can be serious with the worst attacks occurring in mid summer. Reduce the crop's attractiveness by minimising leaf damage when planting or weeding.
- Downy mildew - grey mould on leaves. Ensure air movement by not overcrowding. Crops can grow through less serious cases. For prevention see 8.17.2.
- White rot - lift and burn infected material. It is important not to return any infected material to the soil as white rot survives in the soil for at least twenty years.
- Smut - dark grey stripes on leaves. Lift before the stripes burst.
- Rust - red spots on leaves. Ensure air movement by not overcrowding. Crops can grow through less serious cases.
- Birds - onion sets lifted out of the ground. For bird deterrents see 8.26, 8.27 and 8.28.
- Set division - Avoid planting at the wrong time or growing the bulbs in poor soil. Prolonged dry weather can induce set division.

11.6.8 Harvesting onions
- The onions are ready when the foliage begins to die back naturally.
- Lift by pulling. If the onions are to be stored ensure that they are cured properly (see 12.12.2) after harvesting.
- Before selling it may be necessary to rub off outer skin and dead foliage.

11.6.9 Harvesting leeks

- Harvesting and trimming leeks occurs in all weather conditions. On a large scale this may require the undercutting of beds or levering with a fork.
- In the UK it is traditional to trim the roots off with a sharp knife to leave the hard 'pan' but cutting too high can damage the leeks.
- It may be necessary to strip back the outer layers to remove rust blemishes, although this adds to the workload.

11.7 Intensively grown alliums SHALLOT, GARLIC, SPRING ONION, WELSH ONION (perennial) and CHIVES (perennial)

The fertility and soil conditions discussed in 11.6 for onions and leeks apply to these alliums.

FIGURE 11.9 GARLIC, SPRING ONIONS, CHIVES AND SHALLOTS

11.7.1 Sowing dates

- Shallot
  - April - plant sets.
- Garlic
  - October - plant individual cloves for protected cropping.
  - November- plant individual cloves for outdoor cropping.
- Spring onions
  - Direct sow seeds in drills in September for protected cropping.
  - Direct sow seeds in drills late February to early May OR
  - Eliot Coleman recommends sowing twelve seeds to a plug and at maturity the clumps are already pre-bunched for harvest.
- Welsh onions
  - March - sow for transplants.
  - This perennial produces clumps of hollow leaves up to 60cm long and is an all year round substitute for spring onions.
  - Lift and divide every three years.
- Chives
  - March - sow for transplants.

11.7.2 Spacings
- Shallot - 15cm x 15cm just below the surface like onion sets.
- Garlic -20cm x 30cm / 3cm deep.
- Spring onion -
    - Direct sow 30cm between rows OR
    - Eliot Coleman's method 15cm x 30cm between transplants.
- Welsh onion - plant as required in permanent borders.
- Chives - plant as required in permanent borders.

11.7.3 Harvesting
- Shallots and garlic will need curing (see 12.12.2).
- Eat the spring onions, welsh onions and chives fresh.

11.8 Field scale umbellifers
CARROTS AND PARSNIPS

11.8.1 Rotation position and fertility requirements

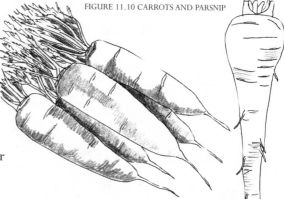

FIGURE 11.10 CARROTS AND PARSNIP

- To prevent fanging carrots and parsnips prefer low fertility situations and so can come later in the rotation after heavy and medium feeders.
- Green manuring
    - Before the crop - carrot and parsnips do not need to be grown after green manure leys.
    - Undersowing - these crops are not suitable.
    - After the crop - as these crops are usually field stored until they are ready for harvest, they are unlikely to have an overwinter green manure sown after them.
- Prefer a pH of about 6.5.
- Carrots are very weed intolerant and so should be planted in a phase of the rotation that has a low weed burden e.g. after crops with large canopies like potatoes and brassicas or after a blanket mulch e.g. after onions grown through black plastic (see 6.2).

11.8.2 Soil conditions

- Most commercial growers grow on peaty or sandy soils with no stones. It is not impossible to grow on other soils, although it will be difficult to get uniform shapes on a stony soil and most growers avoid growing on very heavy clays.
- To achieve a loose fluffy tilth, cultivation equipment such as rotavators or power harrows should be used.
- Ridges are suitable for heavier soils, wet areas and also assist with lifting.

11.8.3 Sowing

- Parsnips
  - To avoid poor germination and canker sow about mid May.
- Carrots
  - First early - sow end of October in polytunnels or under cloches.
  - Second early - sow February (south and east) to late March (north) in polytunnels or under cloches.
  - Main crop strategic planting - sow in early June to avoid the worst of the carrot root fly. The flies emerge from pupae stage during May and early June, and lay eggs around young carrot plants. The eggs hatch after about seven days, and the larvae burrow into the soil and feed on the young roots. Carrot root fly can decimate an entire crop.

11.8.4 Spacings

All parsnip and carrot seeds should be approximately 1cm deep.

- Parsnip:
  - 5cm spacings on ridges.
  - Precision drill at 9cm x 40cm on a bed system with staggered rows.
  - Tighter spacings for smaller parsnips.
- Carrots:
  - 4cm on ridges.
  - 6cm with double rows on ridges.
  - Precision drill 4cm x 40cm on bed system with staggered rows.

11.8.5 Physical barriers for carrots only

- Placing fleeces or tightly woven meshes over the newly drilled carrot crop will help prevent carrot root fly which can decimate a whole crop. Where covers are used, weed management must not be forgotten and the covers will need to be removed regularly for weeding.

11.8.6 Weed control
- As carrots and parsnips are grown from seed, weeding will be the biggest task and expense of the crop.
- They can be slow to emerge and therefore prepare a stale seedbed ten days ahead of sowing (see 7.3).
- It is standard organic practice for carrot seeds to be sown and then the whole bed to be flame weeded just prior to emergence. To get the timing right growers can lay a pane of glass on wooden blocks (above the soil not on it) to bring on early emergence of a few seedlings knowing that the rest of the seedlings are just chitting under the surface. At this point the whole bed is flame weeded. Many contributors to the Standard Working Group were uncomfortable with the use of flame weeding because it is non-discerning and will kill beneficial insects like beetles. It was decided that it should be a restricted practice under Stockfree-Organic Standard 10.4 (a) in special circumstances, like carrots, where the whole crop may be lost.
- Weeding is critical, as carrot crops can be lost. For commercial growers, if it is obvious that you are loosing the battle, it is better to start again and re-sow.
- Once the parsnip and carrot crop is established, aim for three passes with inter-row weeders. Hand roguing of perennial weeds may also be necessary. Ensure you lift fleeces each week to check weed development.

11.8.7 Watering
- According to the Soil Association[13] germination will be reduced in dry conditions. 12-18mm of water can be applied every 4-12 days before emergence.
- Further irrigation four weeks later will increase yields.
- Regular watering in dry spells will prevent cracking.

11.8.8 Common parsnip and carrot problems
- Wireworm - roots tunnelled. For prevention see 8.16.7.
- Carrot root fly - leaves reddish that later turn yellow, roots tunnelled. For prevention use strategic planting dates (see 8.13) and fleece (see 8.15).
- Violet root rot - covered with purple mould. Parsnips, red beetroot and

potatoes carry the fungus and ploughing can increase levels. Practice long rotations.

- Sclerotinia rot - collapsed leaf stalks or white mould on roots. Practice long rotations.
- Canker in parsnip - blackened roots. Lime the soil. Do not sow too early, choose resistant varieties.
- Roots split - heavy rain or copious watering after a dry spell. Adopt a 'little and often' watering policy in dry spells.
- Roots fanged - soil is too fertile. Practice a long rotation, placing carrots and parsnips after heavy and medium feeders (see 6.2).
- Roots green topped - sunlight on exposed crowns. Not harmful if it occurs. Prevent by earthing / ridging up.
- Roots very small - hitting areas of compaction (see 2.8) or too closely crowded (see 11.8.4).

11.8.9 Harvesting and storage
- Lever with a fork or undercut with machinery, making hand harvesting easier.
- There are machines for mechanical harvesting.
- Growers often leave parsnips in the soil until they are needed, as they are the hardiest of root crops. Carrots may require some frost protection e.g. straw or plastic mulch.
- Lifted carrots or parsnips need to be topped. They should only be kept in storage for a couple of weeks or they tend to go rubbery.

11.9 Intensively grown umbellifers
CELERY, CELERIAC, FENNEL

11.9.1 Rotation position and fertility requirements
- Celery, celeriac and fennel are not as demanding, in terms of nitrogen, as other leafy crops but will still need a fairly rich soil and are generally grown in warmer countries.
- They prefer a richer soil than for carrots and parsnips (see 11.8.1) and are more difficult to grow successfully.
- Green manuring
  - Before the crop - can follow a one-year green manure ley.
  - Undersowing - not suitable because they do not like the root competition.

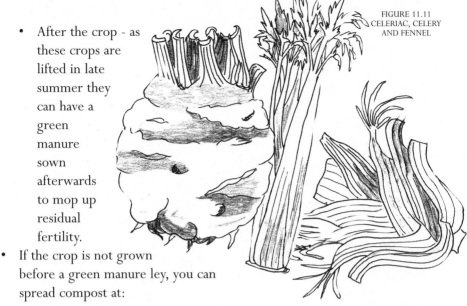

FIGURE 11.11
CELERIAC, CELERY
AND FENNEL

- After the crop - as these crops are lifted in late summer they can have a green manure sown afterwards to mop up residual fertility.
- If the crop is not grown before a green manure ley, you can spread compost at:
  - Ten tonnes per acre;
  - one barrow load per ten metre square.
- Celery, celeriac and fennel like slightly acidic conditions at about 6.5.
- These umbellifers are very weed intolerant and so should be planted in a phase of the rotation that has a low weed burden e.g. after crops with a large canopy e.g. leaf beets (see 6.3).

11.9.2 Sowing for Transplants
- Celery - there are self-blanching, green and red types. Sow the seed with heat in March for pricking into modules.
- Celeriac - sow the seeds with heat in March for pricking into modules. Do not plant the seedling deep in the module because extra rooting from the bulb makes it more difficult to lift.
- Fennel - Sow in monthly succession from the end of April through to August.

11.9.3 Soil conditions
- These are marshland plants and therefore a moisture retentive soil is essential with lots of organic matter mixed into the soil (see 11.9.1).
- Wait until at least May when the soil is warmer.
- A fine tilth is required for good root establishment.
- Cultivate to a depth of 10cm.
- Ensure that the bed is level.

11.9.4 Spacings
- Celery - 25cm x 30cm.
- Celeriac - 30cm x 35cm.
- Fennel - 25cm x 50cm.

11.9.5 Crop care
- Ensure that the plants do not dry out, as they tend to run to seed.
- Hoe regularly when the weeds are just emerging and they are their white stringy stage when they are easily killed.
- Water regularly.
- Hollow out the soil around the bulb of celeriac to prevent extra rooting (this will make them easier to lift).

11.9.6 Common celery, celeriac and fennel problems
- Celery leaf spot / blight - caused by the fungus Septoria apiicola. Leaves covered with brown spots. It is important to select resistant varieties but unfortunately in wet seasons whole celery crops can be unsaleable. This has proved to be such a problem that many growers in 2004 decided to avoid growing celery and celeriac altogether.
- Cutworm - eaten at ground level. For prevention see 8.16.6.
- Carrot root fly - roots eaten. Fleece to prevent.
- Celery fly - leaves tunnelled and blistered, stalks tough and bitter. Pinch out badly affected leaves.
- Sclerotinia rot - mouldy at the base of plants. Long rotations are recommended.
- Cucumber mosaic virus - yellow not withered leaves. Destroy affected plants and wash hands and tools thoroughly before touching other plants.
- Boron deficiency - yellow withered leaves. Apply borax with permission from the certifying body.
- Split or pithy - dry soil, correct accordingly.
- Bolting - irrigate during drought conditions. Avoid planting out seedlings which have grown too large or have been checked by cold or dryness.

11.9.7 Harvesting
Lift before the onset of the frosts. It is possible to store celeriac in clamps, over the winter (see 12.14).

11.10 Field scale cucurbits
COURGETTES, MARROWS AND SQUASHES

FIGURE 11.12 SPAGHETTI SQUASH,
PATTY PAN SQUASH AND COURGETTES

11.10.1 Rotation position and fertility requirements
- Courgettes, marrows and squashes like a fairly rich and moist soil.
- Green manuring
  - Before the crop - can follow a one-year green manure ley or should follow an overwinter green manure (see 6.2) which has been able to develop in the spring.
  - Undersowing - these crops are very suitable for undersowing with any clover. At Tolhurst Organic Produce we undersow squashes in the field with red clover and allow this to grow for thirty months with regular mowing to perform the function of the main fertility-building ley (see 6.2).
- If the crop is not grown before a green manure, you should spread compost at:
  - Ten tonnes per acre;
  - one barrow load per ten metre square.
- pH of about 6.0.

11.10.2 Raising transplants
- Courgettes are immature marrows and both are grown in the same way. You can grow courgettes for most of the season and at the end allow a few fruits to grow into marrows. It is advisable to use courgettes with a bush habit.
- Squashes divide into summer and winter storage types. Summer squashes

can be eaten as courgettes (choose bush habits) and the storage squashes can be cured (see 12.13.3 and 12.15) and stored for up to eight months (choose trailing varieties).

- They can be grown in 9cm pots in the greenhouse and then hardened off for transplanting outside:
  - one seed per pot OR
  - two seeds per pot and thin out the weaker seedling.
- In the warmer southern counties the seeds can be direct sown.
- Sow from March for an early crop of courgettes or summer squashes in the polytunnel or under cloches.
- Sow late April / early May for maincrop courgettes and winter squashes.

11.10.3 Soil conditions

- The soil must not be cold and damp. In northern areas it may be necessary to grow field scale cucurbits under cloches or grow them through black plastic. Certified growers in these circumstances will need to apply to the certification body for permission to use black plastic.
- Make certain that the soil is firm enough to anchor roots but to give good porous structure to permit air to reach the roots.
- Because of deep roots it will be necessary to have non-compacted subsoil (see 2.8).
  - 60 to 90% of roots will be in the top 30cm of soil.
  - 20 - 25% will be 30 - 50cm.
  - The tap root will penetrate deeper.

11.10.4 Planting out

- Transplant in mid to late May.
- For bush habits plant in two rows with staggered spacings 125cm apart and green manure paths in between.
- For trailing (squashes and pumpkins) spacings should be 90cm x 120cm. Weeding is difficult, so it is necessary to undersow the clover before they become rampant with growth in early July.

11.10.5 Cucurbit problems

Fortunately courgettes and squashes tend to be relatively trouble-free, suffering at worst from mildew (see 8.17.3) and slugs (see 8.16.1). The biggest issue is regular picking of courgettes and finding the winter squashes in the clover.

11.10.6 Harvesting

- Once the courgettes and summer squashes are in full flush they should be picked through every day.
- If the winter squashes have been undersown with clover, then by the time of harvesting it is necessary to find the crop under the leaves of the plant and the clover.
- Harvest winter squashes just before the onset of the frost. Remove the mature fruits with a small knife and cure (see 12.13.3 and 12.15).

11.11 Protected cucurbits CUCUMBERS AND MELONS

11.11.1 Rotation position and fertility requirements

- Cucumbers and melons are heavy feeders, requiring the highest level of fertility of all protected crops.

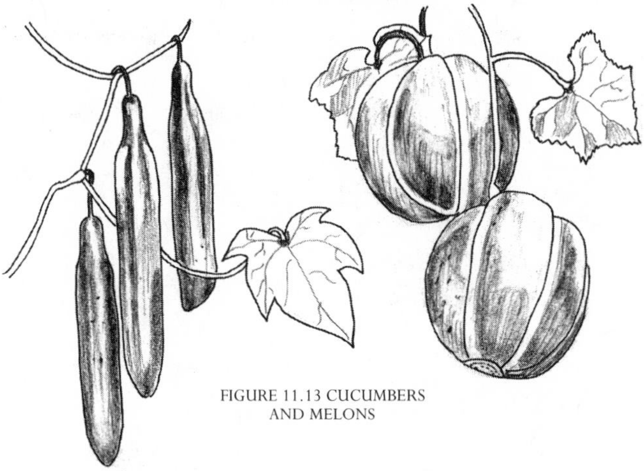

FIGURE 11.13 CUCUMBERS AND MELONS

- Green manuring
  - Before the crop - will benefit from growing after a one-year ley.
  - Undersowing - they are suitable for undersowing with low growing, shade tolerant green manure, e.g. yellow trefoil or Kent wild white clover, although their dense foliage may mean that growing green manure in the paths between the crops is more likely.
- However, a one-year ley is impractical in protected cropping as commercial growers cannot afford it. With normal cropping dig in ten litres / two buckets full of year-old compost for each square metre.
- pH level 6.0.
- Potash requirements same as tomatoes (see 11.2.2).

11.11.2 Raising transplants

- To aid fertility choose all-female protected cucumbers.
- When choosing melons choose small-fruited varieties.

- A minimum temperature of 15°C is needed for satisfactory growth, so in unheated greenhouses or polytunnels sowing should be in mid April.
- Sow one seed (or two seeds and thin the weaker seedling) into a 9cm pot.
- Sow at a temperature of 18°C.

11.11.3 Soil conditions
- Create a warm, moist soil at planting time of 15°C.
- Make it firm enough to anchor roots but also have a porous structure to permit air to reach the roots.
- Because of deep roots it will be necessary to have non-compacted subsoil (see 2.8).
- 60 to 90% of roots will be in the top 30cm of soil.
- 20 to 25% will be between 30 and 50cm.
- The tap root will penetrate deeper.

11.11.4 Planting out
- Plant in two rows with staggered spacings 75cm apart and green manure paths in between.

11.11.5 Atmospheric conditions
- Cucumbers and melons prefer hotter and more humid conditions than the protected solanaceae (see 11.2).
- Damp down the paths and plants at least twice a day in the morning and early afternoon.
- Vent to keep the temperature between 18-24°C during the day and keep the vents shut at night at least until the early summer.

11.11.6 Pollination
- Female flowers have miniature fruit behind them, males do not.
- In cucumbers, male flowers need to be removed. Fertilised fruit is bitter.
- Fortunately many modern varieties are all-female but these tend to favour warmer conditions and are not suitable for growing outside.
- Hand pollination will be necessary for melons. Wait until 6 female flowers are open. Each on a separate lateral. Remove a mature male flower, fold back the petals and push gently into the heart of each female flower. Do this at midday - one male flower will fertilise 4 females.

11.11.7 Supporting and training

- The plants will grow past two metres.
- Cucumbers will grow 25 fruits per plant.
- Melons will grow between four and six fruits per plant.
  - Support cucumbers and melons either the same way as tomatoes (see 11.2.7), but be careful when twisting the strings as they are delicate and can easily break OR
  - Using a trellis stretched across a wooden frame.
- The climbing shoots should be trained on vertical wires and pinched out when the leader reaches the roof.
- Check whether the cucumber fruit mature on the main stem or on side shoots. Generally each side shoot is pinched out at two leaves beyond a female flower.
- For melons pinch out the growing point after three leaves to encourage side shooting. Stop the side shoot at three leaves. Leave one melon per lateral shoot.
- Melons will need nets attached to wires to support the fruit from tennis-ball size to maturity.

11.11.8 Watering

- Little and often is the golden rule. The soil should be constantly moist but not waterlogged. It may be necessary to water twice a day.
- Growth checks due to irregular watering results in fruits drying and entrance spots for infection.

11.11.9 Common protected cucurbit problems

- Aphids - for prevention see 8.16.2.
- Red spider mite - mottled leaves and silken webbing. For prevention see 8.16.4.
- Eelworm - wilted leaves, roots covered with galls. For prevention see 8.16.8.
- Powdery mildew - mouldy patches on leaves, and stems. For prevention see 8.17.3
- Botrytis - grey mouldy patches on stems, grey mould on fruits. For prevention see 8.17.4.
- Cucumber mosaic virus - mottled yellow and green leaves, misshapen and warty fruit. For prevention choose resistant varieties and prevent its spread by aphids (see 8.16.2). Once the crop has the virus there is no treatment.

Destroy affected plants and wash hands and tools thoroughly before touching other plants.

- Basal stem rot - soft brown rot at the base of stems, leaves wilted. Avoid overwatering and keep water away from the base of the stem. Remove affected plants.
- Root rot - blackened and rotten roots. This fungal disease thrives in cold conditions. Remove affected plants.
- Verticillium wilt - wilted leaves. Practice long rotations. Remove affected plants.
- No flowers - lack of humidity.

11.11.10 Harvesting
- For cucumbers cut with a small knife and do not let them become over-ripe. It is better to cut small.
- For melons cut the fruits with a small knife as soon as they feel soft when you press the ends.

11.12 Field scale edible grasses
SWEETCORN

11.12.1 Rotation position and fertility requirements
- Sweetcorn likes a fairly rich and moist soil.
- Green manuring
  - Before the crop - can follow a one-year green manure ley or an overwinter green manure which has been able to develop in the spring (see 6.2).
  - Undersowing - These crops are very suitable for undersowing with any clover. At Tolhurst Organic Produce we undersow sweetcorn in the field with red clover and allow this to grow for 30 months with regular mowing to perform the function of the main fertility-building ley.
- If the crop is not grown before a green

FIGURE 11.14 SWEETCORN

manure, you should spread compost at:
- Ten tonnes per acre;
- one barrow load per ten metre square.

11.12.2 Sowing dates for transplants
- For a continuous supply plant three varieties to mature at different times.
- Sweetcorn germinates reliably at 13°C.
- In the southern and eastern counties transplants can be sown in the greenhouse from late April with outdoor direct sowings occurring from mid May to mid June.
- In the northern and western counties sow as transplants from mid May to mid June. Sweetcorn can now be grown in the colder, wetter counties thanks to the breeding of early F1 hybrids.
- Grow in 9cm pots and do not keep for longer than three weeks once the seedlings have emerged.
- Wait until the danger of frosts has passed before planting out.

11.12.3 Soil conditions
- Sweetcorn like to be planted into a well-consolidated seedbed, where they can anchor their roots. If there is rocking in the root zone, a poor crop will result.
- The soil must not be cold and damp. In northern areas it may be necessary to wait until late June before planting out.
- Roots will appear at the base of the stems. These must be covered with further soil or compost. Alternatively grow the sweetcorn on ridges.

11.12.4 Spacings
- 40 cm x 125cm.
- Grow in rectangular blocks and not in single rows to ensure the wind pollination of the female flowers.

11.12.5 Pollination
- The tassels at the top of the adult plant are the male flowers.
- The female flowers are the silks above the immature cobs.
- The side shoots that develop should not be removed.
- Tapping the male tassels when the plants are fully developed will help pollination.

11.12.6 Weed control
- Weed ten days after planting.
- Weeding with machinery - aim for three passes with inter-row weeders. Ensure you lift fleeces each week to check weed development.
- Weeding by hand - hoe when the weeds are just emerging, at their white stringy stage, and are easily killed.
- Before undersowing - ensure a clear seedbed before undersowing.

11.12.7 Watering
- Water during dry spells and especially at flowering time.

11.12.8 Sweetcorn problems
- Smut can appear in hot weather. These galls must be cut off to prevent their release of black spores.
- Frit fly maggots bore into the growing points of the sweetcorn, resulting in stunted growth.
- Blackfly - for prevention see 8.16.2.
- Earwigs - cultivating in early spring can disturb their overwinter habitat and bring eggs to the surface for predators.

11.12.9 Harvesting
- Each plant should produce two cobs.
- Test for ripeness when the tassels are blackening.
- Peel the husk back and press your thumb nail into the first few kernels.
- If a watery liquid squeezes out, it is not ready.
- If the liquid is creamy, it is ready to harvest.
- If the liquid is thick and doughy, they may be over ripe.
- Twist off the ripe cob from the stem.
- Sweetcorn is a type of maize which has been bred for its high sugar and low starch content. Once the cob has been picked, the sugar in the kernels is steadily converted into starch. That is why they should be eaten fresh.

11.13 Legumes
BROAD BEANS, RUNNER BEANS, FRENCH BEANS, MAINCROP PEAS, SUGAR SNAP PEAS.

11.13.1 Rotation position and fertility requirements
- Legumes like a fairly rich soil.
- Green manuring
    - Before the crop - should follow a non-leguminous overwinter green manure which has been able to develop in the spring.
    - Undersowing - These crops

FIGURE 11.15 BROAD BEANS, PEAS, FRENCH BEANS AND RUNNER BEANS

are very suitable for undersowing with the clover forming paths.
- Legumes supply their own nitrogen but require a good supply of potash in the soil (see 3.3.2).
- If the crop is not grown before a green manure, you should spread compost at:
    - Five tonnes per acre;
    - Twenty metre square area - one barrow load.
- Legumes prefer a pH between 6.5 and neutral. Lime the previous winter if necessary.

11.13.2 Sowing dates
- Broad bean
    - Overwinter crop - direct sow in October / November for a June crop.
    - Main crop - direct sow in late March for a July / August crop.

- Runner beans
    - Earlies - sow as transplants with heat in mid March for a late July crop.
    - Main crop - sow as transplants mid April or direct sow mid May when the soil is at least 10°C for an August / September crop.
    - Autumn crop - sow as transplants mid May or direct sow early June for cropping into October.

- Peas
    - First earlies (early protected crop) - direct sow from early March for a

June crop. You may wish to avoid this crop if protected cropping space is at a premium as the crop value to work ratio is negative on a small scale.
- Second earlies - direct sow in early April for a July crop.
- Main crop - direct sow outside from early May for an August crop.
- Autumn crop - direct sow outside in early June for a September / October crop.

French beans and sugar snap peas are only half hardy and will yield better when grown under a protected structure, especially in north and westerly counties.

- French beans
  - Suited to growing under a protected structure.
  - Earlies - sow as transplants with heat in mid April for a July crop.
  - Main crop - direct sow in late May for an August / September crop.
- Sugar snap peas
  - Same dates as earlies, second earlies and main crop peas.
  - Suited to growing under a protected structure or outdoors. You may wish to avoid this crop if protected cropping space is at a premium.

11.13.3 Soil conditions
- The key to legumes is good porous structure rather than fine cultivation. Because of deep roots it will be necessary to have non-compacted subsoil (see 2.8).
- They also like a firm, well consolidated seedbed to prevent rocking in the root zone. Finding a sheltered spot with protection from the wind will also prevent rocking.

11.13.4 Spacings and support structures

Supporting vertical growing broad beans and peas
- Sow broad beans 20cm apart in staggered double rows, 5cm deep.
- Sow peas 5cm apart in staggered triple rows, 5cm deep, in a figure of 5 on a dice formation.
- Support the double or triple rows with wooden stakes driven into the ends of rows and along the rows if needed. Tie twine, fencing mesh or netting between the wooden posts.

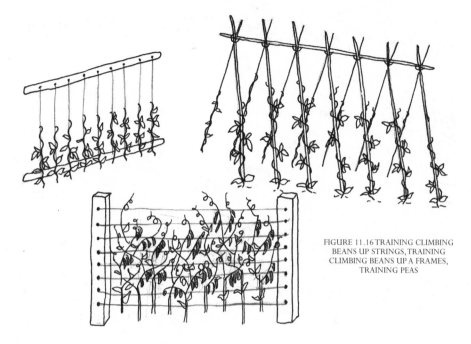

FIGURE 11.16 TRAINING CLIMBING
BEANS UP STRINGS, TRAINING
CLIMBING BEANS UP A FRAMES,
TRAINING PEAS

Training climbing beans

- Plant two bean plants at the foot of each cane.
- Runner beans
  - 'A' frame - use 8ft bamboo canes to form an 'A' frame structure. Make the first row by pushing canes 20cm into the ground with a 30cm space in between. Directly opposite and parallel to the first row of canes place another row of canes 60cm away. Where they cross tie with twine that goes the length of the row. The twine is eventually fastened to a post in the ground at each end.
  - Wigwam - use 8ft x 8ft bamboo canes to form a wigwam. Place each cane in a circle formation 20cm into the ground, 30cm apart. Tie all the canes at one point.
- French beans (climbing)
  - Structures same as runner beans with 15cm between individual plants.

11.13.5 Weed control

- Weed ten days after planting.
- Weeding by hand - hoe when the weeds are just emerging, at their white stringy stage, and are easily killed.
- Before undersowing - ensure a clear seedbed before undersowing.

11.13.6 Watering
The critical watering times are when the flowers are just opening and as the pods are swelling.

11.13.7 Common legume problems
- Black bean aphid - to avoid the worse of the black bean aphid (in broad beans) pinch out tops once four trusses have formed. For aphid prevention see 8.16.2.
- Pea and bean weevil - notched leaves but never seems to cause much harm and most cases can be ignored. For prevention see 8.16.10.
- Pea moth - tunnelled pea pods with maggots present. Use strategic planting dates see 8.13.
- Birds, rabbits and mice these competing animals adore the young shoots. For advice on suitable barriers see 8.23, 8.24 and 8.25.
- Downy mildew - white or brown moulds that occur in cool wet seasons. For prevention see 8.17.2.
- Powdery mildew - white or brown moulds that occur in dry seasons. For prevention see 8.17.3 and the use of strategic planting dates see 8.13.
- Botrytis - grey mould. For prevention see 8.17.4.
- Chocolate spot - brown streaks on leaves, stems and pods. Largely a cosmetic disease.
- Fusarium wilt - stunted growth and brown streaks inside the stems. Avoid over watering. Remove badly affected plants.
- Absent flowers - too much nitrogen in the soil. Practice long rotations and place after heavy feeders.

11.13.8 Harvesting
- It may be necessary to harvest up to three times a week.
- Broad beans should be picked before the scar on each shelled bean has become discoloured.
- Runner beans should be picked when they are young and have not developed stringiness. This will stimulate further production.
- French beans should be picked when they are about 10cm long.
- Peas and sugar snap peas are better picked when young.
- When harvesting has finished, cut the main stem 5cm above the soil so that the nitrogen can be released back to the soil. Leave the foliage for several months before trying to remove it from cane and twine structures. In this time the undersown clover can be allowed to grow on.

11.14 Chenopods - the beets
BEETROOT, ANNUAL SPINACH, PERPETUAL SPINACH, CHARD

11.14.1 Rotation position and fertility requirements

- Beets are moderate feeders and can make do with the residual fertility of a previously heavily composted crop or should follow a one-year green manure ley see 6.3.
- Green manure

FIGURE 11.17 ANNUAL SPINACH, BEETROOT AND SWISS CHARD

  - Before the crop - a one-year green manure ley is suitable. At Tolhurst Organic Produce we grow bare root leek transplants (see 5.4) the previous year and then, as soon as they are lifted, put the soil into a green manure to accumulate moderate nitrogen for the following crop.
  - Undersowing - beets are not suitable for undersowing because they do not like the root competition.
  - After the crop - a green manure can be sown after the beetroot and annual spinach are lifted. The perpetual spinach and chard remain in the soil overwinter so that a spring crop can be harvested.
- pH between 6.5 and 6.8.
- If the beets are directly sown, they will be very weed intolerant and so should be grown in a phase of the rotation that has a low weed burden e.g. after a green manure ley.
- Beets are very sensitive to a lack of boron - light soils and wetter soils in the west may need borax additions with certified growers needing to apply to the certification body for permission to use this. This information will be available from soil analysis.

11.14.2 Sowing dates

All beets are suitable for direct sowing, although you may find more reliable results and easier weeding if you raise them as transplants.

- Bunch beetroot

- Three seeds to a plug. Sow in February and March with heat.
- Continue to sow as transplants at monthly intervals until early May.
- Main crop beetroot
  - Direct sow in mid May.
- Annual spinach
  - Direct sow OR one seed per plug.
  - Summer varieties - sow every few weeks from mid March to late April (under protection) and outdoors until the end of May.
  - Winter varieties - sow in August and September.
  - New Zealand varieties - are not true spinach but less prone to bolting. Sow in late May for picking between July and September.
- Perpetual spinach (leaf beet)
  - Direct sow OR one seed per plug.
  - Sow in mid April.
- Chard
  - Direct sow OR one seed per plug.
  - Sow in mid April.

11.14.3 Soil conditions
- Beetroots prefer a shallow tilth whereas as the leaf crops will need a deeper bed.
- Annual spinach may need some shading to prevent it running to seed.

11.14.4 Spacings
- Bunch beetroot - 20cm x 35cm.
- Main crop beetroot - 10cm x 35cm.
- Annual spinach - 15cm x 35cm.
- Perpetual spinach (leaf beet) - 30cm x 35cm.
- Chard - 30cm x 35cm.

11.14.5 Weed control
- Use a stale seedbed (see 7.3) to reduce weed competition before sowing or transplanting modules.
- Weed ten days after planting.
- Weeding with machinery - aim for three passes with inter-row weeders. Ensure you lift fleeces each week to check weed development.
- Weeding by hand - hoe when the weeds are just emerging, at their white stringy stage, and are easily killed.

11.14.6 Watering

- Especially if sowing directly, water before drilling to ensure uniform germination.
- Avoid dry soil with beetroots as this will lead to woody bulbs.
- The deeper rooting leaf crops can withstand drought conditions to some extent.

11.14.7 Common beet problems

- Slugs - seedlings eaten. For prevention see 8.16.1.
- Cutworm - beetroots eaten. For prevention see 8.16.6.
- Downy mildew - mouldy patches on leaves. For prevention see 8.17.2.
- Heart rot - beetroots blackened inside. Boron deficiency. Apply borax with permission from the certifying body.
- Manganese deficiency - leaves rolled, yellow or mottled. Do not over lime.
- Bolted - caused by dry soil, lack of shade or lack of organic matter. Grow resistant varieties and practice sound rotations with careful attention to fertility regimes.
- Small and leathery beetroots - caused by dry soil and lack of organic matter. Practice sound rotations with careful attention to fertility regimes.
- Large and leathery beetroots - harvest delayed for too long.
- Split beetroots - caused by heavy rain or too much watering after a prolonged dry spell. Try a 'little and often' watering policy.

11.14.8 Harvesting

- Lift the beetroot when you have the required size. Small beetroot with high quality leaves can be lifted as a two-in-one crop with the leaves acting as spinach. Ensure the last of the crop are lifted before severe frosts in early November and clamped (see 12.14).
- Pick annual spinach over time. With New Zealand spinach pinch out the growing point.
- Treat perpetual spinach and chard as a cut-and-come-again crop, aiming for four cuts. They can get tough, so pick when they are quite young. If the leaf quality is high, you can cut it off with a knife above the growing point. Otherwise individually pick leaves (with chard the enlarged midribs are part of the harvest) by sliding the hand down to the base of the stem and using a swift downward breaking off movement ensuring that you do not uproot the plants. If you are uncertain about uprooting, use scissors.
- By late October ensure that the perpetual spinach and chard are completely picked back to the growing point and cover them with fleece,

cloche or straw to protect from the frost and to ensure a subsequent crop the following spring.

11.15 Lettuce

The following information is taken from the Soil Association Technical Guide for Organic Lettuce Production.

11.15.1 Rotation position and fertility requirements

*   It is standard practice on commercial holdings for lettuces to be double-cropped in the same year.
*   Place in a later part of the rotation with a low weed burden.
*   Green manuring

FIGURE 11.18 BUTTERHEAD LETTUCE, COS LETTUCE, CONTINENTAL LEAF, CRISP LETTUCE

    *   Before the crop - lettuces should NOT be grown after a green manure ley since there might be too much nitrogen in the soil leading to tipburn, rots and the lush growth attracting aphids. EU regulation (194/912) lays down maximum nitrate levels in lettuces.
    *   Undersowing - as lettuces are short-lived crops and because of double cropping they are not suitable for undersowing.
    *   After the crop - after harvesting an overwinter green manure can be planted.
*   Lettuces tend to get squeezed in where there is a gap. Therefore, additions of well-rotted (at least over a year-old) compost will assist with fertility. Spread compost at
    *   Five tonnes per hectare;
    *   Twenty metre square area - one barrow load.
*   pH between 6.5 and 6.8.

11.15.2 Sowing dates for transplants

- Sow as transplants with one seed per plug.

There are four types of lettuce:

- Butterhead types - loose leaf presented with minimum trimming.
- Cos - upright, tougher, waxier leaves (variety Little Gem becoming increasingly popular).
- Continental leaf e.g. Lolla Rossa, Red oak leaf, Salad bowl.
- Crisp / Iceberg - with solid hearts, presented with minimum trimming or, in the case of icebergs, with the outer leaves removed.

Table 11.2 Continuity of supply – butterhead / cos and Continental lettuce planting programme[14]

Sowing date		Planting date		Harvesting date	
Jan	13th (with heat)	March	10th	May	15th (with fleece)
	30th (with heat)		20th		22nd (with fleece)
Feb	15th (with heat)		30th		29th (with fleece)
March	6th (with heat)	April	9th	June	5th (with fleece)
	25th (with heat)		25th		12th
April	10th	May	8th		19th
	25th		20th		26th
May	2nd		30th	July	3rd
	8th	June	5th		10th
	15th		12th		17th
	27th		18th		24th
June	3rd		25th		31st
	12th	July	3rd	Aug	7th
	19th		10th		14th
	27th		18th		21st
July	5th		26th		28th
	12th	Aug	2nd	Sept	4th
	23rd		13th		18th
	27th		17th		25th

Table 11.3 Continuity of supply – crisp / iceberg lettuce planting programme

Sowing date		Planting date		Harvesting date	
Jan	1st (with heat)	March	5th	May	29th (with fleece)
	15th (with heat)		15th	June	5th (with fleece)
	30th (with heat)		30th		12th (with fleece)
Feb	20th (with heat)	April	5th		19th
March	10th (with heat)		10th		26th
	25th (with heat)		30th	July	3rd
April	5th	May	6th		10th
	19th		20th		17th
May	5th	June	2nd		24th
	16th		12th		31st
	30th		20th	Aug	7th
June	5th		26th		14th
	10th	July	1st		21st
	15th		6th		28th
	22nd		13th	Sept	4th
	29th		20th		11th
July	3rd		24th		18th
	6th		27th		25th

11.15.3 Soil conditions

- A fine tilth is required for good root establishment.
- Cultivate to a depth of 10cm.
- Ensure that the bed is level.
- Lettuces prefer some level of shade and are suitable for intercropping with slower growing crops e.g. brussel sprouts. The soil preparation should be for the main crop and the lettuces should take their chances[15].
- Do not plant the transplants too deeply. The growing point should be at the level of the soil. Treat them carefully, so that the leaves of the seedlings are not torn and so that soil does not get in their hearts.
- Ensure that compost is moist at the time of planting.

11.15.4 Spacings
- Little gem - 20cm x 25cm.
- Cos, butterheads, continental - 30cm x 30cm.
- Crisp / iceberg - 35cm x 35cm.

11.15.5 Crop care
- The key to successful lettuce cultivation is quick growth.
- Fleeces
    - advance early crops by 12 -14 days;
    - give frost protection;
    - protect from competing animals.
- The fleece covers need to be removed when watering.
- Covers can be left on until harvest except for crisp / iceberg types that need to 'harden off' a week before harvest.

11.15.6 Weed control
- Lettuces are a short-lived crop and are generally grown on a high density spacing to out compete the weeds.
- Early lettuces under fleece should be monitored each week.
- Main season lettuces need to be checked once a fortnight.
- Weed ten days after planting.
- Weeding with machinery - aim for two passes with inter-row weeders.
- Weeding by hand - hoe when the weeds are just emerging, at their white stringy stage, and are easily killed.

11.15.7 Watering
- Water before transplanting.
- Water four days after transplanting if the lettuces have not begun rooting out.
- A lettuce grows most in the last three weeks before harvest, so ensure that it is not checked by dry conditions at this time.
- Bolting (premature running to flower) is induced by high temperatures (over 21°C) and dry conditions.
- Trickle irrigation is the ideal. Where a sprinkle irrigation system is used, ensure that there is a fine spray to prevent soil splash making the lettuces no longer presentable.

11.15.8 Common lettuce problems
- Slugs - seedlings eaten or leaves with holes. For prevention see 8.16.1.
- Aphids - for prevention see 8.16.2.
- Root aphid - leaves wilted and roots covered with white patches. Root aphid over winters in lombardy and black poplars and migrates in June. Later lettuce crops tend to escape worst effects.
- Cutworm - seedlings severed or leaves wilted. For prevention see 8.16.6.
- Eelworm - leaves wilted and roots covered will gall like swellings. For prevention see 8.16.8.
- Lettuce root maggot - leaves wilted with the roots tunnelled with maggots. No treatment, remove affected plants. Avoid growing on land used for chrysanthemums in previous years.
- Downy mildew - mouldy or powdery patches on leaves. For prevention see 8.17.2.
- Botrytis - grey mould on leaves or base of plant. For prevention see 8.17.4.
- Tipburn - brown edged leaves. Tipburn is a calcium deficiency and can be caused by irregular watering, nutrient imbalance, too much nitrogen and / or compaction.
- Poor germination - seeds too warm during propagation. Keep temperatures between 15°C and 21°C.
- No hearts - caused by lack of organic matter and other checks to growth.
- Bolting - ensure that you do not delay transplanting. Avoid overcrowding and dryness at the roots.

11.15.9 Harvesting
- Lettuce will mature over a fortnight, so two or three selective harvests will need to be made.
- In hot weather lettuces may mature nearly all at the same time and will need to be cut within a few days.
- Harvest with a sharp knife at the base of the stem. Trim outer leaves.
- It will be necessary to reduce field heat by harvesting early in the morning and / or cooling within half an hour of cutting (see 12.11).

11.16 Protected non-brassica salad leaves
LETTUCE, CHICORIES, ENDIVES, CORN SALAD, CLAYTONIA, SORREL, SALAD SPINACH, LEAF AMARANTH

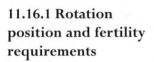

11.16.1 Rotation position and fertility requirements

- All leaves can be grown as main season salads or

FIGURE 11.19 NON-BRASSICA SALAD LEAVES: CHICORY, ENDIVE WITLOOF, CORN SALAD, CLAYTONIA, RED VEINED SORREL AND LEAF AMARANTH

winter salads. There are, however, two different techniques recommended depending on the time of year you are growing with main season leaves being directly sown and overwinter crops being raised as transplants, after another crop.
- Non-brassica salad leaves need a moderate soil and can make do with residual fertility of a previously heavily composted crop.
- Difficulties with protected cropping rotations are discussed in section 6.4.

- Green manuring
  - Before the crop - green manuring is not always possible because of 'back-to-back' cropping in protected cropping. Winter salad leaves (all the leaves except lettuce) can be grown in the autumn after other main greenhouse crops.
  - Undersowing - salad leaves are not suitable.

11.16.2 Characteristics of the leaves
- Lettuce leaves (see 11.15)
- Chicories
  - Endive - bitter tasting so add sparingly to mixed salads. Direct sow in the main lettuce season or as transplants (one seed per plug) in late July / early August for winter salads.
  - Sugar loaf chicory - again lettuce shaped but winter hardy. Direct sow in the main lettuce season or as transplants (one seed per plug) in late

July / early August for winter salads.

- Radicchio (Red chicory) - Direct sow in the main lettuce season or as transplants (one seed per plug) in late July / early August for winter salads. Some heads need to be cut back for winter re-growth.
- Belgian Endive (witloof) - Eliot Coleman[16] suggests forcing chicons (tightly bunched groups of leaves) grown from stored endive roots that were started previously from seed transplants in late May. The roots grow during the summer months and are harvested in October. Discard any thin (below 3cm diameter) or forked roots. Cut off the leaves to within 2cm, cutting off the bottom of the root so that they are 15cm long. Store in a black, light excluding bucket, filled with dry sand until you want to start forcing them. At regular intervals plant roots with the crown above the soil in 23cm pots filled with wetted sand. Keep in a dark, humid environment so that they are blanched. The chicons should take three weeks to develop.
- Corn salad (lambs lettuce) - this truly winter crop can be directly sown or raised as transplants (three seeds per plug) from early September through to early November. As it is a relatively bland taste you may just want to reserve it for winter salads. It germinates best in shade.
- Claytonia (miners lettuce) - Direct sow in the main lettuce season or as transplants (three seeds per plug) in late July to early August for winter salads.
- Sorrel - this perennial plant can be propagated by means of seed (sow late July to early August as transplants) or root division. Sorrel adds a lemony zest to mixed salads.
- Spinach salad (as a winter salad) - see 11.14.2 for main sowing season or direct sow in late August and September for winter salads.
- Leaf amaranth - Direct sow in the main lettuce season or as transplants (three seeds per plug) in late July to early August for winter salads.

11.16.3 Sowing dates
- Spring and summer salad bags
  - Non-brassica salad leaves can be directly sown for main season salad bags where the leaves are harvested small and the crop is redrilled after each picking. It will be worthwhile choosing pelleted lettuce seed to aid drilling. Johnny's Selected Seeds have designed two seeders specifically for this purpose[17] and recommend this technique.
  - Direct sow weekly from late February to mid June.

- It is not appropriate to use spring and summer salad leaves as cut and come again (CCA) crops as they will bolt, are likely to suffer tipburn and the growth may also be more fibrous due to plant stress.
- Overwinter salad bags
  - For an overwinter crop CCA salad leaves should be sown as transplants after the longest day (i.e. from mid June).
  - All non-brassica salad leaves are particularly well suited to the UK autumn / winter climate with the exception of lettuce.

11.16.4 Spacings
- Directly sown - 5cm x 5cm.
- Transplants for overwinter
  - Chicories - 30cm x 30cm.
  - Curly endives - 40cm x 40cm.
  - Corn salad - transplant at 10cm x 10cm with three seeds per module.
  - Claytonia - 10cm x 30cm.
  - Sorrel - 10cm x 30cm.
  - Spinach - 10cm x 30cm.
  - Leaf amaranth - 10cm x 30cm.

11.16.5 Transplanting technique
- Ensure that the soil is level and well rolled and consolidated.
- To prevent the leaves becoming contaminated with soil, the transplant plugs are planted so that the base is at the surface of the soil and no deeper than 5cm.

11.16.6 Crop care
- Hand hoe transplants regularly.
- Avoid soil splash on the leaves by using a fine spray when watering.
- Avoid overwatering especially from September onwards, as this tends to create favourable conditions for grey moulds.
- All chicories can be blanched by covering with a light-excluding pot. Leave a gap between the soil and the pot's rim to allow for ventilation.

11.16.7 Salad leaf problems
- See 11.15.8.
- Once any chicory has started to run to seed they should not be included in salad bags because they are too bitter to eat.

11.16.8 Harvesting techniques with cut and come again crops

- It is very easy to rip up the plant roots when using a knife, as they are not deeply anchored. Harvest leaves with a pair of scissors.
- Direct sown leaves
  - Harvest the leaves at the desired size before they start to bolt.
- For CCA leaves raised as transplants
  - Harvest corn salad by cutting the whole plant at soil level. They are usually served as whole plants in salads
  - In most seasons it will be necessary to cut almost weekly up until the end of autumn. Growth slows down after November and stops midwinter, starting again early February.
  - Cover the trimmed plants with a fleece between December and January. Place the fleece over a cloche frame, so that it is not resting on the crops.
  - By the end of February you will probably need to cut at least every week in favourable conditions. By mid March some of the crops will probably start to bolt.

1 HDRA (2002) Organic Early Potato Production in Devon. 6.6.02. Kingsbridge, South Devon.

2 Francis Blake (1987) Organic Farming and Growing. Crowood Press.

3 Terry Marshall3 has written 'Organic Tomatoes - the Inside Story', which is an extremely informative read and much of the information in this section is taken from there.

4 MARSHALL T (1999) Organic Tomatoes the Inside Story. Harris Associates.

5 COLEMAN E (1995) The New Organic Grower - A Masters Manual of Tools and Techniques for the Home and Market Gardene. Chelsea Green Publishing Company.

6 This latter technique was seen at the Schofield's Growing with Nature, Bradshaw Lane Nursery, Pilling, Preston.

7 MARSHALL T (1999) Organic Tomatoes the Inside Story. Harris Associates.

8 MARSHALL T (1999) Organic Tomatoes the Inside Story. Harris Associates.

9 Personal communication with Alan Schofield, Growing with Nature (2004).

10 FINCH S & EDMONDS GH (1994) Undersowing Cabbage Crops with Clover - Effects on Pest Insects, Ground Beetles and Crop Yields. IOBC / WPRS Bulletin 17(8) 159 - 167

11 Johnny's Selected Seeds, 955 Benton Avenue, Winslow, Maine 04901-2601 USA. www.johnnyseeds.com

12 This technique is used by Alan Schofield at Growing with Nature, Lancashire.

13 SOIL ASSOCIATION (1999) Organic Carrot Production - Soil Association Technical Guides.

14 SOIL ASSOCIATION - Organic Lettuce Production. Soil Association Technical Guides.

15 Advice from COLEMAN E (1995) The New Organic Grower - a Masters Manual of Tools and Techniques for the Home and Market Gardener. Chelsea Green publishing company.

16 COLEMAN E (1995) The New Organic Grower - a Masters Manual of Tools and Techniques for the Home and Market Gardener. Chelsea Green publishing company.

17 Johnny's Selected Seeds, 955 Benton Avenue, Winslow, Maine 04901-2601 USA. www.johnnyseeds.com

Chapter Twelve

Season extension and crop storage

Under Stockfree-Organic Standard 16.1 it is a standard principle that:
In order to minimise fossil fuel use and avoid compromising the freshness of the stockfree-organic food consideration must be given to the 'food miles' and the produce should be consumed as close to source as possible.

The Stockfree-Organic Standards actively encourage local food production. Organic fruit and vegetables are the most widely purchased type of organic food, accounting for 31% of all organic sales. Of this percentage around 55% at the wholesale level are imported. If UK growers grew at either end of the season and made better use of storage techniques, they could gain a larger percentage of the market and there could be a reduction in the amount of food brought in from abroad[1]. Imported food often relies on migrant labour where the workers are paid very badly and work in poor conditions.

12.1 Spring and autumn season extension
Spring and autumn season extension techniques aim to improve frost protection. The benefits of season extension include[2]:

1. year round supply;
2. reduced reliance on imports;
3. higher yields for the whole year;

4. insect pest exclusion;
5. greater selection of vegetables to offer the customer.

At a workshop organised in 2003 by the Soil Association[3] the problems of season extension were discussed by commercial organic growers. Whilst promoting early transplant raising through heating and lighting is economically viable, attempting to raise the soil temperature in a greenhouse or polytunnel (e.g. under soil or above soil heating) is likely to be too expensive for growers who are not monocropping[4]. For this reason, the rest of the chapter looks at affordable season extension techniques. Discussions are based on a talk given by Alan Schofield[5] at the above workshop, the paper 'Season Extension Techniques for Market Gardeners' and the work of Eliot Coleman.

Winter salads have been brought to the public's attention by Joy Larkcom in 'Oriental Vegetables – the complete guide for the gardening cook' and 'The salad garden' and Eliot Coleman's the 'Four Season Harvest'. These are a very promising means of producing 'interesting vegetables' when there only seems to be root vegetables or brassicas available. The winter salads with which the authors are familiar are discussed in sections 11.4 protected brassica salad leaves and 11.16 protected non-brassica salad leaves. The varieties described in this book are not intended to be exhaustive and it is worth your while experimenting with different salad leaves as they become available.

12.2 Soil fertility
Soil fertility, the heart of stockfree-organic systems, can present problems for season extension. Previous crops in the polytunnel / greenhouse may have been undersown with a green manure, e.g. yellow trefoil (see 3.5.3) which will be incorporated in the following spring. But the incorporation of a green manure before the early crops, highlighted by an asterix in Table 12.1, may result in too high levels of nitrogen.

Crops take up nitrates very readily and, if they are not utilised immediately in the formation of protein, they are stored in the cells in their original form. When nitrates are ingested or cooked, there is a risk that they will convert to nitrites that can potentially combine with amines to form carcinogenic nitrosamines. There are, therefore, risks when growing vegetables under sub-optimal light conditions.

The food plants most readily affected are cereals, leafy vegetables, turnips, spinach and beets. Fortunately, Elm Farm Research Centre (Stopes et al, 1988[7]) has shown clear differences between nitrate levels in conventional and organic crops, but in sub-optimal light conditions there may still be problems. It is, therefore, important to ensure that there is not too much nitrogen in the soil.

Green manures should only be incorporated before:
• non-leafy season extension polytunnel / greenhouse crops e.g. early courgettes or
• main season crops that are planted in May e.g. tomatoes and peppers.

Green manuring can also be carried out AFTER spring crops are removed e.g. growing crimson red clover between May and June, for an intensive fix of nitrogen to be slotted in during back-to-back cropping (see 6.4).

In all likelihood, when growing in sub-optimal conditions in a polytunnel or greenhouse, the problems of rotations (see 6.4) and back-to-back cropping might lead to insufficient soil fertility. In these circumstances, your finest plant-based compost (see chapter 4) should become the primary source of soil fertility, spread on the soil surface before direct sowing or transplanting. Adding plant-based compost will also have the double benefit of 'topping up' beneficial micro-organisms to the soil which are disease suppressers, keeping the moulds at bay.

12.3 Transplant raising from January to March

Transplants can be grown before it would be safe to direct sow the same crop and can give up to a six-week head start on the season. The biggest problem with early season transplant raising is downy mildew. It is important to reduce humidity; drip irrigation is preferable to an overhead sprinkler or watering can. Foliar treatments with mint oil[8] have also been shown to be beneficial, providing that it is applied soon after infection, although this has not been registered for UK use by the Pesticide Safety Directorate.

You will need propagation equipment to raise early transplants and it can be very expensive. Many stockfree-organic growers have made their own successful DIY systems.

Table 12.1 Vegetable crops suitable for season extension[6]

Season extension technique	Suitable crops	Notes
Outdoor crops		
Traditional autumn and winter crops with good standing (available until May.)	Leeks, carrots, parsnips, cabbage, cauliflower, swede. Brussel sprout available until March.	
Overwinter crops with continual harvesting except December & January (available until early May.)	Kale, chard, perpetual spinach.	In November remove dying foliage and protect with fleece.
Sown from June to October of the previous year for spring cropping (available late April onwards.)	Purple sprouting broccoli, spring greens / cabbage, broad bean, pea, overwinter onions.	Use varieties that mature at different times. See 11.3.4 for extending spring cabbage harvest through double spacing.
Polytunnel / greenhouse crops		
Cut and come again crops with continual harvesting except Dec & Jan (available until early May.)	Winter salads (see 11.4 and 11.16), chard, perpetual spinach.	In November remove dying foliage and protect with fleece supported by hoops.

Polytunnel / greenhouse crops

Sown in August and September of the previous year for early spring cropping (available early April to June.)	Purple sprouting broccoli, spring greens / cabbage, spring onions, annual spinach, turnip.	See 11.3.4 for extending spring cabbage harvest through double spacing. Use fleece supported by hoops.
Sown in October of the previous year for early spring cropping. (available - April to June)	Carrots, overwinter onions, garlic.	Use fleece for added frost protection.
See section 12.3 Transplants grown from January with heat and light for same season cropping (available May onwards.)	*Lettuce (see 11.15), *beetroot, *spinach, courgette, cucumber.	Use fleece for added frost protection. The cucurbit transplants can be raised in large pots to avoid planting into cold soils.
Direct sow from early March for same season cropping (available May onwards.)	*Beetroot, *turnip, *radish, *spinach, carrot, spring onion, bunching onions.	Use soil warming techniques. Use fleece supported by hoops for added frost protection.
Late autumn crops (available late September onwards.)	Pak choi, chinese cabbage, celery, other winter salads (see 11.4 and 11.16)	Use fleece supported by hoops for added frost protection.

* = Crops that may take up nitrates too readily if grown after a green manure

12.3.1 Germination units / chitting sheds

Germination units are enclosed, darkened and heated spaces with tightly packed shelves. It is possible to make a germination unit from a small garden shed, bubble wrapped on the interior and without a window. Once in there the transplants are not watered and therefore their stay has to be short. Forcing blocking transplants (see 5.3.6) is easier than transplants in module trays because the moisture lasts longer and the seeds can be seen in the indents.

- Immediately after sowing, place the transplants on the shelves. Transplants that require warmer temperatures - peppers, aubergines, melons and cucumbers[9] should be put on the higher shelves and others on the lower.
- Seal the unit so that the heat cannot escape, but ensure that the fumes of the heater are exhausted.
- Check the germination unit twice a day and once the seed cases have started to crack remove to the propagating bench.

12.3.2 Heating propagation benches

The use of soil warming cables (with a thermostat) provides a stable bottom heat on propagating benches especially when used in conjunction with mist irrigation. The cables are often laid in a sand tray to provide steady heat. The sand should be underlain with a thermal barrier to reduce heat loss and to encourage a more economical use of the heating. A bench temperature of 21° - 24°C is ideal and the cables will maintain this temperature providing that the surrounding air is not too cold. At night and on particularly cold days supplementary heating must be considered which can range from the humble greenhouse paraffin heater up to large fan-assisted propane heaters.

12.3.3 Supplementary lighting for propagating benches

Camplex™ produce a range of lights for propagation. These produce light as close to daylight and yellow spectrum light that are good for germinating seeds. The lights should be switched on, with a time switch, in the mornings and late afternoons so that the transplants think that the days are longer. Depending on the size of lamp they should not be situated less than 1.5m away from the plants.

12.3.4 Choosing suitable varieties for season extension

As this is a newly developing area, the information as to suitable varieties for season extension does not yet exist.

The stockfree-organic grower should be looking for:

- suitability to an early market;
- resistance to bolting;
- resistance to moulds e.g. mildew and botrytis;
- resistance to frost damage;
- ability to stand.

Interestingly, at the Soil Association workshop the origin of the seed was also cited as a factor in season extension. For example, using English potato seed rather than Scottish will bring the season forward by to up two weeks.

12.4 Warming the soil through cultural practices

If seedlings are transplanted into cold soil, they will either sit there or perish. Therefore it is important to warm the soils.

- *Elevation* - hot air rises and cold air will sink to a valley bottom. A site on the brow of a hill, with unimpeded down-slope air drainage to the valley below may be ideal providing a 4–6 week longer season.
- *South facing slopes* – south facing slopes warm up quicker in the spring. The closer to the perpendicular the southern slope is to the angle of the sunlight, the more quickly it warms. Windbreaks should be placed to the north of structures sited on south facing slopes.
- *Solar chimneys* – greenhouses / polytunnels on the vertical of a slope will draw air through them. If both doors are open, the hot air will circulate through the structure and escape; however, if the upper door is closed then the structure will become a passive solar collector. This can be enhanced with long narrow structures.
- *Soil types* – light sandy soils that drain fast will warm up more quickly than heavier clay soils in spring.
- *Soil colour* – dark soils will warm up more quickly than light coloured soils.
- *Windbreaks placed perpendicular to the prevailing wind* will increase soil temperatures. These can be made of commercially available wind break materials, willow, hedges or planted crops e.g. Jerusalem artichoke.

12.5 Warming the soil with plastic mulches

The environmental costs of the manufacture and disposal of plastic mulches are discussed in section 10.3.8. The benefits of black plastic mulches include[10]:

- earlier crop production (7 to 21 days);
- warmer soils;
- higher yields;
- reduced soil splash;
- weed suppression;
- more efficient use of irrigation water;
- decrease in disease;
- better management of certain insect pests.

For successful plant establishment with black plastic mulch, it is important that beds are level, plastic is tightly laid and that irrigation is used. Whilst clear plastic mulches will further increase the soil temperature, weeds will tend to grow underneath it and therefore black plastic mulch is more commonly used by organic growers.

12.6 Warming the soil with paper mulches

Due to its biodegradable nature, the use of a paper mulch can have benefits similar to plastic, but without the disposal problems. However, on organic soils, with their active soil life, the paper can break down too quickly where it is buried. An innovative group in Virginia, US[11] carried out experiments into alternatives to plastic and retarded the degradation of paper mulch by oiling it. This resulted in a transparent mulch and, as with clear plastic, soil temperatures were higher than under black plastic. To combat the weed problem and to prevent the soil from becoming too hot they laid a mulch of hay on the oiled paper mulch several weeks later after the transplants had been planted.

12.7 Season extension in a greenhouse

It is beyond the scope of this book to discuss what constitutes a sound greenhouse structure. Terry Marshall in *Organic tomatoes: the inside story*[12] discusses the direction and angle of structures to capture the winter light following on from research by WJC Lawrence at the John Innes Horticultural Institute in 1948.

- A north to south direction is suitable for main season growing to provide equal light to beds.
- However, an east to west direction is more suitable for season extension as the structure will gain 27% more winter light.
- (For the E to W direction) when glass on the south side is angled at 60°, the light transmission is increased by 63%.

Terry has designed a greenhouse that incorporates these features and discusses all the techniques for making the best use of light.

12.8 Season extension in a polytunnel

Again polytunnel technologies are evolving all the time and so a description of different structures may be out-of-date within just a couple of years. The following generalisations can be made:

- The structure needs to be strong enough to resist the force of the wind and the weight of snow.
- Similar to the greenhouse capturing winter sun the polytunnel should also run from east to west so that one of its curved surfaces captures the southern sun[13].
- The polytunnel should not get too much shade from nearby hedges or trees.
- The polytunnel should not be too large to inhibit air circulation. 7m x 22m with side venting and double doors has been described as an ideal size[14].
- Roll up sides provides a simple method for providing ventilation and shading to assist with the control of temperature and humidity. There are now polytunnels available that can fully open on hot days[15].
- 'Close down' of the sides (if they have vents) and the doors for season extension is important to retain all the heat available in early spring, autumn.

12.9 Fleece protection

These covers are made of spun-bonded polyester and spun-bonded polypropylene and are so light that they float on the crops and do not need to be supported. However, in protected cropping fleeces are better supported with wire hoops to encourage air circulation.

The fabric of fleece is permeable to sunlight, water and air and underneath it provides a microclimate similar to the interior of a greenhouse. The heavier the fleece, the more frost protection afforded and the less likely that it is to rip. Each fleece should last for four years if carefully looked after. It can be used in spring to bring on transplants early or laid over mature autumn crops to reduce frost damage.

- Lay fleeces after transplanting.
- Protected cropping – attach the fleece to wire hoops with clothes pegs.
- Outdoors - weight or bury the edges (although burying can shorten the life of the fleece).
- Ensure that there is enough slack in the fleece to allow for the crop to grow (unless it is already supported by hoops).
- Harden off the crop by gradual removal of the fleece at between four and six weeks.
- Finally remove the fleece on a cloudy day just before rain to avoid shock.
- In self-pollinated crops or leafy vegetables, like outdoor lettuce or cabbage, the covers can be left until harvesting.

The drawbacks of fleeces include:

- the need to lift for overhead irrigation;
- the need to lift for weeding;
- a favourable environment for weed growth;
- a favourable environment for aphids;
- wet fleeces create the ideal habitat for slugs;
- wet fleeces sitting on crop leaves and growing points can damage them (hence the need for supports).

12.10 Air circulation and disease prevention

Poor air circulation in early spring or late autumn can lead to botrytis and other moulds. It is important to use resistant varieties so that the crops have better standing ability in less than ideal conditions.

- Use greenhouses and polytunnels with side vents / side flaps to encourage air circulation low to the ground.
- Air circulation will be poor if the structure is situated in a very sheltered site.
- Vent each morning to remove the overnight moisture.
- Locate the greenhouse or polytunnel on a south-facing slope to encourage

the chimney effect for air circulation (see 12.4).
- Use fans.
- Use drip irrigation rather than overhead sprinklers to reduce humidity.

12.11 Extending storage life of vegetables through removing 'field heat'

According to Josie Bevan[16], after a crop has been harvested it is easy to forget that it is still alive and respiring. The higher the temperature a crop is stored in, the quicker it will respire and degrade. When vegetables are put into storage, the respiration process needs to be slowed down but not stopped altogether. In general, crops which have higher respiration do not store for long and should reach the final consumer as soon as possible. These include:

- fruiting vegetables e.g. tomatoes;
- cauliflower;
- broccoli;
- stem vegetables;
- leafy vegetables;
- root vegetables sold with their leaves.

It is very important to harvest these types of crops in the cool of the morning, below 10°C but even then it may be necessary to remove the field heat from them. The easiest way to remove field heat is to cool the produce using a refrigerated cool store fitted with fans for air circulation. The cooling needs to be carried out as rapidly as possible, without causing chilling injury which will occur at 0.5°C. Once a temperature between 4-8°C is achieved, air movement should be reduced to a lower level. This not only helps to restore a humid layer round the vegetables, preventing drying out, but also allows heat and excess water to vapourise. Perishable vegetables should then be sold fresh.

12.12 Curing vegetables before storage
12.12.1 Maincrop potato curing
- the ideal temperature for curing is between 15°-20°C;
- at a humidity of 85–90 for five to ten days and then stored in their optimum conditions (see 12.15).

12.12.2 Onion and garlic curing

At the simplest level onions and garlic that are grown though black plastic can be cured by uprooting and sitting on top of the plastic or put in chitting trays staked outside in the field. This method will work even in wet autumns but will take longer. Alternatively, they can be laid out on a bench in a greenhouse or polytunnel.

- the ideal temperature for curing is between 30°-40°C;
- at a humidity of 60-75 for four to seven days and then stored in their optimum conditions (see 14.15).

The idea of bulb curing is to remove excess moisture from the crop and therefore ventilation is required. Condensation during this phase is likely to be high and therefore the moisture should be removed quickly and not recycled. The curing also dries the neck of the onion or garlic, leaving the bulbs well sealed with a good skin finish. Onion skins must be dry before loading into ambient barn storage, and they can be stored on the floor up to 50cm deep.

According to Ric Bowers[17], grain drying facilities may be adapted to suit onion drying. Small-scale onion dryers can be built for relatively little capital investment. A main-duct along the outside length and lateral vents running under the drying crop at regular intervals will provide sufficient airflow. The airflow may be regulated to each lateral duct by means of sliding doors. This coupled to an intake fan and heat source is all that is required. Small-scale production systems may use inexpensive space heaters, provided that only paraffin fuel in used in the drying process.

12.12.3 Winter squash curing

Curing winter squashes and pumpkins is achieved by exposing the fruits to the sun for seven to ten days in a protected structure, which will allow the skin to dry and toughen. Fruits will not store if they are exposed to frost in this period.

If this is not possible they should be stored in chitting trays stacked up in a insulated building and subjected to a temperature of around 15°C for ten to fourteen days then reduced to 10-12°C. Regular ventilation is essential during the first two weeks. With ideal conditions and suitable varieties they can be kept until the following May, even June on occasions.

12.14 Storage clamps and ambient barn storage

In the case of crops that naturally store for a long time the stockfree-organic grower can work with nature. Carrots, parsnips, artichoke, celeriac, cabbage and swede can be left in the field until they are needed, although they may need some frost protection e.g. thick straw mulch. These should be harvested prior to sale and should not be barn stored for more than a couple of weeks.

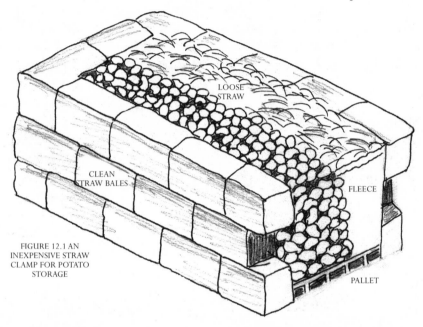

FIGURE 12.1 AN INEXPENSIVE STRAW CLAMP FOR POTATO STORAGE

LOOSE STRAW

CLEAN STRAW BALES

FLEECE

PALLET

Potatoes and beetroot can be stored for longer periods in clamps. Onions, shallots and garlic can be stored in barns. Crops stored in clamps and barns are susceptible to frost damage, so it is important to insulate them with straw and fleece. The heat generated by the crop can be put to good use, which will reduce the risk of frost damage. Unfortunately, insulating has the disadvantage of restricting air flow and enabling temperatures to rise above the optimum for long term storage. Clamps and ambient stores should, therefore, have a means of ventilating cool air from outside into the store. Straw clamps can be set up at little expenses and should store potatoes and beetroot adequately until the end of March. To carry storage vegetables into April and beyond requires refrigerated storage (see 12.15).

12.15 Optimum conditions for storage vegetables[18]

Whatever the type of storage and whatever the vegetable, it is vital that only good quality, disease-free crops are used. Rots are likely to occur where there is freestanding water in a refrigeration unit, so efforts should be made to vent condensation or to absorb it[19].

Table 12.2 Optimum storage for season extension vegetables

Vegetable	Temperature °C	Relative Humidity %	Storage life
Potato main crop	3 – 5	90 – 95	5 – 10 mths
Swede	0	98 - 100	4 – 6 mths
Kohl rabi	0	98 - 100	2 – 3 mths
Onion	0	65 - 70	1 – 8 mths
Shallot	0	65 - 70	6 – 7 mths
Garlic	0	65 - 70	6 – 7 mths
Parsnip	0	98 - 100	4 – 6 mths
Carrot maincrop	0	98 - 100	7 – 9 mths
Celeriac	0	97 -99	6 – 8 mths
Winter squash	10	50 - 70	up to 8 mths
Pumpkin	10	50 - 70	2 – 3 mths
Main crop beetroot	0	98 - 100	4 – 6 mths

1   Soil Association personal communication. Chapter 14 discusses developing local markets and chapter 15 discusses food access through community development initiatives.
2   BACHMANN J & EARLES R (2000) Season Extension Techniques for Market Gardeners. ATTRA – Horticulture Technical notes.
3   SOIL ASSOCIATION (2003) - Extending the Season 15.10.03, Growing with Grace, Clapham, Lancashire.
4   Under stockfree-organic standard 7.3(a) greenhouse and polytunnel monocropping of annual crops is restricted.
5   SCHOFIELD A (2003) Extending the Season. Workshop 15.10.03 organised by the Soil Association.
6   This section does not include storage vegetables for season extension.
7   STOPES C et al (1988) The Nitrate Content of Vegetable and Salad Crops Offered to the Consumer as from Organic and Conventional Production Systems.
8   MOWATT H Healthy Vegetable Transplants. Organic Farming. 64: 22-23
9   Personal communication with Alan Schofield of Growing with Nature, Pilling, Preston.
10 Adapted from BACHMANN J & EARLES R (2000) Season Extension Techniques for Market Gardeners. ATTRA – Horticulture Technical notes.

11 SCHONBECK M (1995) Mulching Choices for Warm Season Vegetables. The Virginia Biological Farmer. Spring 16-18. and ANDERSON DF et al (1995) Evaluation of a Paper Mulch made from Recycled Materials as an Alternative to PlasticFilm Mulch for Vegetables. Journal of Sustainable Agriculture. Spring 16-18.
12 MARSHALL T (1999) Organic Tomatoes the Inside Story. Harris Associates.
13 WELLS OS (1995) High Tunnels for Early Spring or Late Fall Production of Tomatoes and Other Crops. New England Vegetable and Small Fruit Newsletter. March 5-7.
14 SCHOFIELD A (2003) Extending the Season. Workshop 15.10.03 organised by the Soil Association.
15 Haygrove Tunnels were sponsors of the Soil Association workshops.
16 BEVAN J (1997) Storage-Extending Availability. New Farmer and Grower. Summer 23-25.
17 BOWERS R (1999) Elm Farm Bulletin 43.
18 Adapted from MAYNARD DN & HOCHMUTH GJ (1997) Knott's Handbook for Vegetable Growers. Fourth Edition. John Wiley and Sons Inc.
19 e.g. when cold storing potatoes place a loose layer of straw 50cm thick over the stack to absorb the moisture.

Chapter Thirteen

The marketing of stockfree-organic produce

13.1 Conversion Periods

Once you have rented or bought land, before produce can be sold as stockfree-organic it needs to go through a 24-month conversion period. This is an opportunity for you to allow the soil to rebuild its organic matter levels and fertility, especially if it has been under an intensive conventional cropping regime. After a period of twelve months the produce can be sold as 'in conversion', but this is not recommended. As the stockfree-organic system that you will be operating in the future will not generally rely on outside inputs, it is the recommendation of organic advisors that the land is put into a fertility-building ley for two years to allow successful and self-sustaining cropping in Year Three.

Whilst a two-year delay may seem frustrating, it is important to look on it as a time to build up your experience, visit other organic farmers, attend seminars and conferences, discuss with advisors and farmers and read available literature. Many other growers keep paid employment, so that they can fund the building of the farm's infrastructure and wildlife habitats for predator / pest balance in the future. It is better to start the project with as little debt as possible.

The rest of the chapter presumes that the grower is in a position to sell their produce.

13.2 Why direct marketing

In the UK the area for organic fruit and vegetable production accounts for only 2% of all organic land. However, sales of organic fruit and vegetables make up about 31% of all organic sales in the UK with around 55% at the wholesale level being provided for by imports from abroad[1]. Food from abroad, coupled with the associated 'food miles', indicates the potential for more home growing and more direct marketing. This chapter outlines different marketing options and weighs up their advantages and disadvantages, ranking them in terms of level of involvement, time and resources.

13.3 Selling to the wholesale market (least involved)

In the past 50 years the fresh produce marketing system has become highly sophisticated, with wholesalers, packers, multiple retail outlets and the supermarkets becoming worldwide operations[2]. Improved transportation and communication systems, as well as uniform grading and packing standards, has allowed wholesale buyers to shop throughout the world to find the produce and price they desire.

It cannot be emphasised enough that it is essential to secure a market outlet prior to growing a crop, as growing on speculation carries a high risk to the grower. If you are selling large volumes or do not have an existing market, it will be necessary to sell wholesale. Wholesalers will be looking for:

- a grower who will specialise, providing a consistent flow of produce over the entire growing season. Buyers often prefer not to deal with a seller on an occasional basis;
- specific quality and volume;
- low prices;
- the grower to act as a knowledgeable salesperson, who can provide future supply information, help arrange transportation and answer questions.

When selling wholesale, your enterprise will depend on your skills as a seller. If you are new to this form of marketing, it is important that you agree the following with the wholesaler:

- desired characteristics (variety, grade, size);
- ordering procedures;
- packaging. If it is organic it may need pre-packing;
- weekly purchase volume;

- preferred transportation methods;
- prices paid;
- payment schedule.

Setting the price is one of the most important skills you must acquire, as you must earn an acceptable return. You must know, by speaking to other growers and other wholesalers:

- break-even price and the related volume you must sell to achieve it;
- prevailing market prices;
- your produce quality relative to your competitors;
- purchasing options of buyers.

13.4 Direct selling to restaurants, schools and shops

Selling directly to restaurants, schools and shops eliminates one or two middlemen. By assuming this traditional wholesaler function, the grower can keep the profit that normally goes to the wholesaler. Chefs and restaurant owners may be willing to make the extra effort to get high-quality and speciality items, but they demand the same consistent quality and service from the grower that they can get from a wholesaler i.e. different vegetable lines, frequent deliveries, convenient ordering and expert advice.

Advantages for the grower include:

- price higher than selling to wholesalers;
- possible outlet for speciality produce;
- more precise production planning.

Disadvantages for the grower include:

- high level of off-farm customer service;
- competition from wholesalers who have speciality sales staff;
- need for wide variety of produce;
- low per-customer sales volume.

13.5 Farmers' markets

Farmers' markets are a gathering point for farmers to sell locally grown and other speciality produce (e.g. jams and pickles) to local consumers.

Advantages for growers include:

- collective selling attracts more customers, because of the convenience of having a variety of produce;
- selling large volumes very quickly;
- publicity for other ventures e.g. to recruit more box scheme members;
- direct contact with consumers;
- entertainment e.g. street artists to attract more customers.

Disadvantages for growers include:

- downward competitive pressure because price comparison is easy and many customers are 'bargain hunters' especially when it comes to vegetables;
- time away from growing;
- difficult to get salespeople with good people skills;
- limited market days mean that farmers' markets are not likely to be the only selling strategy.

13.6 Farm shops

The farm stall or shop is the classic way of adding value to farm produce. Retail outlets can range from a temporary stall selling seasonal produce to a full-scale, full-time 'supermarket'. Location is all important, but so too is the commitment to retailing. The public expect farm shops to be open at weekends and on summer evenings and good service and image are essential. This can therefore represent a severe intrusion to a grower's privacy.

Quality, attractiveness and freshness are major selling points of the farm shop, as is the need to adhere to stringent hygiene measures. Location is essential to the success of a farm shop, but a good location may mean local competition from other farm shops. Shops near villages or towns are more likely to get regular custom than sites off the beaten track.

The ideal site will have:

- a visible entrance from a busy road;

- good access and car parking;
- attractive buildings, e.g. converted traditional farm;
- distinctive selling points e.g. speciality produce, seasonal produce or below average price bulk goods.

Before getting established the farm shop may require:

- planning permission if products are bought in to resell;
- planning permission for a building's change of use;
- planning permission for signposting;

and will require the observance of the Health Regulations, Food & Hygiene Acts and the Weights & Measures Act.

Financing a farm shop also needs careful consideration. A high turnover will be needed to repay the following investments and costs:

Capital costs:

- Building conversion / construction.
- Counters / chill cabinets / freezers.
- Till.
- Van, if goods need to be collected or delivered.
- Connection of services.

Revenue costs:

- Permanent staff.
- Casual labour.
- Council tax.
- Heat and light.
- Insurance.
- Stock wastage.
- Loss leaders.
- Maintenance.

Trade may also prove to be highly seasonal, with implications for cash flow.

13.7 Share schemes and box schemes (most involved)
13.7.1 Defining Community Supported Agriculture (CSA)

According to the Centre for Integrated Agricultural Systems (USA), unlike conventional agriculture, in which farmers bear the risks of weather, pests and the market place alone, in CSA the entire community shares both bounty and scarcity. In its simplest term CSA is a partnership between farmers and consumers.

Community supported agriculture began in the early 1950s in Germany, Switzerland and Japan as a response to concerns about food safety. Japan, for example, has more than 600 producer-consumer co-operatives that supply food to more than eleven million people. In Britain CSA has been slower to take off. The Soil Association runs a support service to CSAs available at www.cuco.org.uk. The *Cultivating Communities*[3] website is a resource for all community-based local food initiatives. It is intended as a networking tool to encourage CSA practitioners to share their experiences and information.

CSAs are well known for fostering connections between rural and urban communities. Many could not function without core support from committed volunteers. Members can visit their CSA farms and help plan and harvest crops. Many farms host open days, produce newsletters and hold workshops that educate members about sustainable farming.

13.7.2 Share schemes
There are several versions of CSA – the two most popular in the UK are the 'share scheme' and the traditional 'box scheme'. In the former members become shareholders paying a fee (between £100 and £500) at the beginning of the growing season to meet a holding's operating expenses for the forthcoming year. In return members receive a box of produce throughout the growing season, distributed via the usual box scheme routes.

The directors of NyKA, the Open Garden Foundation, Hungary, have produced the definitive 'CSA: a farmer's manual – how to start up and run a CSA' which has recently been translated from Hungarian[4]. If you are considering share farming you will really need to read this. Chapter 3 looks at How to get started and urges growers to:

1. Decide what kind of farmer you are.
2. Decide on what you have to offer.
3. Have you thought of going organic?
4. Finding your customers.
5. Get help.
6. Decide on the best-fit CSA.
7. Timing.
8. Preparing promotional materials.
9. Launching your CSA.
10. Preparing lists of consumers.
11. Producing the harvest.
12. Distribution.
13. Feedback and communication.

13.7.3 Box schemes

Box schemes are different from share schemes because customers tend to have less input into the farm enterprise. Instead they pay for their vegetables on a weekly basis in a traditional retailer / consumer relationship. In this situation it is the farmer who takes the risk. However, from an operational point of view there are many similarities between share schemes and box schemes and the two can be examined in the same way.

According to Tim Deane[5] advantages for growers include:

- control - direct contact with customers;
- very fresh produce reaching customers;
- breadth of cropping - reduced financial risk from individual crop failures;
- diversity of cropping - advantages for rotation;
- reduction of pest and disease problems;
- utilisation of all farm produce - allows sales of irregular amounts of minor crops;
- reduced waste - allows sale of what may be classed otherwise as out-grades;
- financial security - defaults on payments (unlikely) would not be catastrophic;
- financial stability - projections of income can be made with confidence;

- maximised income - cut out middle man and receive a fairer return;
- reduced costs - packaging, transport, commission;
- absence of continual marketing, once customer base is established;
- grower satisfaction - positive feedback as opposed to neutral or negative when trading wholesale, socialising with customers;
- steady enterprise growth - a scheme should allow for expansion if that is the goal;
- direct sales possible without need for major road frontage.

Disadvantages for growers include:

- complexity of cropping required to ensure enticing boxes all year;
- requirement for personal involvement, imagination and attention to detail;
- high labour demand and no economies of scale, therefore high variable costs;
- length of season - harvest not confined to peak periods;
- space required for packing and storage;
- dealing with a lot of individual customers - growers often complain that they spend more time with administration and packing duties than growing;
- need for a core group of organisers and often voluntary help.

The Soil Association has produced two very useful publications: '*Setting up an organic box scheme*' and '*Growing organic vegetables for a box scheme*'.

13.8 Tips for a successful CSA

The rest of the chapter aims to help you to decide your CSA policies and is based on the experience of several different schemes in the UK. Throughout the discussions the growing is separated from the marketing which includes packing, distribution and promotion.

Experienced box scheme operatives have collectively come up with the following assumptions about growing:

1. One acre produces enough produce to fill 25 - 30 boxes a week (Tim Deane).
2. One person full-time can manage 2.5 acres of market garden with machinery (Eliot Coleman).
3. That same person can manage the picking and packing for a hundred customers with part time help on packing days (Tim Deane) or fifty customers without help (Organic Growers of Durham).

4. One acre of crops (including intensive and protected cropping) could provide a turnover of at least £9,000 per annum.

Working on these assumptions it should be possible to predict whether it is feasible for you to start a CSA. However, be warned that the marketing can instantly erode any financial returns you make on the growing, if it is not carefully planned:

1. Aim to set a price that will give a fair return to the growing enterprise (horticultural costs and wages for growing and harvesting) and the marketing (packhouse, van and wage costs for packing and distribution).
2. If you wish to make your organic vegetable boxes affordable, e.g. a small box for around the £6 mark (2005 prices), then you must ensure packing and distribution costs are about 10% of the total cost. When those costs approach 30% you will need to put up to an extra delivery charge for each box.

Other considerations that will effect the assumptions are:

*   allowing preferences - instantly incurs an administration charge and adds to the work load of the packers for larger schemes;
*   whether to weigh produce - many schemes fill by eye but this may incur trading standards implications;
*   buying in produce from other growers or from wholesalers will affect returns. Aim to add between 70 to 100% on bought-in produce to cover your handling and distribution costs;
*   hungry gap (late April, May and early June) - will you run throughout the year or close during the hungry gap? Running during the hungry gap will reduce the financial viability of the marketing side because you may need to buy in produce. However, to stop supply may mean that valuable customers are lost.
*   distribution policy – delivery to collection points will inevitably be cheaper than door to door deliveries (see 13.10.1).

13.9 Budgeting for a CSA
To illustrate the financial planning for a fully operational box scheme, a fictional case study Joe Bloggs Organics is described. Roger and Lily have rented ten acres of land on a ten year lease and have put it into stockfree-organic conversion (see

13.1) in 2002. During this time they have employed contractors to keep the fertility building ley (red clover and rye) regularly mowed and have carried on in their regular paid employment to provide capital investment in the project.

£	Scenario 1 200 customers	Scenario 2 250 customers	Scenario 3 300 customers	Assumptions
Table 13.1 Projected sales and costs[6]				
Projected sales for 45 weeks closing during the hungry gap	63,000.00	78,750.00	94,500.00	Mean price of a bag £7.00
Start up costs spread over 5 years with 10% interest	7913.40	7913.40	7913.40	See Table 15.2
Annual growing costs	60,997.60	60,997.60	60,997.60	See Table 15.2
Annual marketing costs	18656.40	18656.40	18656.40	See Table 15.2
Gross margin before tax	- 24,567.40	- 8,817.40	+ 6,932.60	

They have split the field into three distinctive areas:

1. protected cropping (0.5 acre) where they have put a large polytunnel;
2. garden crops (1.5 acre) surrounded by a windbreak and newly planted hedge
3. the field (nine acres) with wildlife strips, a fence and newly planted hedge.

During the conversion period Roger and Lilly have offered their time

Table 13.2 Costings (2001-2003)

Type	Description	Cost	Subtotal
Start up costs spread over five years with 10% interest			
	Clover seed	375.00	
	Contractors establishment	225.00	
	Contractors three mowings for two years	270.00	
	Fencing	5,000.00	
	Hedges	1,000.00	
	Trees	500.00	
	Windbreak	2,000.00	
	30ft x 100ft Polytunnels	3,200.00	
	2nd hand small greenhouse for transplant raising	500.00	
	Rotavator	800.00	
	Transplant raising equipment	400.00	
	2nd hand tractor	6,000.00	
	Tractor implements	2,000.00	
	Manual tools	400.00	
	Hoes and seed drill	300.00	
	Wheel barrows and carts	200.00	
	Building for packing	3,500.00	
	Benches	300.00	
	Scales	500.00	
	Irrigation	2,500.00	
	Promotional leaflets	500.00	
	2nd hand caravan / canteen	500.00	
	2nd hand van	5000.00	35970.00
	Add 10% interest on borrowed money	3597.00	39567.00
	TOTAL PER ANNUM		7913.40
Annual growing costs			
	Rent for five acres	500.00	
	Certification	600.00	
	Insurance	400.00	

Type	Description	Cost	Subtotal
	90% of Roger's wages	11,754.00	
	90% of Lilly's wages	11,754.00	
	90% of two employees wages	23,508.00	
	National insurance	4,701.60	
	Insurance	400.00	
	Pensions	1410.00	
	Seeds	400.00	
	Compost	300.00	
	Water	1000.00	
	Heating and lighting	100.00	
	Fertilisers e.g. seaweed	100.00	
	General services and repairs	500.00	
	Fuel	500.00	
	Plastic mulches and fleeces	150.00	
	Miscellaneous horticultural expenses	200.00	
	Depreciation on machinery 20%	1760.00	
	Depreciation on polytunnel 30%	960.00	60,997.60
Annual marketing cost			
	10% of Roger's wages	1306.00	
	10% of Lilly's wages	1306.00	
	90% of two employees wages	2612.00	
	National insurance	522.40	
	Pensions	160.00	
	Heat for pack house	50.00	
	Packaging	500.00	
	Fuel	500.00	
	Newsletters	100.00	
	Phone	300.00	
	Postage	300.00	
	Depreciation on van 20%	1000.00	
	Buying in vegetables	10,000.00	18656.40
	TOTAL		87,567.40

voluntarily to the project.

In 2003 they begin cropping and employ two members of staff. They have set a pricing policy of veggie bags for £6 and £10 and expect to sell more of the smaller bag. They anticipate that they can grow enough for 270 – 300 bags a week and may need to buy in occasional produce.

Roger and Lily can make the Joe Bloggs Organics box scheme financially viable between 280 and 300 bags of vegetables. To gain more income they could always raise the price of the bags, charge visitors for educational visits or try to extend production during the hungry gap. Conversely, to reduce costs they could accept a lower wage, reduce staffing by cultivating a smaller acreage, not invest as much in the initial start up costs, 'muddling through' (which is what most growers do) or buy less bought in vegetables. However, they might need to pay for extra help, especially on packing and harvesting days, and so this would affect the annual marketing costs.

13.10 Case studies of selling mechanisms for stockfree-organic growers featured in Growing Green International
Interestingly, none of the growers featured in Growing Green International are currently selling through the wholesale, packers or supermarket routes. Many of them started out this way, but actually found direct marketing through CSA, box schemes or restaurants to be the lifeblood of their enterprises.

Stockfree-organic systems are not suited to the specialist growing of a few crops. Wholesale selling requires some level of monoculture and probable high percentage of grade-outs. Because the Stockfree-Organic Standards restrict the use of biological insecticides, stockfree-organic systems cannot withstand the same level of monoculture as can some traditional organic systems selling in bulk quantities. It is difficult to see how stockfree-organic growing systems can operate without complex rotations and cropping variety (e.g. usually about 50 different vegetables) to spread the risk of pest attack and other failures. When growing organically, if diversity (as opposed to monoculture) is the key, the produce is better suited to marketing locally.

13.10.1 Example of collection points -Tolhurst Organic Produce, Reading
We never considered doing a doorstep delivery service when we were starting

up because so much of the effort would need to go into marketing and the price of the organic vegetables would rise. At Tolhurst Organic Produce only 10% of the labour time goes into marketing and that is why we can sell our vegetable bags so cheaply (2006 prices) - £5.50 (5-7 items), £7.25 (6-8 items) and £10.00 (10+ items).

The growers liaise with two co-ordinators - one in Reading and one in Oxford. The co-ordinators get 5% of sales and in turn they liaise with the neighbourhood representatives.

The neighbourhood reps were found by placing adverts in health food shops, libraries and community centres (anywhere where likely supporters congregate). Each neighbourhood rep takes a delivery of between twelve and fifteen bags at their house and then individual customers collect them from there. This brings in the social element of the box scheme.

A van driver, with his own van, is paid £5 a drop off. All customers have to pay one week in advance, so that, if they fail to collect the bag, the neighbourhood rep already has the money. They do not have any difficulty in recruiting new neighbourhood reps, who are paid in vegetables, and, if they make sales of over £100, they are also paid a 2.5 percentage. The commitment from the neighbourhood rep involves between a half and one hour's work a week.

13.10.2 Example of doorstep deliveries - Growing with Grace, North Yorkshire

Based on the model of doorstep deliveries pioneered by Growing with Nature, Lancashire, the Growing with Grace bag scheme provides organic vegetables to parts of Northern and Eastern Lancashire, as well as some of the Yorkshire Dales (Ribblesdale and part of Wharfedale). The scheme is an invaluable resource to these rural communities. There has been much success with a multi-drop initiative in partnership with local post offices, winning Growing with Grace a prestigious National Food Award. This scheme not only saves on delivery miles but also supports small businesses and gets the local community more involved.

13.11 Need for pyramid structures within direct marketing

If you decide to set up a CSA scheme, the first step is to carry out some research to find out about similar schemes that already exist locally. There are grants to help with feasibility studies and marketing outlined in the *Organic Farm Management Handbook*[7]. Then providing that you are happy to go ahead, it is time to promote your idea locally. Speak to potential customers - playgroups, gardening groups, health groups (e.g. cancer support) and environmental groups. The best way is to get several articles in the local newspaper or even a spot on the regional news programme.

Even if you do not decide to go down the share scheme route it is important to set up pyramid structures, rather than delivering to each customer individually. Your aim must be to create a quality product that is something more than just a box of vegetables. Our system at Tolhurst Organic Produce involves 'neighbourhood representatives', who are given free vegetables in return for finding customers and acting as multiple drop points, thus adding a social dimension. What we have found is that the vegetables have become a catalyst for encouraging community spirit.

1 SOIL ASSOCIATION (2003) Personal communication.
2 PACIFIC NORTHWEST EXTENSION PUBLICATION. Marketing Alternatives for Speciality Produce.
3 Soil Association, Bristol House, 40-56 Victoria Street, Bristol, BS1 6BY. Tel: 0117 9142425, Email:csa@cuco.org.uk
4 Available from the Soil Association Publications.
5 Adapted and reprinted with kind permission from Elm Farm Bulletin.
6 The costs incurred are intended to be illustrative as opposed to exhaustive.
7 OFMH is regularly updated by LAMPKIN N, MEASURES M and PADEL S and is produced by the University of Wales, Aberystwyth and the Organic Advisory Service at Elm Farm.

Chapter Fourteen

Conclusion

As stated in the introduction sustainability depends on three things: perpetuity, reproducibility and education. The techniques in this book: animal-free food production combined with local consumption, are a toolkit for sustainability. Its comprehensive nature means that it can be used as a constant reference guide becoming any grower's best friend. Once established the stockfree-organic system will reward you with healthier crops, less weeds, pests and diseases.

Nothing in agriculture can be assured to last forever. However, the systems-based approach to soil health, which is essentially a third of this book, is a significant advancement in setting up agricultural systems that can last a long time. Eliminating brought-in fertility is a wonderful way to concentrate your mind on sustaining fertility. It has become increasingly difficult to obtain suitable sources of animal manure for organic systems: its transport, composting and subsequent application is awkward and expensive for the small grower. Future organic legislation is likely to require that the majority of the fertility is created on the holding. This will increase this burden further and for many growers will make the buying in of fertility almost impossible. No sensible self-sustaining organic farmer will be reckless enough to sell his own fertility.

No longer will organic farmers be able to prop up leaky and poorly managed nutrients systems by external inputs. More sustainable rotations, increased use of green manures, better tillage practice, soil management and where appropriate plant-based composts and chipped branch wood are much more sustainable alternatives to poaching other farms fertility. It has been clearly shown that the use of green manures as a primary fertility builder will make significant improvements to soil organic matter levels. You will get a real buzz seeing small earthworms thriving under the mulch of green manures. The health of the soil is central to the whole system.

To achieve these tremendous advances organic producers will need the latest up to date information. This book is invaluable to growers, students and researchers alike. The chapters about fertility, propagation, rotations, weed, pest and disease, environmental conservation, crop care and season extension are at the cutting edge of organic innovation. Organic growers can now conserve fossil fuel resources and have the tools to measure and prove it.

The public are becoming aware of the limitations of increasing global consumption of animal products. If we are to feed a growing world population then we have to reduce animal consumption, there simply is not enough land to go around. Imagine in the UK if every horticultural and cereal growing holding were to convert to organic production and rely on animal inputs or if the Chinese population were to consume as much animal produce as the average American - then there simply would not be enough land to go around. Stockfree-organics is all about optimising land use.

The organic market is still driven primarily by fruit and vegetables and therefore organic growers are the life blood of the organic movement. They have often been responsible for bringing about big changes in the way the movement operates and the policy it adopts, striving for innovation in both marketing and standards. Organic growers have pioneered many aspects of organics over the years and continue to adapt and survive with the ever increasing pressures that the market place thrusts upon us. So we are confident that some of you will wish to bring about this exciting new aspect of organic production. Sure you will have questions and maybe even some doubts but the dawn of a new era for agriculture is upon us.

Iain Tolhurst and Jenny Hall
January 2006

Stockfree-Organic Services
20 Hawthorn Avenue, Orrell, Wigan, WN5 8NQ. Tel: 01942 621769
Email: sowandgroworganics@phonecoop.coop

Appendix 1

About the Vegan Organic Network – sponsors of this book

www.veganorganic.net

In 1996 a small group active in horticulture and community action started an informal group called the Vegan Organic network known as VON. This group aimed to co-operate in providing practical information about vegan-organic growing which can be broadly defined as growing food in a:

"sustainable environmentally friendly way without the use of any animal manures or slaughterhouse by-products or other animal remains and without the use of artificial chemicals or genetically modified material."

From the outset they saw vegan organics not as a single issue campaign, but as an integrated international movement. Their vision went beyond the central aim of vegan cultivation; it also embraced an alternative view of market economics, of cooperation, and a movement for land reform and redistribution.

In order to increase public awareness, VON members established a charitable trust in May 2000. The Vegan Organic Network is registered with the Charity Commission, registration number 1080847. Whilst VON is registered in the UK, its constitution allows for operation in any part of the world. The stated object of the charity is:

"to advance the education of the general public in the principles of vegan organic horticulture and agriculture, in particular but not exclusively through the undertaking of research into such horticulture and agriculture and disseminating the results of this research for the public benefit."

The Vegan Organic Network is a non-profit making registered charity (1080847) and a company limited by guarantee (3869080). The annual report and accounts are available and these list the names of the trustees / directors, officers, and financial structure. The Articles and Memorandum of the Charitable Company allow for the usual powers of such organisations, including the facility to acquire property, co-operate with other bodies including other charities. In keeping with their ethical concerns VON banks with Triodos Bank and can reclaim tax paid on certain donations in the UK and some other countries. Annual accounts are examined by independent accountants, and a copy of the latest accounts is available.

Achievements to date of VON have been done on an unpaid voluntary basis.

- *International network of supporters* - Growing Green International (biannual 40-paged magazine) and a regular news bulletin are informative growing-centred publications sent to 500 worldwide supporters who pay their subscriptions. They also have an email discussion group with daily postings. VON has supporters in most EU countries including France, Germany, Ireland, Spain, Portugal, Denmark, Sweden, Hungary, and Greece and worldwide in the USA and Canada. There are also a German-speaking network Biovegan and a French-speaking network Végéculture. VON has arranged support and publicity for projects in Sierra Leone, Uganda, Gujerat and Malawi.
- *Stockfree-Organic Symbol* - VON made a subtle change from the term most widely used in animal free agriculture which is stockless to stockfree. This change was considered to be more positive and progressive. The world's first commercial holding Tolhurst Organic Produce was inspected to the Stockfree-Organic Symbol on the 8th November 2004. VON has contracted the inspection and certification functions to Soil Association Certification Ltd so that it is possible for growers to hold the Soil Association and Stockfree-Organic symbols simultaneously in accordance with EU regulations. VON has now set up a new department, Stockfree Organic Services – 20 Hawthorn Avenue, Orrell, Wigan, WN5 8NQ. Tel: 01942 621769 Email: sowandgroworganics@phonecoop.coop
- *Educational material* - As well as Growing Green International VON produces fact sheets on every aspect of stockfree-organic systems. These are available from the website at www.veganorganic.net VON has also co-operated with HDRA - the Organic Association to produce a publication for the Third World Organic Support Group. For commercial growers VON has produced a twenty-paged booklet on stockfree-organic

techniques and is currently making a video to accompany this book.

- *Establishing an education, research and demonstration centre* – It is a long-term aim for VON to establish a purpose-built centre. In 2003, the Movement for Compassionate Living offered VON a substantial legacy towards a building. Since then VON has been fortunate to have received other donations.
- *Local food growing training* - VON has provided 4 weekend courses for growers and gardeners which have been held in Manchester, Darlington, Bolton and Wigan. The courses have covered composting, green manuring, rotation planning, how to grow 60 different vegetables, propagation, greenhouse care, pest and disease control, weed control, gardening for wildlife, agroforestry and permaculture design. VON has also assisted in the publicity of courses run by its members.
- *Farm visits and farm networks* - Seeing is believing! 2005 will see the seventh year of farm visits. VON has arranged for many students to get fulfilling and practical work experience with farmers. Many of whom have gone onto set up their own projects.
- *Professional advisors* – VON has an advisory panel to assist commercial growers to convert to stockfree-organic. VON's work follows on from that of Elm Farm Research Centre, ADAS Terrington and Co-operative Wholesale Society at Leicester. VON particularly recommends the consultancy services of Iain Tolhurst.

VON is now trying to create the demand for animal free food grown in accordance with their Standards. It can only do so successfully through widespread publicity and with the cooperation of like minded people and organisations. The task involves creating the demand from growers. Currently the main source of such food is via box schemes. These will continue to grow and make a crucially important contribution both in supplying need, involving the community, generating employment and by demonstrating an alternative system of marketing. It is, nevertheless, important that stockfree-organically grown food is also made widely available.

The Stockfree Organic Standards offer an ethical and pragmatic beacon of light for the future of food production. However, food production is but one aspect of a dynamic culture which embraces justice for people, animals and the environment in a sustainable balance. To achieve this VON perceives that we must change our lifestyles and introduce a philosophy which will continue to maintain our unique planet. Members of VON are motivated by the awareness of a great unease in society that we are moving towards a world that can no longer sustain life in the natural way it has always evolved. Thus supporters attempt to come to grips with politics and ethics in everyday living. It has been said that until compassion embraces all living beings we will not find peace.

Appendix 2

Select bibliography

- BACHMANN, J & EARLES, R (2000) Season extension techniques for market gardeners. ATTRA – Horticulture Technical notes.
- BALSARI, P et al (2002) Mechanical and physical weed control in maize. 5th European Weed Research Society workshop on Physical Weed Control.
- BLAKE, F (1987) Organic farming and growing. Crowood Press.
- BLEEKER, P et al (2002) Experiences and experiments with new inter row weeders. 5th European Weed Research Society workshop on Physical Weed Control.
- BURNETT, G Permaculture – a beginner's guide. Permanent publications.
- COLEMAN, E (1995) New Organic Grower. A master's manual of tools and techniques for the home and market gardener. Chelsea Green publishing.
- COLEMAN, E (1999) Four Season Harvest. Chelsea Green publishing.
- DALZIEL OBRIEN, R (1956) Intensive gardening. Faber.
- DURNING, AH and BROUGH, HB (1992) Reforming the Livestock Economy in BROWN, LR (ed) State of the World. WorldWatch Institute.
- ELM FARM RESEARCH CENTRE (1984) The Soil.
- FERN, K (1997) Plants for a Future. Edible & useful plants for a healthier world. Permanent publications.
- FINCH, S & EDMONDS, GH (1994) Undersowing cabbage crops with clover – effects on pest insects, ground beetles and crop yields. IOBC / WPRS Bulletin 17(8) 159 – 167.
- HART, R (1997) Forest Gardening. Green Books.
- HAYES, M and KINGA, M (2001) Community Supported Agriculture (CSA): a farmer's manual – how to set up and run a CSA. Godollo.
- HILLS, L (1977) Organic Gardening. Penguin Books.
- JANNAWAY, K Abundant living in the coming age of the tree. Movement for Compassionate Living.
- JANNAWAY, K Self-reliant tree-based autonomous vegan villages (STAVV). Movement for Compassionate Living.
- KING, J (1997) Reaching for the Sun: How Plants Work. Cambridge University Press.
- KUEPPER, G & ADAM, K (2002) Organic Potting Mixes for Certified Production. Horticulture Technical Note of ATTRA.
- LAMPKIN, NH (1990) Organic Farming. Farming Press.

- LAMPKIN NH, MEASURES, M and PADEL, S (regular updates) Organic Farm Management Handbook. University of Wales, Aberystwyth and the Organic Advisory Service at Elm Farm.
- LANGLEY, G (1995) Vegan Nutrition. Vegan Society.
- LARKOM, J (1998) Oriental Vegetables. John Murray.
- LARKOM, J (1995) Salads for small gardens. Hamlyn.
- LEAKE, AR (2001) Performance of organic arable rotations: a UK experience. Available at www.teagasc.ie/publications/2001/tillageconference/paper06.htm
- MARSHALL, T (1999) Organic Tomatoes the inside story. Harris Associates.
- MERFIELD, C (2002) Organic weed management: a practical guide. Available at www.merfield.com/research/organic-weed-management-a-practical-guide.pdf
- PACIFIC NORTHWEST EXTENSION PUBLICATION. Marketing Alternatives for Speciality Produce.
- PEARCE, B et al (2004) Alternative non-animal based nutrient sources, for organic plant raising. Elm Farm Bulletin 71: 7-10
- PEARS, P & STICKLAND, S (1995) Organic Gardening: The Royal Horticultural Society Encyclopaedia of Practical Gardening. Mitchell Beazley.
- PIMENTEL, D & M (1979) Food Energy and Society. Resources & Environmental Science Series.
- PIMENTEL, D (1980) Handbook of Energy Utilisation in Agriculture. CRC Press.
- PRETTY, J (1988) The Living Land. Earthscan publications.
- PULLEN, M (2004) Valuable Vegetables: Growing for Pleasure or Profit. Eco-logic books.
- RYRIE, C (2001) Pests. Gaia books.
- SOIL ASSOCIATION - Organic Lettuce Production. Soil Association Technical Guides.
- SOIL ASSOCIATION - Setting up an organic box scheme. Soil Association Technical Guides.
- SOIL ASSOCIATION - Growing organic vegetables for a box scheme. Soil Association Technical Guides.
- SOIL ASSOCIATION (1999) Organic Carrot Production – Soil Association Technical Guides.
- SOIL ASSOCIATION (2002) Improving biodiversity on organic farms. Soil

Association Technical Guides.
- STOUT, R (1961) Gardening without work.
- WALKER, J (2003) Weeds an earth friendly guide to their identification, use and control. Cassell Illustrated.
- WALSH, S (2003) Plant based nutrition and health. The Vegan Society.

Select journals
- GROWING GREEN INTERATIONAL – magazine of the Vegan Organic Network
- INFORMATION LEAFLETS from the VEGAN ORGANIC NETWORK
- ELM FARM RESEARCH CENTRE BULLETIN
- NEW LEAVES – magazine of the Movement for Compassionate Living
- ORGANIC FARMING – magazine for producers of the Soil Association
- ORGANIC WAY – magazine of HDRA (the Organic Association)
- THE VEGAN – magazine of the Vegan Society
- THE VEGETARIAN – magazine of the Vegetarian Society
- VEGAN VIEWS – magazine independent of the Vegan Society but shares the same aims

Useful organisations
Stockfree-Organic Services – for application packs and commercial growers enquiries
20 Hawthorn Avenue, Orrell, Wigan, WN5 8NQ, UK. Tel: 01942 621769
Email: sowandgroworganics@phonecoop.coop

Vegan Organic Network – www.veganorganic.net
10 Charter Road, Altrincham, Cheshire, WA15 9RL, UK. Tel: 0845 2235232
Email: info@veganorganic.net

Animal Aid - www.animalaid.org.uk
The Old Chapel, Bradford Street, Tonbridge, Kent, TN9 1AW, UK.
Tel 01732 364546

Ballyroe Vegan Organic Horticulturalists (Ireland) -
http://homepage.eircom.net/~ballyroe/
Email: ballyroe@eircom.net

Biovegan (Austrian-based) – www.biovegan.org
Altenmarkt 95, 8333 Riegersburg, Österreich. Tel: +43/(0)676/922 14 33
Email: dialog@biovegan.org

Centre for Vegan Organic Education (US-based) - www. veganorganiced.org
P.O. Box 13217, Burton, WA, 98013, US. Email: info@veganorganiced.org

Coswinsawsin Farm, Duchy of Cornwall - www.organicstudiescornwall.co.uk
Organic Studies Centre, Duchy College, Rosewarne, Camborne, Cornwall,
TR14 0AB, UK. Tel: (01209) 722155

Cultivating communities – www.cuco.org.uk
Soil Association, Bristol House, 40-56 Victoria Street, Bristol, BS1 6BY, UK.
Tel: 0117 914 2425 Email: csa@cuco.org.uk

Danish Institute of Agricultural Sciences -
http://web.agrsci.dk/pvf/Gronsager/ktk/index_uk.shtml
Department of Horticulture, Kirstinebjergvej 10, P.O. Box 102, DK-5792
Aarslev. Tel: +45 6390 4128
E-mail: Kristian.ThorupKristensen@agrsci.dk

Ecoforest Education for Sustainability (Spanish-based) -
www.ecoforest.org
Apdo 29, Coin 29100, Malaga, España. Tel: (+34) 661 079 950 Email:
info@ecoforest.org

Elm Farm Research Centre – www.efrc.com
Hamstead Marshall, Newbury, Berkshire, RG20 0HR, UK. Tel: 01488 658298
Email: elmfarm@efrc.com

Farm Animal Reform Movement (US) - www.farmusa.org
10101 Ashburton, Bethesda, MD 20817, US. Email: info@farmusa.org

HDRA – the Organic Organisation – www.hdra.org.uk
Ryton Organic Gardens, Coventry, Warwickshire, CV8 3LG, UK. Tel: 024
7630 3517
Email: enquiry@hdra.org.uk

HIPPO (Food aid with a purpose) - www.ivu.org/articles/net/hippo.html
The Old Vicarage, Llangynog, Carmarthen, SA33 5BS, U.K. Email:
HIPPOCHARITY@aol.com

Institute of Plant-based Nutrition - www.plantbased.org
333 Bryn Mawr Avenue, Bala Cynwyd, PA, 19004-2606, USA.

Khadigar Farm (US-based) - http://www.navs-online.org/voice/newart.html
Box 1167, Farmington, ME 04938, USA.

Le Guerrat (French market garden and guest house) -
http://vegan.port5.com/flashvegangite2.html
Sue Morris & Trevor Warman, 09420 Esplas de Serou, Rimont, France.
Tel: +33 (0)5 61 96 37 03
Email: leguerrat@aol.com

Movement for Compassionate Living – www.mclveganway.org.uk
105 Cyfyng Road, Ystalyfera, Swansea SA9 2BT, UK.
Email: mcl@unisonfree.net

Real food – www.realfood.org.uk
PO Box 339, Wolverhampton, West Midlands, WV10 7BZ, UK.
Tel: 0845 458 0146

*Permaculturacañadulce (Vegan-organic permaculture centre in Spain
with emphasis on yoga)* - www.permaculturacanadulce.org/en
Buzón 14 La Charca, 29100 Coin, Malaga, Spain. Tel: (+34) 951 16 50 37
Email: info@permaculturacanadulce.org

Plants for a Future – www.pfaf.org
Tel: 01208 872963 Email:webmaster@pfaf.org

Soil Association – www.soilassociation.org.uk
Bristol House, 40-56 Victoria Street, Bristol, BS1 6BY, UK.
Tel: 0117 314 5000
Email: info@soilassociation.org

Spiral Seed (vegan friendly permaculture) - www.spiralseed.co.uk
Spiralseed, 35 Rayleigh Avenue, Westcliff On Sea, Essex, SS0 7DS.
Email: landandliberty@ukonline.co.uk

Steward Community Woodland (vegan organic project Devon) -
www.stewardwood.org
Affinity Woodland Workers Co-op, Steward Community Woodland,
Moretonhampstead, Newton Abbot, Devon, TQ13 8SD, UK.
Tel: 0845 458 1926 Email: affinity@stewardwood.org

Stockless Arable Organic Project, ADAS Terrington -
www.stocklessorganic.co.uk
ADAS, Woodthorne, Wergs Road, Wolverhampton, WV6 8TQ, UK. Tel: 0845
7660085

Stockless Organic Research at the University of Nottingham -
www.nottingham.ac.uk/biosciences/ah/Organic/organic.html
Division of Agricultural & Environmental Sciences, School of Biosciences,
University of Nottingham, Sutton Bonington Campus, Loughborough, Leics.
LE12 5RD, UK. Tel: 0115 951 6074.

VEGA (Vegetarian Economy and Green Agriculture) –
www.vegaresearch.org
14 Woodland Rise, Greenford, Middlesex, UB6 0RD. Tel: 020 8902 0073
Email: info@vegaresearch.org

Vegan News – http://www.btinternet.com/~bury_rd/sumfive.htm

Veganodling (Swedish-based vegan organic group) -
http://on.to/veganodling
c/o Staffan Melin, Möllevångsgatan 43A, SE-214 20, Malmö, Sweden.
Tel: +46 (0)40 786 27
Email: staffanmelin@home.se

Vegan Society – www.vegansociety.com
Donald Watson House, 7 Battle Road, St Leonards-on-sea, East Sussex,
TN37 7AA, UK. Tel: 0845 458 8244 Email: info@vegansociety.com

Vegan Views – www.veganviews.org.uk
Flat A15, 20 Dean Park Road, Bournemouth, Dorset, BH1 1JB, UK.
Email: info@veganviews.org.uk

Vegan Village (web-based community) – www.veganvillage.co.uk

Végéculture (Canadian french speaking vegan organic group) –
www. vegeculture.net
1177, boul. de la Montagne, St-Casimir, Québec G0A 3L0, Canada.

Végéculture (France) – www. vegeculture.net
18 Square de Provence, 35000 Rennes Bretagne, France.

Vegetarian Society – www.vegsoc.org
Parkdale, Dunham Road, Altrincham, Cheshire, WA14 4QG, UK.
Tel: 0161 925 2000
Email: info@vegsoc.org

Vegfam - www.veganvillage.co.uk/vegfam
The Sanctuary, Nr Lydford, Okehampton, Devon, EX20 4AL, UK.
Tel: 01822 820 203
Email: vegfam@veganvillage.co.uk

Vegfamily (web-based community) – www.vegfamily.com

Veggies catering campaign - www.veggies.org.uk
Sumac Centre, 245 Gladstone Street, Nottingham, NG7 6HX, UK.
Tel: 0845 458 9595
Email: info@veggies.org.uk

VIVA! – www.viva.org.uk
Vegetarians International Voice for Animals, 8 York Court, Wilder Street,
Bristol, BS2 8QH, UK. Tel: 0117 944 1000 Email: info@viva.org.uk

Welsh College of Horticulture – www.wcoh.ac.uk
Northop, Mold, Flintshire, CH7 6AA, UK. Tel: 01352 841000 Email:
info@wcoh.ac.uk

Index

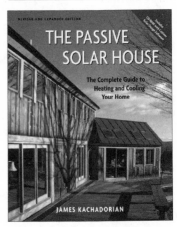